Dynamic Learning:
Dreamweaver CS3

with Video Tutorials and Lesson Files

Fred Gerantabee & AGI Creative Team

AGI   O'REILLY®   Dynamic Learning™

BEIJING · CAMBRIDGE · FARNHAM · KÖLN · PARIS · SEBASTOPOL · TAIPEI · TOKYO

Dynamic Learning: DreamweaverCS3
By Fred Gerantabee & AGI Creative Team

Additional writing: **Jeremy Osborn, Jeff Ausura, Sean McKnight, Greg Heald**

Series Editor: **Christopher Smith**

Technical Editors: **Caitlin Smith, Cathy Auclair, Haziel Olivera, Linda Forsvall**

Additional Editing: **Edie Freedman**

Video Project Manager: **Jeremy Osborn**

Cover Design: **Edie Freedman, O'Reilly Media**

Interior Design: **Ron Bilodeau, O'Reilly Media**

Graphic Production: **Lauren Mickol**

Additional Production: **Aquent Studios**

Indexing: **Caitlin Smith**

Video Editor: **Trevor Chamberlin**

Proofreading: **Jay Donahue**

Published by O'Reilly Media, Inc., 1005 Gravenstein Highway North, Sebastopol, CA 95472.

O'Reilly books may be purchased for educational, business, or sales promotional use. Online editions are also available for most titles (*safari.oreilly.com*). For more information, contact our corporate/institutional sales department: 800.998.9938 or *corporate@oreilly.com*.

Please report any errors by sending a message to errata@aquent.com.

Print History: September 2007, First Edition.
ISBN 10: 0-596-51057-8
ISBN 13: 978-0-596-51057-2
[F]

Printed in Canada.

Dynamic Learning:
Dreamweaver
CS3

with Video Tutorials and Lesson Files

Contents

Lesson 2: Creating a New Site

Lesson 3: Adding Text and Images

Lesson 4: Styling Your Pages with CSS

Lesson 5: Creating Page Layouts with Tables

Lesson 6: Creating Page Layouts with CSS

Lesson 7: Fine-Tuning Your Workflow

Lesson 8: Working with Frames

Lesson 9: Adding Flash, Video, and Sound Content

Lesson 10: Getting Modular with Reusable Items

Lesson 11: Under the Hood: Editing in the Code View

Lesson 12: Building Web Forms

Lesson 13: Managing Your Web Site: Reports, Optimization & Maintenance

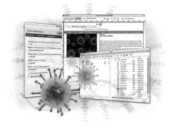

DVD Contents

Resources on the DVD

The *Dynamic Learning: Dreamweaver CS3* Digital Classroom DVD that is included with this book is loaded with useful information, video tutorials that accompany each lesson, and the lesson files that you'll need to complete the exercises contained in this book.

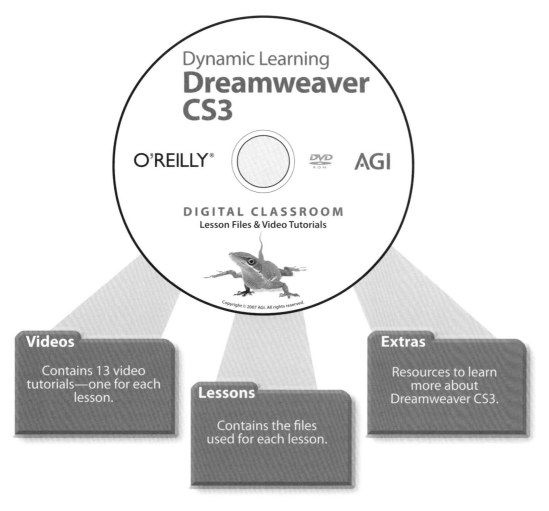

The included video tutorials play on both Windows and Mac OS computers using the free Adobe® Flash® player available at adobe.com/products/flashplayer.

Starting up

About Dynamic Learning

Adobe® Dreamweaver® CS3 lets you design, develop, and maintain web sites and web pages. Both designers and developers use Dreamweaver CS3 which lets you create and edit content using a visual layout or a coding environment. Dreamweaver CS3 also provides tight integration with other Adobe products such as Photoshop® CS3 and Flash® CS3 Professional.

Dynamic Learning: Dreamweaver CS3 is like having your own personal instructor guiding you through each lesson while you work at your own speed. This book includes 13 self-paced lessons that let you discover essential skills and explore the new features and capabilities of Dreamweaver CS3. Each lesson includes step-by-step instructions and lesson files, along with video tutorials that complement the topics covered in each lesson. These accompanying files are provided on the included *Dynamic Learning: Dreamweaver CS3* DVD, developed by the same team of Adobe Certified Instructors and Dreamweaver experts who have created many of the official training titles for Adobe Systems.

Prerequisites

Before you start the lessons in *Dynamic Learning: Dreamweaver CS3,* you should have a working knowledge of your computer and its operating system. You should know how to use the directory system of your computer so that you can navigate through folders. You need to understand how to locate, save, and open files. You should also know how to use your mouse to access menus and commands.

Before starting the lessons files in *Dynamic Learning: Dreamweaver CS3*, make sure that you have installed Adobe Dreamweaver CS3. The software is sold separately, and not included with this book. You may use the 30-day trial version of Adobe Dreamweaver CS3 available at the *Adobe.com* web site, subject to the terms of its license agreement.

System requirements

Before starting the lessons in *Dynamic Learning: Dreamweaver CS3*, make sure that your computer is equipped for running Adobe Dreamweaver CS3, which you must purchase separately. The minimum system requirements for your computer to effectively use the software are listed below and on the following page.

System requirements for Adobe Dreamweaver CS3:

Windows OS

- Intel® Pentium® 4, Intel Centrino®, Intel Xeon®, or Intel Core™ Duo (or compatible) processor
- Microsoft® Windows® XP with Service Pack 2 or Windows Vista™ Home Premium, Business, Ultimate, or Enterprise (certified for 32-bit editions)

- 512MB of RAM (1GB recommended)
- 1 GB of available hard-disk space (additional free space required during installation)
- 1,024x768 monitor resolution with 16-bit video card
- DVD-ROM drive
- Internet or phone connection required for product activation

Macintosh OS

- 1GHz PowerPC® G4 or G5 or multicore Intel® processor
- Mac OS X v.10.4.8 or later
- 512MB of RAM (1GB recommended)
- 1GB of available hard-disk space (additional free space required during installation)
- 1,024x768 monitor resolution with 16-bit video card
- DVD-ROM drive
- Internet or phone connection required for product activation

Starting Adobe Dreamweaver CS3

As with most software, Adobe Dreamweaver CS3 is launched by locating the application in your Programs folder (Windows) or Applications folder (Mac OS). If necessary, follow these steps to start the Adobe Dreamweaver CS3 application:

Windows

1 Choose Start > All Programs > Adobe Dreamweaver CS3.

2 Close the Welcome Screen when it appears. You are now ready to use Adobe Dreamweaver CS3.

Mac OS

1 Open the Applications folder, and then open the Adobe Dreamweaver CS3 folder.

2 Double-click on the Adobe Dreamweaver CS3 application icon.

3 Close the Welcome Screen when it appears. You are now ready to use Adobe Dreamweaver CS3.

Menus and commands are identified throughout the book by using the greater-than symbol (>). For example, the command to print a document would be identified as File > Print.

Fonts used in this book

Dynamic Learning: Dreamweaver CS3 includes lessons that refer to fonts that were installed with your copy of Adobe Dreamweaver CS3. If you did not install the fonts, or have removed them from your computer, you may substitute different fonts for the exercises or re-install the software to access the fonts.

If you receive a Missing Font Warning, press OK and proceed with the lesson.

Resetting the Dreamweaver workspace

To make certain that your panels and working environment are consistent, you should reset your workspace at the start of each lesson. To reset your workspace, choose Window > Workspace Layout > Designer (Windows) or Window > Workspace Layout > Default (Mac OS).

Loading lesson files

The *Dynamic Learning: Dreamweaver CS3* Digital Classroom DVD includes files that accompany the exercises for each of the lessons. You may copy the entire lessons folder from the supplied DVD to your hard drive, or copy only the lesson folders for the individual lessons you wish to complete.

For each lesson in the book, the files are referenced by the file name of each file. The exact location of each file on your computer is not used, as you may have placed the files in a unique location on your hard drive. We suggest placing the lesson files in the My Documents folder (Windows) or at the top level of your hard drive (Mac OS).

Copying the lesson files to your hard drive:

1 Insert the *Dynamic Learning: Dreamweaver CS3* Digital Classroom DVD supplied with this book.

2 On your computer desktop, navigate to the DVD and locate the folder named dwlessons.

3 You can install all of the files, or just specific lesson files. Do one of the following:
   - Install all lesson files by dragging the dwlessons folder to your hard drive.
   - Install only some of the files by creating a new folder on your hard drive, named dwlessons. Open the dwlessons folder on the supplied DVD, select the lesson you wish to complete, and drag the folder(s) to the dwlessons folder you created on your hard drive.

Macintosh users should see the important note on the next page.

Macintosh users may need to unlock the files after they are copied from the DVD. This only applies to MacOS computers. After copying the files from the DVD to your computer, select the dwlessons folder, then choose File > Get Info. In the dwlessons info window, click the You can drop-down menu labeled Read Only, which is located in the Ownership section of this window. From the You can drop-down menu, choose Read & Write. Click the arrow to the left of Details, then click the Apply to enclosed items... button at the bottom of the window. You may need to click the padlock icon before the Mac OS allows you to change these permissions. After making these changes, close the window.

Working with the video tutorials

Your *Dynamic Learning: Dreamweaver CS3* Digital Classroom DVD comes with video tutorials developed by the authors to help you understand the concepts explored in each lesson. Each tutorial is approximately five minutes long and demonstrates and explains the concepts and features covered in the lesson.

The videos are designed to supplement your understanding of the material in the chapter. We have selected exercises and examples that we feel will be most useful to you. You may want to view the entire video for each lesson before you begin that lesson. Additionally, at certain points in a lesson, you will encounter the DVD icon. The icon, with appropriate lesson number, indicates that an overview of the exercise being described can be found in the accompanying video.

DVD video icon.

Setting up for viewing the video tutorials

The DVD included with this book includes video tutorials for each lesson. Although you can view the lessons on your computer directly from the DVD, we recommend copying the folder labeled *Videos* from the *Dynamic Learning: Dreamweaver CS3* Digital Classroom DVD to your hard drive.

Copying the video tutorials to your hard drive:

1   Insert the *Dynamic Learning: Dreamweaver CS3* Digital Classroom DVD supplied with this book.

2   On your computer desktop, navigate to the DVD and locate the folder named Videos.

3   Drag the Videos folder to a location onto your hard drive.

Viewing the video tutorials with the Adobe Flash Player

To view the video tutorials, you need the Adobe Flash Player 8 or later (Adobe Flash Player 9). Earlier versions of the Flash Player will not play the videos correctly. If you're not sure that you have the latest version of the Flash Player, you can download it for free from the Adobe web site: *http://www.adobe.com/support/flashplayer/downloads.html*

The accompanying video files use the Adobe Flash Video format to make universal viewing possible for users on both Windows and Mac OS computers. The most recent versions of the free Adobe Flash Player software generally improve playback performance of these video files.

Playing the video tutorials:

1   Make sure you have at least version 8 of the Adobe Flash Player.

2   On your computer desktop, navigate to the Videos folder on your hard drive or DVD.

3   Open the Videos folder and right-click (Windows) or Ctrl+click (Mac OS) on the Dynamic_Learning_DW_CS3.swf file.

4   Choose Open > Open With > Flash Player. If there is no Flash Player option available, you may need to install the latest version of Flash Player.

Macintosh users on the new Intel-based Mac OS computers may need to download the standalone Flash Player from Adobe.com *to see this option. If the Flash Player is installed, you can just double-click the video tutorial file you wish to view.*

5   The video tutorial opens, using the Flash Player, and begins to play. The Flash Player has a simple user interface that allows you to control the viewing experience, including stopping, pausing, playing, and restarting the video. You can also rewind or fast-forward, and adjust the playback volume.

*A. Go to beginning. **B**. Play/Pause. **C**. Fast-forward/rewind. **D**. Stop. **E**. Volume Off/On. **F**. Volume control.*

Playback volume is also affected by the settings in your operating system. Be certain to adjust the sound volume for your computer, in addition to the sound controls in the Player window.

Additional resources

The Dynamic Learning series goes beyond the training books. You can continue your learning online, with training videos, and at seminars and conferences.

Video training series

Expand your knowledge of the Adobe Creative Suite 3 applications with the Digital Classroom video training series that complements the skills you'll learn in this book. Learn more at *agitraining.com* or *oreilly.com*.

Seminars and conferences

The authors of the Dynamic Learning seminar series frequently conduct in-person seminars and speak at conferences, including the annual CRE8 Conference. Learn more at *agitraining.com* or *oreilly.com*.

Resources for educators

Visit *oreilly.com* to access resources for educators, including instructors' guides for incorporating Dynamic Learning into your curriculum.

Images and animations used in this book

The files provided on the DVD are to be used only in connection with the tutorials in this book. They are copyrighted, and may not be reproduced, copied, or used by you for any other purpose without first obtaining permission from the copyright owner.

What you'll learn in this lesson:

- Exploring Dreamweaver's primary features

- Introducing new features in CS3

- Understanding how web sites and web pages work

- Coding HTML/XHTML: the basics

Dreamweaver CS3 Jumpstart

Whether you are a novice web designer or an experienced developer, Dreamweaver is a comprehensive tool you can use for site design, layout, and management. In this lesson, you'll take a tour of Dreamweaver's key features and get a better understanding of how web pages work.

Starting up

Before starting, make sure that your tools and panels are consistent by resetting your workspace. See "Resetting the Dreamweaver workspace" on page 3.

You will work with several files from the dw01lessons folder in this lesson. Make sure that you have loaded the dwlessons folder onto your hard drive from the supplied DVD. See "Loading lesson files" on page 3.

See Lesson 1 in action!

Use the accompanying video to gain a better understanding of how to use some of the features shown in this lesson. Open the Dynamic_Learning_DW_CS3.swf file located in the Videos folder and select Lesson 1 to view the video training file for this lesson.

What is Dreamweaver?

Dreamweaver is an excellent coding and development tool for new and experienced users alike, and has quickly become the preferred web site creation and management program, providing a creative environment for designers. Whether you design web sites, develop mobile phone content, or script complex server-side applications, Dreamweaver has something to offer.

Design and layout tools

Dreamweaver's many icon-driven menus and detailed panels make it easy to insert and format text, images, and media (such as video files and Flash movies). This means that you can create great-looking and functional web pages without knowing a single line of code—Dreamweaver takes care of building the code behind the scenes for you. Dreamweaver does not create graphics from scratch; instead, it is fully integrated with Adobe Photoshop CS3, so you can import and adjust graphics from within the application.

The Insert bar features icons in several categories that let you easily add images, web forms, and media to your page.

Site management and File Transfer Protocol (FTP)

Dreamweaver has everything you need for complete site management, including built-in file transfer (FTP) capabilities between a server and your local machine, reusable objects (such as page templates and library items), and several safety mechanisms (such as link checkers and site reports) so you can ensure that your site works well and looks good. If you're designing your pages with Cascading Style Sheets (CSS), the new Browser Compatibility Check and CSS Advisor features will help you to locate and troubleshoot any potential display issues that may occur across different web browsers.

Coding environment and text editor

Dreamweaver lets you work in a code-only view of your document, which acts as a powerful text editor. Edit HTML code directly and switch views to see the results of your code as you work. Enhancements such as color coding, indentation, and visual aids make Dreamweaver a perfect text editing or coding environment for web designers of any level.

For more experienced developers, Dreamweaver also supports popular coding and scripting languages, such as JavaScript, and several server-side languages, including ColdFusion, PHP, and ASP.NET. Specialized insert menus and code panels help you to build pages and applications in the language of your choice.

```
BasicHTML.html                                                    _ ▢ ✕
[🔲 Code] [◪ Split] [🔳 Design]  Title: Put a title here    ⇕. ⊙.  C ▤. ▨.  ▷°. ☰ Check Page

1   <!DOCTYPE html PUBLIC "-//W3C//DTD XHTML 1.0 Transitional//EN"
    "http://www.w3.org/TR/xhtml1/DTD/xhtml1-transitional.dtd">
2   <html xmlns="http://www.w3.org/1999/xhtml">
3   <head>
4   <meta http-equiv="Content-Type" content="text/html; charset=utf-8" />
5   <title>Put a title here</title></head>
6
7   <body>
8   My text and pictures go here...
9   <p><b>My Bold Title</b></p>
10
11
12  <p>This text will appear inside of its own paragraph.</p>
13
14
15  </body>
16  </html>
```

Code view is a full-featured text editor that color-codes tags and scripts for editing that's easier to decipher.

Scripting languages, such as those used to build interactive web pages or e-commerce sites, fall into two categories: client-side and server-side. Client-side languages (such as JavaScript) run in your browser, while server-side languages (such as ColdFusion) require special software installed on the server to run.

Who uses Dreamweaver?

Dreamweaver's popularity is a result of its diversity. Its ability to take a site from conception through launch—and maintenance afterward—makes it a preferred tool among industry professionals, businesses, and educational institutions. However, it remains easy and accessible enough for novice designers to get up and running quickly. It's not unusual to see Dreamweaver utilized for personal projects or by small businesses and media professionals, such as photographers and painters, to maintain a web presence.

What's new in Dreamweaver CS3?

CS3 introduces many innovative design and coding features as well as improvements to Dreamweaver's flagship features. Now that Dreamweaver is part of the industry-standard Adobe Creative Suite, it has been engineered to work as seamlessly as possible with files from other CS3 applications, offering native support for Photoshop files and the ability to edit placed images directly in Adobe Photoshop CS3.

Spry Widgets and the Spry framework for Ajax

Asynchronous JavaScript and XML (AJAX) is a popular combination of technologies used to create highly interactive web applications, or Rich Internet applications (RIAs). The Spry framework for Ajax is a JavaScript library for web designers that enhances user interactivity through navigation and form components as well as XML data-driven objects. Users of all levels can add visual effects, create intuitive menus, and develop within the Spry framework without having to climb the steep learning curve normally required to create these advanced features from scratch.

The Insert bar features a new Spry Widgets category with XML data-driven objects, self-validating form components, and enhanced navigation items, such as drop-down and accordion-style menus that you can easily customize and format with CSS (Cascading Style Sheets).

The new Spry Widgets section of the Insert bar.

To view and customize a navigation bar created using the new Spry Widgets pane, follow these steps:

1   Launch Dreamweaver CS3.

2   Choose File > Open, or press the Open button (📁) on the Welcome Screen.

3   When the Open dialog box appears, navigate to the dw01lessons folder and select SpryWidgets.html. Press Open.

4   Preview the document by choosing File > Preview in Browser, or by pressing the Preview/Debug in browser button (◉) in the Document toolbar. Choose the default web browser or pick from a list of browsers installed on your computer. The document will open in a browser window. You can roll over the menu elements to see them expand to reveal more menus.

    If you are using Internet Explorer on the Windows platform, you may need to select the *Allow Blocked Content* option under the toolbar and press OK. This is a security feature in this browser which prevents the external javascript file used in this widget from automatically running.

A customized Spry menu bar with pop-up submenus.

5 Close the browser and return to the document in Dreamweaver. Customizing Spry menus is easy. In the Document window, click on the tab at the top of the menu that reads *Spry Menu Bar: MenuBar1*. In the Property inspector at the bottom of your screen, locate and select Your Links in the first column to expand the menu.

Select the entire menu by its label; you can view and modify all of the menu options in the Property inspector.

6 In the Property inspector, Link 1, Link 2, and Link 3 represent locations in the menu where you can place any links you want. Select Link 1. In the text field labeled Text, enter the words **Adobe Dreamweaver**.

7 In the text field labeled Link, type **http://www.adobe.com/dreamweaver** in place of the pound sign (#). Press Enter (Windows) or Return (Mac OS) to commit the change.

Use the Property inspector to create a link on your page.

8 Choose File > Save to save the page, and preview the new changes you made by choosing File > Preview in Browser or by pressing the Preview/Debug in browser button in the Document toolbar. The new link you added appears when you move the cursor over *Your Links*; you can now click the link to jump to the Adobe site.

The method is the same to customize the other two links—try it to see how easy it is to create interactive menus to navigate around your web site or other web sites.

9 Close the browser and return to Dreamweaver. Choose File > Close to close the document.

See Spry effects in action!

Use the video that accompanies this lesson to gain a better understanding of how to take advantage of Spry effects. Open the Dynamic_Learning_DW_CS3.swf file located in the Videos folder and select Lesson 1 to view the video training file for this lesson.

Spry effects

Elements on a page can adopt some very cool behaviors—boxes can fade in and out, shrink and grow; menus and images can slide in when a user loads a page. Spry effects make all this possible. Take a look at some of the new Dreamweaver Spry effects through the Behaviors panel (open by going to Window > Behaviors). Choose the plus-sign symbol > Effects and check out the Spry effects options.

The new Effects group contains highly interactive Spry effects.

1   Choose File > Open. When the Open dialog box appears, navigate to the dw01lessons folder. Select the file named SpryEffects.html, then Press Open.

2   Choose File > Preview in Browser or press the Preview/Debug in browser button (⊜) on the Document toolbar. The page will launch in a new browser window.

3   Use your cursor to roll over and select the different boxes on the page to see how Spry effects can make objects disappear, highlight, and fade to bring life and interactivity to an otherwise simple web page.

Each box uses a different Spry effect for some very cool interactivity.

4   Close the browser and return to Dreamweaver. Choose File > Close.

Photoshop CS3 integration

Users of the industry-standard Adobe Photoshop CS3 application can now easily bring designs and components they've created in Photoshop into Dreamweaver for use in their web pages. The new Optimization panel lets you specify settings for how to import a Photoshop document. Editing the document later is a snap; just double-click it and edit the original layered .psd file directly in Photoshop CS3. You can even select portions of documents in Photoshop CS3 and paste them directly into a document in Dreamweaver.

Now you will see how easy it is to import Photoshop images in the .psd file format into your web pages.

1 Choose File > Open. When the Open dialog box appears, navigate to the dw01lessons folder and select the file named PhotoshopDoc.html. Press Open.

2 Locate the Insert bar above the Document window, and select the Image icon (⬜).

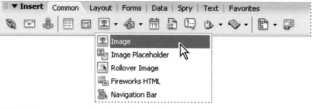

Click the image icon on the Insert bar and choose Insert Image to choose an image for your page.

3 The Select Image Source dialog box appears, prompting you to locate an image file to place in your page. Navigate to the images folder within the dw01lessons folder and select the image named Discover.psd. Press OK (Windows) or Choose (Mac OS) to place the image. If the Image Tag Accessibility Attributes dialog box appears, choose Cancel.

4 The Image Preview dialog box appears. Here's where you can set the quality, file type, and other options for the image file that you're about to place. Leave the default settings at JPEG, Quality 80%. Press OK.

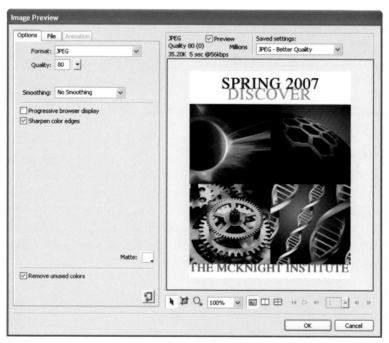

The Image Preview window saves your Photoshop file into a web-ready format before you place it in the page.

5   Now you must save the converted image. In the Save Web Image dialog box that appears, navigate to the images folder within the dw01lessons folder. In the Name field, type **Discover.jpg**, then press Save.

Choose a save location for the converted image.

6   Next, the Image Tag Accessibility Attributes dialog box appears. Press OK. The image is placed in your document.

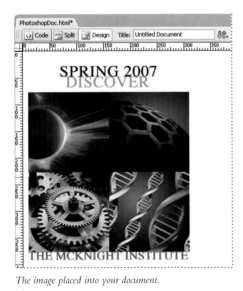

The image placed into your document.

7   Choose File > Save to save your work, then choose File > Close.

You can also drag and drop .psd files from a folder on the Desktop directly into a Dreamweaver document. Give it a try!

CSS layouts

The continuing efforts of web designers to find the best design practices have resulted in a migration from table-based to CSS-based layouts. The use of tables for web page layouts is an old technique, preferred for their easy grid-like structure and guaranteed compatibility in most older browsers. However, the positioning flexibility that only CSS offers has made it the standard for today's web designers.

If you're a CSS novice but you want to get started on the right foot, the new CSS layouts in Dreamweaver will quickly get you up and running. Extensive inline comments included in the code will help you learn so that you can sharpen your CSS expertise while being creative and productive.

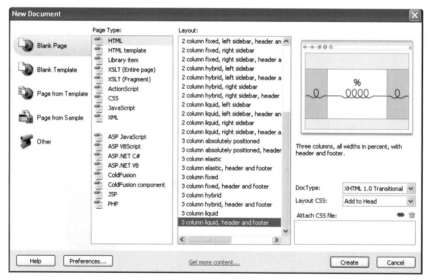

Choose from lots of ready-to-customize CSS layouts that you can modify with your own content, colors, and images.

1 Choose File > New. Under Blank Page > HTML, you will see dozens of preconstructed layouts that take full advantage of the flexibility and power of CSS. Press Cancel.

2 To see an example of a page based on one of these layouts, Choose File > Open. Navigate to the dw01lessons folder and select the CSSLayouts.html document. Press Open. This page is based on the three-column liquid-header and footer CSS layout, which you can find under New Document > HTML.

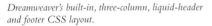

Dreamweaver's built-in, three-column, liquid-header and footer CSS layout.

A customized version of this CSS layout with some basic formatting.

3 Leave this file open, as you will use it in the next exercise.

Browser compatibility check

For years, web site designers have battled with consistency issues across different browsers, which often leads to sites being geared toward one specific browser or another. This is especially true of CSS-dependent web pages, where varying standards among browsers means lots of testing, trial, and error. Dreamweaver's new Browser Compatibility Check feature locates any potentially buggy CSS and HTML combinations and displays them in the Results panel. By combining Browser Compatibility Check with the CSS Advisor, you can address and resolve any potential compatibility issues without juggling browsers.

The Manage CSS feature and the CSS Advisor

With CSS you can format, fine-tune, and position text, images, and content boxes creatively and precisely on your web page. Dreamweaver CS3 provides several panels, menus, and helpers to get you up and running with CSS. Not all designers follow the same workflow; some like to create styles before adding content, and others may add and edit styles as they progress further into a project. The Manage CSS feature in Dreamweaver makes it possible to easily adjust, move, and transition styles as you work so that you can add and fine-tune styles across multiple pages.

Meanwhile, the software's CSS Advisor feature flags potential CSS-related problems that may surface during the Browser Compatibility checks. The Results panel shows you the exact issue, the page and line number where it occurs, and an online link to the Adobe CSS Advisor so that you can find the best solutions to the problem. It's like having a CSS expert sitting alongside you, ready to help!

Adobe Device Central

The widespread use of Internet-ready devices, such as mobile phones and PDAs, makes it more necessary than ever to adapt your work for multiple sizes and platforms. Dreamweaver CS3 is now integrated with Adobe Device Central, which displays and simulates the appearance of HTML content in a variety of mobile, PDA, and handheld device skins and environments. Adobe adds new device profiles quarterly so that you can always stay on top of the market and make sure your content looks its best. Small Screen Rendering (SSR) mode shrinks images and text to emulate how they will display in a selected device, making it easier and more intuitive to develop rich mobile content.

To preview a page in Device Central:

1   With the CSSLayouts.html file open, choose File > Preview in Browser > Device Central. Device Central, which is a separate application, launches.

Preview a currently open page in Device Central.

2   The Device Central application shows the page in the default mobile device. To see how this page will look in a popular mobile phone or PDA, double-click a device name from the Available Devices list on the left. Try the Motorola RAZR listing.

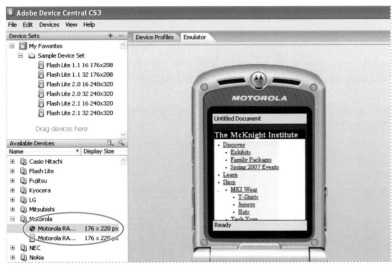

The CSSLayouts.html page, as it would appear in the popular Motorola RAZR phone.

3   Choose File > Close (Windows) or Device Central > Quit (Mac OS) to exit Device Central and return to Dreamweaver. Choose File > Close to close the file.

Adobe Bridge CS3

All editions of Adobe Creative Suite 3 now feature Bridge CS3, a new standalone application designed to provide you with easy access to, and organization and management tools for, files across CS3 applications. Use Dreamweaver with Bridge CS3 for a more fluid workflow between your web site projects and essential resources such as images, stock photos, and source files.

Bridge CS3 provides full search capability and XMP metadata tagging, so you can easily find and add resources within the Dreamweaver environment. If your Dreamweaver site is part of a larger project that spans print, video, and mobile applications, Bridge CS3 keeps you connected to common resources and essential documents across all CS3 applications.

An overview of features

This book is dedicated to exploring, learning, and putting to use all that Dreamweaver has to offer. In this section, we will discuss some of the application's coolest features.

Three different points of view: When you edit a document, Dreamweaver lets you see your work in one of three views: the Design, Split, or Code view. Dreamweaver's easy-to-use Design view lets you build visually and see everything come to life as you create your pages. More experienced web designers and coders can use the Code view to edit a document's HTML code and scripts directly, enhanced with easy-to-read color coding and visual aids.

For those who like something in between, the Split view provides a split-pane Design and Code view all at once. You can easily change views at any time with a single click in the Document toolbar.

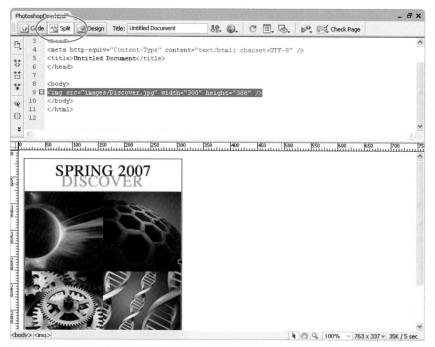

The Split view lets you edit your page visually while seeing the code being created behind the scenes.

Built-in FTP: You can easily upload and download files to your web server from the Files panel's drag-and-drop interface, or use the Get/Put button at any time to post pages you're currently working on. There's no need for separate software. Dreamweaver also provides Check In/Check Out functionality and synchronization features for easy management.

Page and code object Insert bars: You can find intuitive icons for most common web page elements on a categorized Insert bar, from which you can add elements to your page with a single click. You can use additional panels to fine-tune any page element to ensure that you see exactly what you want. Included in the default Insert bar are tools for formatting text, building forms, and creating layouts. Customize a Favorites tab with your most-used icons.

The Insert bar is divided into several categories geared toward specific tasks.

Customizable workspace layouts: You can save combinations and positions of panels and toolbars for easy recall at any time. Save multiple workspace layouts for different users, or create different workspaces for specific tasks, such as coding or designing page layouts.

You can customize the Favorites bar with icons from any of the other Insert bar categories.

Powerful visual aids: Take advantage of the precision you're accustomed to in other design programs through Dreamweaver's guides, rulers, measuring tools, and customizable positioning grid. Dreamweaver's Design-Time style sheets let you customize the look of your page exclusively for the editing process, making layout quicker and easier without permanently altering the page's appearance.

Rulers, a document grid, and guides help you size and position page items with precision.

CSS panel: Take advantage of the vast design and formatting options that CSS provides through Dreamweaver's full-featured CSS panel, which lets you create, edit, and manage styles on the fly from a single panel.

How web sites work

Before embarking on the task of building web pages (and in turn, a web site), it's a good idea to know the basics of how web sites work, how your users view them, and what you need to know to make sure your web site looks and works its best.

A simple flow chart

What happens when you type in a web site address? Most people don't even think about it; they just type in a URL, and a web site appears in a flash. They likely don't realize how many things are going on behind the scenes to make sure that pages gets delivered to their computers so that they can do their shopping, check their email, or research a project.

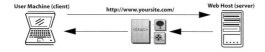

When you type in a URL or IP address, you are connecting to a remote computer (referred to as a server) and downloading the documents, images, and resources necessary to reconstruct the pages you will view at that site. Web pages aren't delivered as a finished product; your web browser (Internet Explorer, Firefox, Safari, etc.) is responsible for reconstructing and formatting the pages based on the HTML code included in the pages. HTML (Hypertext Markup Language) is a simple, tag-based language that instructs your browser how and where to insert and format pictures, text, and media files. Web pages are written in HTML, and Dreamweaver builds HTML for you behind the scenes as you construct your page in the Design view.

An Internet service provider (ISP) enables you to connect to the Internet. Some well-known ISPs include America Online and Earthlink. You view web pages over an Internet connection using a browser, such as Internet Explorer, Firefox, or Safari. A browser can decipher and display web pages and their content, including images, text, and video.

Domain names and IP addresses

When you type in a web site address, you usually enter the web site's domain name (e.g., Ebay.com). The web site owner purchased this domain name and uses it to mask an IP address, which is a numerical address used to locate and dial up the pages and files associated with a specific web site.

So how does the Web know what domains match what IP address (and in turn, which web sites)? It uses a DNS (Domain Name Service) server, which makes connections between domain names and IP addresses.

Servers and web hosts

A DNS server is responsible for matching a domain name with its companion IP address. Think of the DNS server as the operator at the phone company that connects calls through a massive switchboard. DNS servers are typically maintained by either the web host or the registrar from which the domain was purchased. Once the match is made, the request from your user is routed to the appropriate server and folder where your web site resides. When the request reaches the correct account, the server directs it to the first page of the web site, which is typically named index.html, default.html, or whatever the server is set up to recognize as a default starting page.

A server is a machine very much like your desktop PC, but it's capable of handling traffic from thousands of users (often at the same time!), and it maintains a constant connection to the Internet so that your web site is available 24 hours a day. Servers are typically maintained by web hosts, companies that charge a fee to host and serve your web site to the public. A single server can sometimes host hundreds of web sites. Web hosting services are available from a variety of providers, including well-known Internet service companies, such as Yahoo!, and large, dedicated hosting companies, such as GoDaddy. It is also common for a large company to maintain its own servers and web sites on its premises.

The role of web browsers

A web browser is an application that downloads and displays HTML pages. Every time you request a page by clicking a link or typing in a web site address, you are requesting an HTML page and any files it includes. The browser's job is to reconstruct and display that page based on the instructions in the HTML code, which guides the layout and formatting of the text, images, and other assets used in the page. The HTML code works like a set of assembly instructions for the browser to use.

An introduction to HTML

HTML is what makes the Web work; web pages are built using HTML code, which in turn is read and used by your web browser to lay out and format text, images, and video on your page. As you design and lay out web pages in Design view, Dreamweaver writes the code behind the scenes necessary to display and format your page in a web browser.

Contrary to what you may think, HTML is not a programming language, but rather a simple text-based markup language. HTML is not proprietary to Dreamweaver—you can create and edit HTML in any text editor, even simple applications such as Windows Notepad and Mac OS X's TextEdit. Dreamweaver's job is to give you a visual way to create web pages without having to code by hand. If you like to work with code, however, Dreamweaver's Code view, discussed earlier, is a fully featured text editor with color-coding and formatting tools that make it far easier to write and read HTML and other languages.

Tag structure and attributes

HTML uses tags, or bracketed keywords, that you can use to place or format content. Many tags require a closing tag, which is the keyword preceded by a forward slash (/).

1   Choose File > Open. When the Open dialog box appears, navigate to the dw01lessons folder. Select BasicHTML.html and press Open.

2   Select the Split button (⊞) in the Document toolbar to see the layout as well as the code that makes up the page.

Take a look at line 9 (indicated at the left edge of the Code panel). The text *My Bold Title* is inside a Bold tag, which is simply the letter *b* contained within angled brackets. Any words or characters inside these tags will be formatted in bold, and will appear as shown in the Design view.

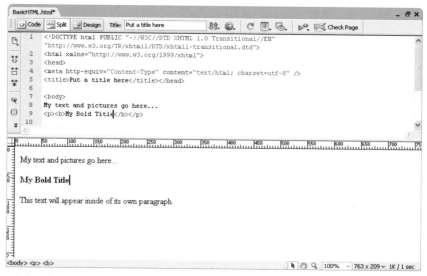

A look at the code reveals the tags used to format text in your page.

Tags can also accept attributes that specify additional information for how the tag should display the content. Attributes are always placed inside the opening tag, and very often they can take a number of different values, such as a size, a color, or a direction in which to align something. Take a look at the line that reads *This text will appear inside of its own paragraph.* This line is enclosed in a *p* (paragraph) tag, which separates it from the other text by a line above and below. You can add attributes to this to align the text in whichever direction you want.

3   Highlight the entire line that reads *This text will appear inside of its own paragraph* at the bottom of the Design view.

4   Locate the paragraph align buttons in the Property inspector. Click the one that centers text (≡).

5   The text is now centered. Take a look at the Code view, and you'll see that the align attribute has been added to the opening *<p>* tag, and has been set to a value of center.

Align or format text in the Property inspector, then see the appropriate tags and attributes created in HTML.

6   Choose File > Save to save your work, then choose File > Close.

The structure of an HTML document

Although you use many HTML tags to format text, certain tags are devoted to establishing structures, such as lists, tables or, most importantly, the HTML documents themselves. The HTML tag is the most fundamental tag. It is used to specify the beginning and end of HTML in a document:

```
<html></html>
```

Inside the main HTML tags are two tags that define the key areas of your web page: the head and the body. The head of your page contains items that are not visible to your user, but are important nonetheless, such as search engine keywords, page descriptions, and links to outside scripts or style sheets. You create the head of the document inside the HTML tags using the *<head>* tag:

```
<html>
<head></head>
</html>
```

The body of your page is where all of the visible elements of your page are contained. Here is where you'll place and format text, images, and other media. You define the body of the page using the *<body>* tag:

```
<html>
<head></head>
<body>
```

My text and pictures go here...

```
</body>
</html>
```

Whenever you create a new HTML document in Dreamweaver, this framework is created automatically before you add anything to the page. Any visual elements you add to the page will be added, using the appropriate HTML code inside the *<body>* tags.

Placing images in HTML

You use some tags in HTML to place items, such as pictures or media files, inside a web page. The IMG tag is the most common example; its job is to place and format an image on the page. To place an image and see the resulting code, follow these steps:

1   Choose File > Open. When the Open dialog box appears, navigate to the dw01lessons folder. Select the Images.html file and press Open to edit the file.

2   Click the Split button (🖳) in the Document toolbar so you're viewing both the layout and the code for your page. In the Design view portion of the Split view, click below the line of text to place your cursor underneath it. This is where you'll place a new image.

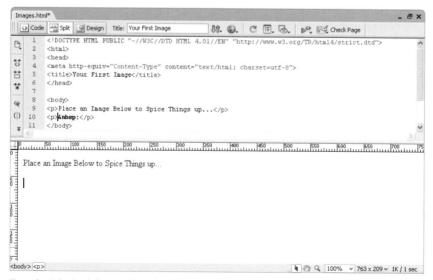

Enter the Split view before you insert the image onto your page.

3   From the Common tab on the Insert bar at the top of the page, press the Image button (▣) and choose Image. When the Select Image Source dialog box appears, select the file named gears.jpg, located under images within the dw01lessons folder.

Choose Insert Image from the Common tab on the Insert bar.

4   Press OK (Windows) or Choose (Mac OS); when the Image Tag Accessibility Attributes dialog box appears, enter the words **Gears Image** in the Alternate text field and press OK to place the image.

Attach alternate text to your image.

The Image Tag Accessibility Attributes dialog box appears when you add images to provide additional information for users with special needs (such as the visually impaired). You should always provide each image with alternative text, but you can disable this panel by choosing Edit > Preferences (Windows) or Dreamweaver > Preferences (Mac OS). In the Accessibility category, uncheck the Images option.

5   The code shows that the HTML *<img>* tag has been used to place the image. Click once on the image in the Document window to select it. The Property inspector at the bottom of the page displays and sets the properties for the image.

6 In the Border box of the Property inspector, type **3** to set a three-pixel border around the image, then press Enter (Windows) or Return (Mac OS). The *<img>* tag now contains the border attribute, which is set to a value of 3, just the way you typed it in the Property inspector.

As you change or add options to a selected image, Dreamweaver changes code behind the scenes.

7 Choose File > Save to save your work, then choose File > Close.

Note that in HTML, images and media are not embedded, but placed. This means that the tags point to files in their exact locations relative to the page. The tags count on those files always being where they're supposed to be in order to display them. This is why HTML pages are typically very lightweight in terms of file size.

Colors in HTML

In Dreamweaver's various panels and in your code, each color is referred to by a six-character code preceded by a pound sign. This code is called hexadecimal code, and is the system that HTML pages use to identify and use colors. You can reproduce almost any color using a unique hexadecimal code. For example, you represent dark red in HTML as #CC0000.

The first, middle, and last two digits of the hexadecimal code correspond to values in the RGB spectrum. For instance, white, which is represented in RGB as R:255 G:255 B:255, is represented in HTML as #FFFFFF (255|255|255). Choosing colors is easy in Dreamweaver, thanks to a handy Swatches panel, which you can find in many places throughout the work area.

The Swatches panel makes it easy to work with colors.

The color pickers in Adobe Photoshop and Illustrator also display and accept hexadecimal codes, making it easy to copy and paste colors between these applications and Dreamweaver.

Case sensitivity and whitespace rules

HTML is a flexible language that has very few rules regarding its own appearance. Based on how strict you wish to write it, HTML can be either very specific about whether tags are written in upper- or lowercase (called case sensitivity) or not specific at all. To see how HTML treats whitespace, follow these steps.

1   Choose File > Open. When the Open dialog box appears, navigate to the dw01lessons folder. Select the Whitespace.html file, then press Open.

2   If your file is not in Split view, press the Split button (▤) in the Document toolbar, so you can view both the layout and the code. You'll notice three seemingly identical tags beneath line 9 in your code:

All of these tags are valid, even though they have very different case structures.

All three tags use a completely different case structure, but all are valid and are treated in the same way. Take a look at the text that reads *This is one sentence. This is another.* The code shows lots of space between the two lines, but the Design view shows no space at all. This is because whitespace or line returns between two pieces of text or tags are not recognized.

Despite the large amount of space between the two sentences, they appear side-by-side in the Design view.

3 To create a line return, or a new paragraph, you need to enter the HTML tags necessary to do so. In the Design view at the bottom, position your cursor after the word *sentence*, then press Shift+Enter (Windows) or Shift+Return (Mac OS) twice. This creates two line returns—you can see that each line return is created in your code by a *
* (break) tag.

To create a line return, hold down the Shift key while pressing the Enter/Return key.

4 To create a new paragraph, position your cursor before the phrase, *This is another*, and press Enter/Return. The text is separated by a line above and below, and is wrapped inside a set of *<p>* (paragraph) tags.

Dreamweaver creates a new paragraph each time you press Enter/Return.

Other than a standard single space (such as the ones used in between words), several consecutive spaces created by the Space bar are ignored, and are still be displayed as only one space in Design view and in a browser.

5 Choose File > Save to save your work then, choose File > Close.

Tag hierarchy

HTML tags follow a certain order of weight, or hierarchy, to make sure everything displays as it should. The tag at the top of the hierarchy is the *<html>* tag; every other tag you create is contained within it. Tags such as the *<body>* tag will always hold smaller tags such as the *<p>* (paragraph), *<img>* (image), and *<strong>* (bold) tags. In addition, structural tags (such as those that create paragraphs, lists and tables) hold more weight than formatting tags such as *<strong>* (bold) and *<em>* (italic). Take this line of code for example:

```
<strong><p>Big bold paragraph</p></strong>
```

Although code such as this may work in certain browsers, it isn't recommended, because the *<strong>* tag technically holds less weight than the *<p>* tag. The following code represents a safer and more proper way to include the bold type:

```
<p><strong>Big bold paragraph</strong></p>
```

Dreamweaver generally does a great job of keeping tags properly nested, or contained within each other. When you choose to manipulate the code by hand, you should always keep good coding techniques in mind.

XHTML 1.0 Transitional

The latest recommended version of HTML is XHTML 1.0, a stricter version of HTML that makes the language more compatible with newer platforms, such as mobile phones and handheld devices, that require code to be perfectly formed. XHTML combines elements of HTML and XML, a language used to describe data. XML, or Extensible Markup Language, has become a popular method of exchanging information among seemingly unrelated applications, platforms, and systems. By default, Dreamweaver creates new web pages using the XHTML 1.0 Transitional standard.

What's the difference?

Although tags and attributes remain the same, the structure of the language changes with XHTML, becoming stricter. Whereas HTML was very forgiving of sloppy coding practices such as overlapping or unclosed tags, XHTML requires all tags to be closed and properly nested. HTML doesn't care which case you use when constructing tags, but in XHTML, all tags must be lowercase.

For example, a *
* (break) tag, which normally doesn't require a closing tag, now must be closed. You can write tags to self-close, using a forward slash—making sure there is a space between the keyword (*br*) and the forward slash—and closing the bracket like so:

```
<br />
```

The result is a well-formed language that takes advantage of newer browsers and device platforms, while remaining compatible with older browsers. Working with XHTML in Dreamweaver requires nothing more than selecting XHTML 1.0 Transitional as the Document Type (DocType) when creating a new page.

Explorations in code

Although this book occasionally refers to the code for examples, hand coding is not a primary goal of the included lessons. The best way to learn how code represents the layouts you are building visually is to switch to the Code view and explore what's happening behind the scenes.

It's important to remember that every button, panel, and menu in Dreamweaver represents some type of HTML tag, attribute, or value; very rarely will you learn something that is unrelated or proprietary to Dreamweaver alone. Think of the Dreamweaver workspace as a pretty face on the HTML language.

A look at the Welcome Screen

A common fixture in most CS3 applications is the Welcome Screen, which is a launching pad for new and recent documents. In Dreamweaver, the Welcome Screen appears when the application launches or when no documents are open. From the Welcome Screen, you can create new pages, create a new site definition, open a recent document, or use one of Dreamweaver's many starter pages or layouts.

The Welcome Screen appears when you launch the application, or when no documents are open.

Here's what you'll find on the Welcome Screen:

Open a Recent Item: A list of the last few documents you worked on appear in the leftmost column, or you can browse to open a different file using the Open button (📁) at the bottom.

Create New: In addition to HTML pages, you can choose from a variety of new document formats such as CSS, JavaScript, and XML. Dreamweaver is not just a web page-building tool, but a superior text editor, making it ideal for creating many non-HTML files. You can also define a new Dreamweaver site using the link at the bottom, or choose the More folder for even more new file options.

Create from Samples: If you're not up to creating a design from scratch, or if you need a little inspiration, Dreamweaver features several starter files, ranging from complete page designs to stripped-down starter layouts. Starter page designs are categorized into several themes, from Health and Fitness to Entertainment, giving you plenty of options for getting started quickly and in style. Basic starter pages include many useful and common layout structures for e-commerce, photo display, and utility forms.

Creating, opening, and saving documents

The lessons throughout this book require that you create, save, and open existing files. You can accomplish most file-related tasks from the File menu at the top, or from the Start page that appears when you launch Dreamweaver.

Creating new documents

Dreamweaver creates text files, commonly in the form of HTML files (or web pages). It can also create files in a variety of text-based languages, including CSS, XML, JavaScript, and even Flash ActionScript.

You can create blank files that you build from the ground up, or get started with a variety of layout templates and themes. You can create new documents from the File menu or from the Start page.

The New Document dialog box gives you a choice of new files in a variety of formats and templates.

1 To create a new document, choose File > New. The New Document dialog box will appear.

2 Select Blank Page > HTML. Under Layout, choose <none> to start a new blank document.

3 To save a document, choose File > Save or File > Save As.

4 When prompted, choose a location for your file and assign it a name. Note that you must save HTML files with an .html extension, or they will not be interpreted properly in a browser. This rule applies for files of any type (.xml, .css, .cfm, etc.).

5 To open an existing document, choose File > Open.

6 Select an existing document and choose Open.

Opening a recently opened document

To open a document you've worked on recently, Choose File > Open Recent or, from the Start page, select a document under the Open a Recent Item column.

Choose a file from the Welcome Screen or choose File > Open Recent to select a recently opened file.

Now that you've seen what Dreamweaver can do, it's time to put what you've learned into practice. Move to the next lesson so you can begin building your first Dreamweaver site!

Self study

Explore the ready-to-use CSS layouts available in Dreamweaver by choosing File > New, then selecting HTML from the Page Type column. Browse the options listed in the Layout column and open a few layouts. Identify some that you'd like to use as a starting point for any future project.

Review

Questions

1   From what two locations in Dreamweaver can a new document can be created?

2   In what three views does Dreamweaver allow you to view and edit documents?

3   True or False: When a web page is requested, it is delivered to a user's browser as a completed, flat file ready for viewing.

Answers

1   From the Welcome Screen or by choosing File > New.

2   Design, Split, and Code views.

3   False. Files are delivered individually; the browser uses HTML code to assemble the resources together to display a finished page.

Lesson 2

What you'll learn in this lesson:

- Creating a site definition
- Establishing local root and remote folders
- Adding and defining pages
- Selecting, viewing, and organizing files with the Files panel
- Uploading and downloading files to and from your remote server

Creating a New Site

Dreamweaver's strength lies in its powerful site creation and management tools. You can use the software to create everything from individual pages to complete web sites. The pages you create within your site can share similar topics, a cohesive design, or a common purpose. And, once your Dreamweaver site is complete, you can efficiently manage and distribute it from within the program itself.

Starting up

Before starting, make sure that your tools and panels are consistent by resetting your workspace. See "Resetting the Dreamweaver workspace" on page 3.

You will work with several files from the dw02lessons folder in this lesson. Make sure that you have loaded the dwlessons folder onto your hard drive from the supplied DVD. See "Loading lesson files" on page 3.

See Lesson 2 in action!

Use the accompanying video to gain a better understanding of how to use some of the features shown in this lesson. Open the Dynamic_Learning_DW_CS3.swf file located in the Videos folder and select Lesson 2 to view the video training file for this lesson.

Creating a new site

In Dreamweaver, the term *site* refers to the local and remote storage locations where the files that make up a web site are stored. A site can also include a testing server location for processing dynamic pages. To take full advantage of Dreamweaver's features, you should always start by creating a site.

The easiest way to create a new site in Dreamweaver is to use the Site Definition wizard. Choose Site > New Site, and the wizard appears.

You can also use the Manage Sites dialog box to create a new site. We discuss this and other functions of the Manage Sites dialog box later in this book.

In this lesson, we begin by using the Site Definition wizard to accomplish the following tasks:

- Define the site
- Name the site
- Define the local root folder
- Set up a remote folder
- Explore advanced settings
- Save the site

By default, the Site Definition wizard opens with the Basic tab selected. The options available here will help guide you through the essentials of defining your site. The Advanced tab allows you to set up local, remote, and/or testing servers directly.

The first screen you see in the Basic tab of the Site Definition wizard allows you to name your site. Avoid using spaces (use underscores instead), periods, slashes, or any other punctuation in your site name, as doing so will likely cause the server to misdirect your files.

To create a new site:

1 Launch Dreamweaver CS3, if it is not already open, then choose Site > New Site. First, you have to name the site. In the Name field, type **museum_site**.

2 If you are working directly on a web server (instead of locally), you can also enter the HTTP address of your server in this window. Because we'll be working locally in this lesson, entering an HTTP address isn't necessary, so leave the HTTP Address field blank and press Next.

The HTTP address can be input into the site definition.

3 You can use Dreamweaver to build web applications using any of five server technologies: ColdFusion, ASP.NET, ASP, JSP, or PHP. Each technology corresponds to a document type in Dreamweaver. Since we won't be using any of these server-scripting environments for this lesson, leave the radio button next to *No, I do not want to use server technology* selected, then press Next to proceed to the next screen in the wizard.

You can build your site using different server technologies.

At this point, you need to set up a local root folder, which is where Dreamweaver stores the files with which you're currently working. The local root folder definition screen allows you to enter information regarding where you'll be working with your files during development.

4   In this lesson, you'll be working locally and uploading to the server when you're ready, so click the first of the two radio buttons listed, labeled Edit local copies on your machine. Dreamweaver asks where you want to store your files locally. You can either create a folder on your hard drive and build your site from scratch, or use a pre-existing folder of content that you've already created for this site. You'll use the second option for this lesson.

To ensure that the links you set up on your computer will work when you upload the site to a web server, it is essential that you store all of the site's resources in one main folder on your hard drive, then identify it within Dreamweaver. This is because the links will only work properly if all of the site's elements remain in the same relative location on the web server as with your hard drive.

5   Click on the folder icon (🗀) to the right of this field to navigate to your prebuilt files.

6   Navigate to your desktop and locate the museum_files folder inside the dw02lessons folder you copied to your desktop earlier.

7   Click Open to open this folder, then press Select (Windows) or Choose (Mac OS) to choose this as your local root folder. The field will now show the path to your newly defined local root folder. Press Next.

Define the path to your local root folder.

8   In most cases, the remote folder is the location on the computer where your web server is running. This is where you'll upload and store your files for deployment to the Web. When you set up a remote folder, you have to choose a method for Dreamweaver to upload and download files to this server. The drop-down menu on this screen offers you a list of access options. Choose FTP (the most commonly used method) from the drop-down menu.

9   Additional fields for FTP address, folder location, login, and password appear. These fields are required to gain FTP access to a server.

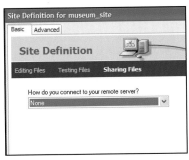

Set up access to your remote folder.

10 You do not have to define your remote folder at this stage. Dreamweaver allows you to define your remote folder at a later time, like when you're ready to upload. In this lesson, you'll work locally now and define your remote folder using the Files panel later. From the drop-down menu, choose None for the remote connection choice. Press Next.

Choose None to define your remote folder later.

11 The final screen in the Basic tab of the Site Definition wizard is a summary of all the settings you just selected. Check that your local information, including the site name and the location of your local root folder (museum_files), are correct. If they aren't, press the Back button to bring you back to the screen containing the error.

Note that the Remote Server and Testing Server options reflect that you'll set them up later.

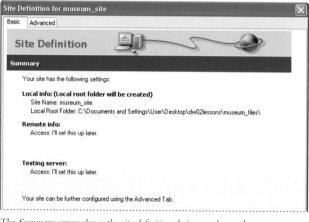

The Summary screen shows the site definition choices you've made.

You've now completed the site definition process, using the Basic interface of the Site Definition wizard. Don't close the wizard yet, though, as you'll now explore the options found under the Advanced tab.

Advanced site-creation options

Don't ignore the Advanced tab of the Site Definition window, as it offers access to many settings that aren't available in the Site Definition wizard.

The Advanced tab also offers access to all of the settings options available in the wizard's Basic tab, so you can go straight to the Advanced tab to create a site when you gain more experience with Dreamweaver.

To create a new site, using Advanced options:

1 Click the Advanced tab in the Site Definition dialog box.

2 From the categories on the left, choose Local Info.

3   Note that the Site Name and the Local Root Folder fields are populated by the
    information you entered using the wizard.

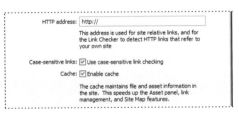

The information you entered using the wizard is reflected here.

The information you set in the Local Info window identifies the site files in Dreamweaver
and enables the software's site management features. One of the more important Local Info
settings is case-sensitive link checking.

The case-sensitive link checking feature ensures that your links will work on a Unix server,
where links are case-sensitive. If you're using a Windows or Mac server, this doesn't matter
as much, but it is a good idea to follow the strict naming and linking conventions of a Unix
system in case you ever move your site to a different server.

4   Click the checkbox next to Use case-sensitive link checking.

Activate the case-sensitive link checking option.

The remaining categories to the left of the Advanced tab of the Site Definition window
help to define your site's production, collaboration, and deployment capabilities. They
include the following:

Remote Info is necessary to upload the site files to the web server. Contact your server
administrator to determine which method to use for your site.

Testing Servers act like public servers in order to test dynamic pages and connections
to the database.

Cloaking allows you to specify file types or specific files that you do not want uploaded to the server.

Design Notes are a collaboration tool that keeps notes regarding the development of the page or site.

Site Map Layout is useful for understanding how your site files connect to one another.

File View Columns is an organizational tool. If you want to share the custom columns with others, you must enable Design Notes as well.

Contribute enables users with basic word processing and web browser skills and little or no HTML knowledge to create and maintain web pages.

Templates can be automatically updated with rewritten document paths using this option.

Spry is a JavaScript library for web designers. It allows designers to build pages that provide a richer experience for their users.

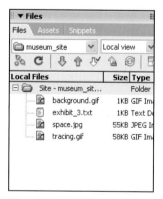

Additional category options found in the Advanced tab.

At this point, you are finished defining your settings, so press OK; Dreamweaver creates a site with the settings you have defined. Note that the Files panel on the right side of your screen displays your local root folder and all of its enclosed content files.

The Files panel shows all of the files in your local root folder.

You are now ready to build pages for your web site.

Adding pages

Dreamweaver contains many features to assist you in building pages for your site. With these features, you can define properties for those pages, including titles, background colors or images, and default text and link colors.

It's important to consider that users will view your pages with different browsers on different platforms (and in different languages). Fortunately, Dreamweaver also includes tools that allow you to create and test pages to ensure compatibility with most users.

To add a page to your site:

1   Choose File > New. The New Document dialog box opens.

Use the New Document dialog box to add a page to your site.

2   You can create a new page using a predesigned layout, or start with a blank page and build a layout of your own. In this exercise, you'll start with a blank page. Click on the Blank Page category on the left side of the New Document window.

Use predefined page layouts to create your page.

3   In the Page Type column, you can select the type of page you want to create (e.g., HTML, ColdFusion, etc.). Select HTML.

Choose the type of page you want to create (HTML).

In the Layout column, you can choose to base your page on a prebuilt design (created using Cascading Style Sheets (CSS), which are discussed in detail earlier in this book). These predesigned layouts fall into one of four categories:

Fixed columns do not resize based on the user's browser settings. They are measured in pixels.

Elastic columns adapt to the user's text settings, but not when the browser window is resized. These columns are measured in ems (a traditional typography measurement).

Liquid columns resize if the user resizes the browser window, but not if the user changes the text settings.

Hybrid columns combine any of the other three options (e.g., three-column hybrid).

4   Click on <none> in the Layout column to build the page without using a prebuilt layout.

Select the type of prebuilt HTML layout you'd like to use.

5   Leave the DocType setting at XHTML 1.0 Transitional. The DocType drop-down menu defines the document type and compliance with different versions of HTML. XHTML 1.0 Transitional is the default setting and is suitable in most cases.

Choose XHTML 1.0 Transitional as your DocType.

The Layout CSS and Attach CSS settings are irrelevant here, since you didn't choose a CSS-based layout for this page.

6   Press Create to create a new blank HTML page.

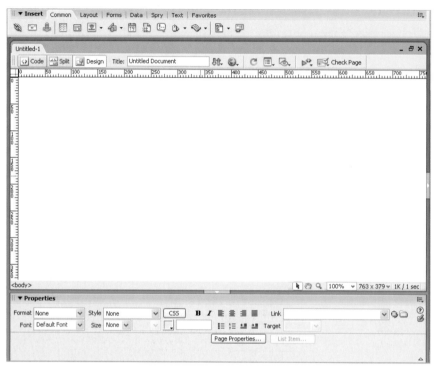

Your new blank HTML page.

Saving a page to your site

You should get accustomed to saving pages to your local root folder early and often. It is very important that you store all of your site's resources in one main folder on your hard drive so that the links you set on your computer will work when your site is uploaded to a server.

1   Choose File > Save.

2   In the Save As dialog box, navigate to your Desktop, and locate the museum_files folder (your local root folder, as defined earlier).

3   In the Name field, name your file **index.html**.

The Internet standard for naming your home page, or the first page users see when they access your site, is index.html. The only time you should not name your home page index.html is if your server administrator requests another name, such as home.html or default.html.

4 Leave the Save As Type field set to All Documents (which includes the .html file extension), and select None from the Unicode Normalization From drop-down menu.

5 Click Save to save the page in your local root folder.

Use the Save As dialog box to save your new page in your site.

Defining page properties

Now that you've created a page in Dreamweaver, you'll use the Page Properties dialog box to specify its layout and formatting properties. You use this dialog box to define page properties for each new page you create, and to modify the settings for pages you've already created.

Dreamweaver uses CSS by default to define settings in the Appearance, Links, and Headings categories of the Page Properties dialog box. You'll start by changing the default page-formatting preferences to HTML formatting.

To specify the layout and formatting properties of your page:

1 Choose Edit > Preferences (Windows) or Dreamweaver > Preferences (Mac OS) to open the Preferences dialog box.

2 In the General category (selected by default), under Editing options, click the checkbox next to *Use CSS instead of HTML tags* to deactivate this feature, then press OK.

Turn off the default CSS formatting in the Preferences dialog box.

3 You use the Page Properties dialog box to set page titles, background colors and images, text and link colors, and other basic properties of every web page. To access the Page Properties dialog box, choose Modify > Page Properties, or use the keyboard shortcut Ctrl+J (Windows) or Command+J (Mac OS). The Page Properties dialog box appears, with the Appearance category selected by default.

The Page Properties dialog box.

4   The Background image field allows you to set a background image for your page. Dreamweaver mimics a browser's behavior by repeating, or tiling, the background image to fill the window. To choose a background image, click the Browse button next to the Background image text field. The Select Image Source dialog box appears.

5   Navigate to the museum_files folder within dw02lessons and select background.gif for your page background, then press OK.

6   Click the Apply button to see the image as the background of your page.

Choose a background image for your page (background.gif).

You can also type the path to your background image into the Background image text field.

7   You use the Background option to choose a background color for your page. If you've also chosen a background image, the color will appear while the image downloads, at which time the image covers the color. If there are transparent areas in the background image, the background color will show through. To choose a background color, click on the color swatch next to the Background text field; the Swatches panel appears. You can choose your background color by clicking on the appropriate swatch from the Swatches panel. Try this by clicking on any color swatch, then press Apply to see the results.

If you click the Apply button, you won't see the background color in your page, as it's covered by the background image you specified earlier.

You can also choose the background color by typing the hexadecimal notation for your desired color into the Background field. Type the hex code **d7d7d7** in the Background text field, then press Enter (Windows) or Return (Mac OS) to specify a light gray as the background color.

Set a background color for your page.

8 The text option allows you to set a default color in which to render type. To set a text color, click on the color swatch next to Text; the Swatches panel appears. You can choose your default text color by clicking on the appropriate swatch from the Swatches panel. Try this by clicking on any color swatch, then press Apply to apply your desired default text color.

As with the background color, you can type the hexadecimal notation for your desired color into the text field. Type the hex code **666666** in the text field to specify a dark gray as the default text color.

You'll see the effects of this change later in this lesson, when you add text to your page using the Files panel.

Set a default text color using the Swatches panel.

9   You can specify the color of linked text in the Appearance category of the Page Properties dialog box. For more information on creating hyperlinks, see Lesson 3, "Adding Text and Images." Set the colors for your different link types in the following fields:

Links: Type **843432** for the default color applied to linked text.

Visited links: Type **666666** for the color applied to linked text after a user has clicked on it.

Active links: Type **CC6500** for the color applied when the user clicks on linked text.

Page Properties					☒
Category	Appearance				
Appearance Title/Encoding Tracing Image	Background image:	background.gif		Browse...	
	Background:	▢ d7d7d7			
	Text:	■ 666666	Visited links:	■ 666666	
	Links:	■ 843432	Active links:	■ CC6500	
	Left margin:		Margin width:		
	Top margin:		Margin height:		
	Help		OK	Cancel	Apply

Choose default colors for links, visited links, and active links.

You can also type the hexadecimal notations for your desired link colors into the respective fields.

10   By default, Dreamweaver places your text and images in close proximity to the top and left edges of the page. To build in some extra room between your page edges and the content on them, use the Margin settings in the Page Properties dialog box. In the Left margin field, type **25** to place your content 25 pixels from the left edge of the page. In the Top margin field, type **25** to place your content 25 pixels from the top edge of the page.

Use the Margin width and Margin height fields to set page margins for viewing in Netscape browsers. For best results, duplicate the settings you entered in the Left and Top margin fields, respectively.

11 Click on the Title/Encoding category to the left of the Page Properties dialog box to
    expose more settings:

- Type **Museum Home** in the Title text field. This sets the title that appears in the title
  bar of most browser windows. It's also the default title used when a user bookmarks
  your page.

- Leave the Document Type (DTD) set to XHTML 1.0 Transitional. This makes your
  HTML document XHTML-compliant.

- Choose Unicode 4.0 (UTF-8) from the Encoding drop-down menu. This specifies the
  encoding used for characters in your document.

- Make sure the Unicode Normalization Form is set to None and that Include Unicode
  Signature (BOM) is unchecked. Both settings are unnecessary for this lesson.

The Title/Encoding category allows you to title your page and/or specify the encoding used.

*The Reload button simply converts the existing document to the encoding you've chosen. It's not
necessary to click this button now.*

12 Click on the Tracing Image category in the left part of the Page Properties dialog box.
    A tracing image is a JPEG, GIF, or PNG image that you create in a separate graphics
    application, such as Adobe Photoshop or Fireworks. It is placed in the background of your
    page for you to use as a guide to recreate a desired page design.

13 Press the Browse button next to the Tracing image field. You can also type the path to your image directly into this text field.

14 In the Select Image Source dialog box, navigate to your dw02lessons folder, and inside the museum_files folder, select the file named tracing.gif, then press OK (Windows) or Choose (Mac OS).

15 Set the transparency of the tracing image to 50% by sliding the Transparency slider to the left.

Place a tracing image in the background of your page.

16 Press Apply to see the results.

17 When activated, the tracing image replaces any background image and/or color you've added to your page, but only in your Document window. Tracing images are never visible when you view your page in a browser. Highlight the path in the Tracing image text field and press the Delete key.

18 Press the Apply button to remove the tracing image and redisplay your background image.

19 Press OK to close the Page Properties dialog box.

20 Choose File > Save. Now that you've finished setting up your page properties, you'll examine your page in Dreamweaver's three different work view modes.

Work views

In this book's lessons, you'll do most of your work in the Design view, as you're taking advantage of Dreamweaver's visual page layout features. You can, however, easily access the HTML code being written as you work in the Design view, and use it to edit your pages via Dreamweaver's other work views. You'll switch views, using the Document toolbar.

The Document toolbar.

1   In the Document toolbar, note that the Design View button (⊞) is activated by default. This means you're currently working with a fully editable, visual representation of your page, similar to what the viewer would see in a browser.

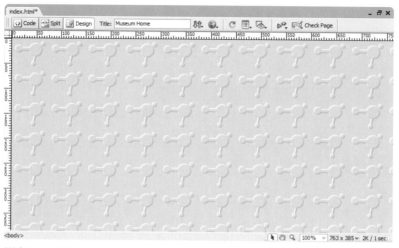

With Design View, you see your page as the viewer will see it.

2   Click on the Code View button (⊙) to switch to the Code view. Your page is now displayed in a hand-coding environment used for writing and editing HTML and other types of code, including JavaScript, PHP, and ColdFusion.

Code View shows the HTML code generated to display your page.

3 Click on the Split View button (🖾) to split your Document window between the Code and Design views. This view is a great learning tool, as it displays and highlights the HTML code generated when you make a change visually in Design mode, and vice versa.

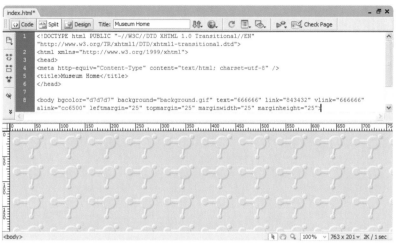

Use Split view to display your page in both modes at once.

4 Switch back to the Design view to continue this lesson.

A look at the Files panel

One of the benefits of working with local files stored in one centralized folder on your hard drive is that they are easy to manage. Dreamweaver provides the Files panel to help you manage files locally and transfer them to and from a remote server. The Files panel maintains a parallel structure between local and remote sites, copying and removing files when needed to ensure synchronicity between the two.

The default workspace in Dreamweaver displays the Files panel in the panel grouping to the right of your Document window.

When you chose to use the museum_site folder as your local root folder earlier in this lesson, Dreamweaver set up a connection to those local files via the Files panel. You should be able to see the entire contents of this folder in the Files panel now.

You have access to the complete contents of your local root folder in the Files panel.

Viewing local files

You can view local files and folders within the Files panel, whether they're associated with a Dreamweaver site or not.

1   Click on the drop-down menu in the upper-left part of the Files panel, and choose Desktop to view the current contents of your Desktop folder.

2   Choose Local Disk (C:) from this menu to access the contents of your hard drive.

3   Choose CD Drive (D:) from this menu to view the contents of an inserted CD.

4   Choose museum_site to return to your local root folder view.

Selecting and editing files

You can select, open, and/or drag HTML pages, graphics, text, and other files listed in the Files panel to your Document window for placement.

1 If it's not already open, double-click on the index.html file, located in the Files panel. The page opens for editing.

2 Click and drag the space.jpg image file from the Files panel to the index.html Document window. (If an Image Tag Accessibility Attributes window appears, press OK to close it.) The image is added to the open page.

If you have Fireworks installed on your computer, you can double-click on the space.jpg image file to open it in Fireworks for editing and/or optimizing.

3 Double-click on the exhibit_3.txt file in the Files panel to open it directly in Dreamweaver.

4 Choose Edit > Select All to select all of the text in this file.

5 Choose Edit > Copy to copy the text to the clipboard.

6 Click on the index.html tab of the Document window to return to the index page. Click on your page to the right of the image to place an insertion cursor.

7 Choose Edit > Paste. The text is added to the open page, beneath the image.

Paste the new text to your page.

Files panel options

The Files panel also offers additional controls for displaying and transferring files. Many of these controls are located in a toolbar at the top of the panel.

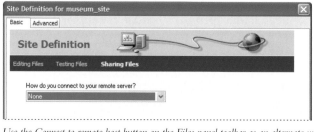

The Files panel toolbar.

1   Click on the Connect to remote host button (🕸) to connect to your remote site at any time. If you haven't specified a remote server yet, the Site Definition wizard will open and prompt you to do so. Close this window to continue.

Use the Connect to remote host button on the Files panel toolbar as an alternate way to access the Site Definition wizard.

2   Click on the Refresh button (ℂ) to refresh Dreamweaver's connection to your local root folder and any remote directories. You should use this button periodically to make sure Dreamweaver recognizes added files.

3   Click on the Get File(s) button (⬇) to copy selected files from your remote server to the local root folder. Because you haven't defined a remote server, Dreamweaver prompts you to do so now. Press No to continue.

Press No to define your remote server later.

4   Click on the Put File(s) button (⬆) to copy selected files from your local root folder to the remote server. Because you haven't defined a remote server, Dreamweaver prompts you to do so now. Press No to continue.

5   Click on the Check Out File(s) button (⬇) to transfer a copy of the file from the remote server to your local root folder, and mark the file as checked out on the server. This option is available only if you've enabled the Check In and Check Out option in the Site Definition dialog box.

6   Click on the Check In button (🔒) to transfer a copy of the file from your local root folder to the remote server, and make the file available to others for editing. This option too is available only if you've enabled the Check In and Check Out option in the Site Definition dialog box.

This option must be checked in order to check files in and out of your server.

7   Click on the Synchronize button (🔄) to synchronize files between your local and remote sites.

Changing the Files panel view

When working with a Dreamweaver site, you can reconfigure the Files panel by changing what appears in it (i.e., local or remote sites) or by expanding and collapsing the panel itself.

Site views

With the Files panel collapsed (the default), you use the Site View drop-down menu to change what's visible in the panel.

The Files panel in collapsed mode.

1 Choose Local View to display only the contents of your local root folder.

2 Choose Remote View to display only the contents of the remote server.

3 Choose Testing Server to display the content of a local server used for trying out pages prior to upload.

4 Choose Map View to display a hierarchical flowchart view of your site.

Expanding and collapsing

The Files panel is collapsed and docked within the panel group by default. You can expand the Files panel to give you a better view of local and remote sites. When the Files panel is expanded, the contents of the local root folder are on one side, and either the remote or the testing server is on the other.

1   With the Files panel collapsed, click on the Expand to show local and remote sites button (⊞) to enlarge and reconfigure the panel.

The Files panel, in expanded mode.

If you expand the Files panel while it's docked (as it is by default), you won't be able to work in the Document window, as the Files panel fills that space. Collapse the Files panel to restore access to the Document window.

2   The toolbar at the top of the expanded Files panel mimics the toolbar when the panel is collapsed, with a slightly different configuration. The view buttons in the center of the toolbar allow you to switch the view displayed on the left side of the panel. By default, the Site Files button (▤) is pushed, which lists the contents of the remote site on the left side of the panel. Press the Testing Server button (▥) to switch this view to a list of files on the testing server, if you've defined one.

3   Press the Site Map button (▦) to display a larger, hierarchical flowchart view of your site on the left side of the panel.

4   All of the other buttons in this toolbar represent the same control options available when the Files panel is collapsed. With the Files panel expanded, click on the Collapse button (▤) to reduce the panel to its default state.

Now that you've learned the basics of creating sites, setting page properties, and managing site files, you'll use these skills in Lesson 3, "Adding Text and Images."

Because you'll be using CSS in other lessons in the book, you'll want to reset Dreamweaver to use the default CSS settings which you disabled earlier in this lesson. Choose Edit > Preferences (Windows) or Dreamweaver > Preferences (Mac OS) to open the Preferences dialog box. Under the Editing options section of the General category, make sure that the Use CSS instead of HTML tags checkbox is checked, then press OK.

Self study

Using your new knowledge of site creation techniques in Dreamweaver, try some of the following tasks to build on your experience:

1   Choose Site > New Site to invoke the Site Definition wizard, and use it to create a new local site called Practice_Site. Click on the Advanced tab, and use the Local Info settings to define the folder practice_site, located in the dw02lessons folder on your desktop, as your local root folder. (Remote/testing server access is not required for this exercise.) Then explore the other categories in the Advanced tab, noting how you can use them to change your site definition in various ways.

2   Use the File > New command to create a new, blank HTML page, and save it to your PracticeSite. Then choose Modify > Page Properties to access the Page Properties dialog box, and experiment with the background, link, margin, and title options available. Finally, switch to the Code and Design view in your Document window to view the code generated by your experimentation.

3   Ensure that the Files panel is collapsed and docked, and refresh its contents. Switch back to the Design view and drag and drop the tubes.jpg image from the Files panel to add it to your page. Then double-click on the text file sticky.txt to open it directly in Dreamweaver. Copy and paste the text from the text file into your Document window, next to the image. Save the page as your home page for this site, and close the Document window.

Review

Questions

1 What characters should you avoid using when naming your site, and why?

2 How is the local root folder essential to the creation of your site?

3 Why is it advisable to set case-sensitive link checking when you're creating a site definition?

4 What happens if you've chosen both a background color and a background image for a page within your site?

5 Where can you view, select, open, and copy files to and from your local root folder, and to and from remote and/or testing servers?

Answers

1 Avoid using spaces (use underscores instead), periods, slashes, or any other unnecessary punctuation in your site name, as doing so will likely cause the server to misdirect your files.

2 It's essential that you store all of your site's resources in your local root folder to ensure that the links you set on your computer will work when your site is uploaded to a server. This is because all of the elements of your site must remain in the same relative location on the web server as they are on your hard drive for your links to work properly.

3 You should use case-sensitive link checking because you want to ensure that your links will work on a Unix server, where links are case-sensitive. If you're using a Windows or Mac OS server, this doesn't matter as much, but it's a good practice to follow the strict naming and linking conventions of a Unix system in case you ever move your site to a different server.

4 If you've added both a background color and a background image for your page, the color will appear while the image downloads, at which time the image covers the color. If there are transparent areas in the background image, the background color will show through.

5 Dreamweaver provides the Files panel to help you not only manage files locally, but also transfer them to and from a remote server. You can view, select, open, and copy files to and from your local root folder and to and from remote and/or testing servers in this panel.

Lesson 3

What you'll learn in this lesson:

- Previewing pages
- Adding text
- Understanding styles
- Creating hyperlinks
- Creating lists
- Using the Text Insert bar
- Inserting images
- Editing images

Adding Text and Images

Text and images are the building blocks of most web sites. In this lesson, you'll learn how to add text and images to web pages to create an immersive and interactive experience for your visitors.

Starting up

Before starting, make sure that your tools and panels are consistent by resetting your workspace. See "Resetting the Dreamweaver workspace" on page 3.

You will work with several files from the dw03lessons folder in this lesson. Make sure that you have loaded the dwlessons folder onto your hard drive from the supplied DVD. See "Loading lesson files" on page 3.

Before you begin, you need to create a site definition that points to the dw03lessons folder from the included DVD that contains resources you need for these lessons. Go to Site > New Site, or, for details on creating a site definition, refer to Lesson 2, "Creating a New Site."

See Lesson 3 in action!

Use the accompanying video to gain a better understanding of how to use some of the features shown in this lesson. Open the Dynamic_Learning_DW_CS3.swf file located in the Videos folder and select Lesson 3 to view the video training file for this lesson.

Typography and images on the Web

Without text and images, most web sites would be pretty sparse. Dreamweaver CS3 offers some convenient features for placing images and formatting text. In this lesson, you'll be building a web site with some photos and tips to help visitors make the most of their summer vacations.

Adding text

You should already have created a new site, using the dw03lessons folder as your root. In this section, you'll be adding a headline and formatting the text on the home.html page.

1   If it's not already open, launch Dreamweaver CS3.

2   Choose Edit > Preferences (Windows) or Dreamweaver > Preferences (Mac OS) to open the Preferences dialog box. Under the Editing options section of the General category, make sure that the Use CSS instead of HTML tags checkbox is checked, then press OK.

3   Make sure your dw03lessons site is open in the Files panel. If not, open it now.

4   Double-click on the home.html file in your Files panel to open it. Without any formatting, the text seems random and lacks purpose. First, you'll add a headline to give the first paragraph some context.

5   Click to place your cursor in front of the word *After* in the first paragraph. Type **My summer on Wyman's Pond** and press Enter (Windows) or Return (Mac OS) to create a line break.

6   Click and drag to highlight the phrase you just typed. In the Property inspector, choose Heading 1 from the Format drop-down menu. The text gets larger and becomes bold.

Use the Format drop-down menu in the Property inspector to make the selected text a level-one heading.

The paragraph and heading options in the Format drop-down menu wrap selected text in HTML tags. In this case, *My summer on Wyman's Pond* has been wrapped in an *<h1>* tag.

7   Choose Edit > Select All or use the keyboard shortcut Ctrl+A (Windows) or Command+A (Mac OS). In the Property inspector, choose Arial, Helvetica, sans-serif from the Font drop-down menu.

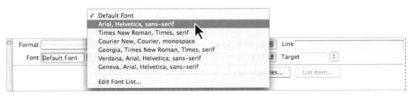

Font options in the Property inspector.

Dreamweaver allows you to format text in a way that is similar to desktop publishing and word processing applications, but there are important differences to keep in mind. Notice that Arial, Helvetica, and sans-serif are listed together as one option in the Font drop-down menu. When a web page is rendered in a browser, it uses the fonts installed on the user's computer. Assigning multiple fonts allows you to control which font is used if the person viewing your page doesn't have a specific font installed. In this case, if the user doesn't have Arial, Helvetica will be displayed instead. Sans-serif is included as the last option in case the user doesn't have Arial or Helvetica. A generic font family is listed at the end of all the options in the Font drop-down menu.

8   Deselect the text by clicking on an empty space in the Document window. Highlight the three lines below *Don't forget to bring:* and choose 14 from the Size drop-down menu in the Property inspector. You'll turn this text into a list later. For now, changing the size will help set it apart from the opening paragraph.

With the three lines of text highlighted, choose 14 from the Size drop-down menu in the Property inspector.

On the Web, font sizes are specified differently than they are in print. The numerical choices in the Size drop-down menu refer to pixels instead of points. Also, the xx-small through larger options may seem oddly generic if you are accustomed to the precision of print layout. Since web pages are displayed on a variety of monitors and browsers, relative measurements can be a useful way for designers to plan ahead for inevitable discrepancies in the rendering of pages.

9 Changing the color of type is just as easy as adjusting the font and size. Highlight *My summer on Wyman's Pond* and click on the Text Color button to the right of the Size drop-down menu. When the Swatches panel appears, select the red labeled #990000.

10 Choose File > Save. Keep this file open for the next part of this lesson.

Understanding styles

After styling all that text so easily, you may be tempted to forget that you're working on a web page. In the Design view, Dreamweaver keeps all of the coding behind the scenes. This can be a convenient way to work, but it's important to remember that every change you make in the Design view creates or modifies code. When you changed the font, size, and color of the main headline, you created CSS code. In the next exercise, you'll open up the hood and tinker with the nuts and bolts of your web page.

1 Click on the Split button ( ) in the Document toolbar to open up the Split view.

2 Highlight the paragraph beneath *My summer on Wyman's Pond* in the Design view. The paragraph appears highlighted in the Code view as well.

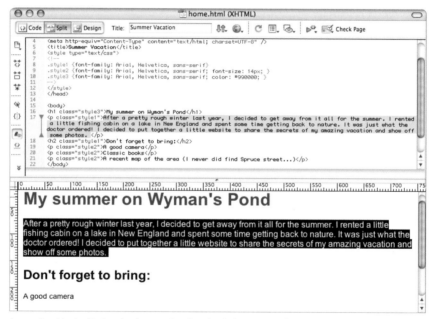

Items selected in the Design view become selected in the Code view as well.

3   In the Property inspector, choose 18 from the Size drop-down menu. Notice that a number of changes were automatically made in the Code view.

```
3   <head>
4   <meta http-equiv="Content-Type" content="text/html; charset=UTF-8" />
5   <title>Summer Vacation</title>
6   <style type="text/css">
7   <!--
8   .style1 {font-family: Arial, Helvetica, sans-serif}
9   .style2 {font-family: Arial, Helvetica, sans-serif; font-size: 14px; }
10  .style3 font-family: Arial, Helvetica, sans-serif; color: #330000; }
11  .style4 {font-family: Arial, Helvetica, sans-serif; font-size: 18px; }
12
13  </style>
14  </head>
15
16  <body>
17  <h1 class="style3">My summer on Wyman's Pond</h1>
18  <p class="style4">After a pretty rough winter last year, I decided to get away from it all for the summer. I rented
    a little fishing cabin on a lake in New England and spent some time getting back to nature. It was just what the
    doctor ordered! I decided to put together a little website to share the secrets of my amazing vacation and show off
    some photos. </p>
19  <h2 class="style1">Don't forget to bring:</h2>
20  <p class="style2">A good camera</p>
21  <p class="style2">Classic books</p>
22  <p class="style2">A recent map of the area (I never did find Spruce street...)</p>
23  </body>
24  </html>
25
```

Changes made in the Design view are immediately reflected in the Code view.

In the *<body>* section, *class="style4"* has been added to the opening *<p>* tag of the highlighted paragraph. As shown in the image above, a new CSS rule has been written for you. The bright pink text that reads *.style4* refers to the class assigned to the *<p>* tag below. The text at the end of line 11 that reads *font-size: 18px;}* is a direct result of selecting 18 from the Size drop-down menu in the Property inspector.

Next, you'll add a little bit of code to see how the Design view and Code view interact with each other.

4   Click between the semicolon and the curly brace following 18px. Enter the following text, making sure to include the colon, semi-colon, and pound sign:

```
color: #003366;
```

When you're finished, click the Refresh button in the Property inspector. The paragraph changes from black to blue.

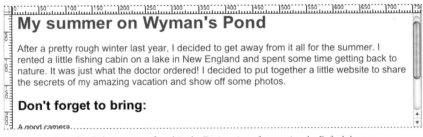

My summer on Wyman's Pond

After a pretty rough winter last year, I decided to get away from it all for the summer. I rented a little fishing cabin on a lake in New England and spent some time getting back to nature. It was just what the doctor ordered! I decided to put together a little website to share the secrets of my amazing vacation and show off some photos.

Don't forget to bring:

A good camera

Changes made in the Code view are reflected in the Design view after pressing the Refresh button.

5   Click inside the paragraph in the Design view. The text field to the right of the Text Color button displays the hexadecimal value that you specified in step 4. The Style drop-down menu above and to the left displays the name of the style applied to the currently selected text. Notice that besides indicating the name of the style, this menu gives you a preview of the style's appearance.

Working in the Split view can be a great way to learn about hand-coding without diving in head-first. Even if you're not quite comfortable editing code, keeping an eye on the code Dreamweaver writes for you can give you a better understanding of how things like CSS affect your web pages.

6   Choose File > Save. Keep this file open for the next part of this lesson.

Previewing pages in a web browser

Viewing your pages in the Design view is helpful, but visitors to your site will be using a web browser to access your site. In Lesson 1, "Dreamweaver CS3 Jumpstart," you learned how browsers use HTML code to render a page. Unfortunately, not every browser renders HTML code exactly the same way, so it's important to test-drive your pages in a number of different browsers to check for inconsistencies and basic functionality.

Next, you'll use Dreamweaver's Preview in Browser feature to see how the Summer Vacation site looks in a web browser.

1   With home.html open in Dreamweaver, choose File > Preview in Browser and select a browser from the available options. This list varies, depending on the browsers you have installed on your hard drive.

Preview in Browser allows you to see how your page would be rendered by a selected browser.

The options found under File > Preview in Browser can be customized by choosing File > Preview in Browser > Edit Browser List.

2   When home.html opens in the browser of your choice, look for differences between the Design view preview and the version rendered by your browser. At this stage there shouldn't be anything too surprising, but there may be subtle differences in spacing and font weight.

It's important to remember that pages might be rendered differently depending on your visitor's browser. As you become more skilled at styling your pages with CSS, you'll learn how to compensate for some of these discrepancies.

3   Close the browser window and return to Dreamweaver CS3 for the next part of this lesson.

Understanding hyperlinks

When people visit a web site, they usually expect to see more than one page. Imagine trying to shop for a new book by your favorite author on a site that consisted of nothing more than a single order form with every book offered by a retailer like *Amazon.com*. This might seem absurd, but without hyperlinks you wouldn't have much choice.

Hyperlinks make the Web a truly interactive environment. They allow the user to freely navigate throughout a web site or jump from one site to another. There are a number of ways to create links in Dreamweaver, but before you get started, you should be aware of some fundamentals.

Links rely on directory paths to locate files. This is simply a description of a file's location that can be understood by a computer. A classic, real-world example is addresses. If you wanted to send a letter to your friend Sally in Florida, you would have to specify the state, city, street, and house where Sally can be found. If Sally lived at 123 Palm Street in Orlando, the path would be:

Florida/Orlando/123 Palm Street/Sally

This simply means that inside Florida, inside Orlando, in the house numbered 123 on a street named Palm Street, you can find a person named Sally. Hyperlinks follow the same logic:

www.somewebsitesomewhere.com/photos/mydog.jpg

This URL address is a link to a JPEG image named mydog.jpg which is inside a folder named *photos* on a web site named somewebsitesomewhere.com.

Creating hyperlinks

Later in this lesson, you'll be creating a gallery page to showcase some of those summer vacation photos mentioned in the main paragraph. Before you work on that page, you'll link it to the home page by creating a hyperlink.

1   Click on the Design button in the Document toolbar to collapse the Split view.

2   In the main paragraph, highlight the word *photos* at the very end of the paragraph.

3   In the Property inspector, type **gallery.html** in the Link text field. Press Enter (Windows) or Return (Mac OS). The highlighted word *photos* automatically becomes underlined.

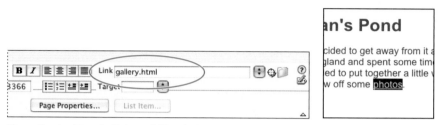

*Type **gallery.html** into the Link text field in the Property inspector.*

4   Choose File > Save and then File > Preview in Browser.

5   Click on the new *photos* link. The gallery page appears in your browser window.

Now visitors can easily navigate to the gallery page, but what happens when they want to go back to the home page? It looks like you'll need another link.

6   Go back to Dreamweaver and double-click on gallery.html in the Files panel. Click to the right of the word *Clouds* and press Enter/Return to create a new line. Choose Insert > Hyperlink to open the Hyperlink dialog box.

The Hyperlink dialog box is one of the many ways to create a link in Dreamweaver. It offers all of the options found in the Property inspector, with a few additions.

7   Enter **Home** in the Text field.

The Hyperlink dialog box is one of the many ways to create links in Dreamweaver.

8   Click on the Browse button to the right of the Link text field to open the Select File dialog box. The dw03lessons folder you defined as the root for this site should be selected for you by default. If not, locate it on your hard drive. Select home.html and press OK (Windows) or Choose (Mac OS).

9   Press OK in the Hyperlink dialog box. A link to home.html has been created for you, using the text entered into the Text field in the Hyperlink dialog box. Choose File > Save and keep this file open for the next part of this lesson.

Relative vs. absolute hyperlinks

After reading about the fundamentals of hyperlinks and directory paths a few pages ago, you may have been surprised by the simplicity of linking home.html and gallery.html. Instead of entering a long directory path in the Link text fields, you merely typed the name of the file. This kind of link is called a relative link. Let's go back to the address example to see how this works.

Remember Sally from Orlando? Imagine you were already standing on Palm Street, where she lives. If you called her for directions to her house, she probably wouldn't begin by telling you how to get to Florida. At this point, all you need is a house number. Relative links work the same way. Since home.html and gallery.html both reside in the dw03lessons folder, you don't need to tell the browser where to find this folder.

Now you'll create an absolute link that will allow visitors to access the Adobe web site to learn more about Dreamweaver CS3—maybe they'll want to make their own summer vacation web sites.

1   Click on the home.html tab above the Document toolbar to bring the home page forward. Create a new line at the bottom of the page after text that reads *(I never did find Spruce Street...)* and type **This page was created with Adobe Dreamweaver**.

2   Highlight the words *Adobe Dreamweaver* and click the Hyperlink button in the Common tab of the Insert bar.

The Hyperlink button in the Insert bar is another convenient way to create links.

3   The Hyperlink dialog box opens. Notice that Adobe Dreamweaver has been entered into the Text field for you. In the Link field, enter the text **http://www.adobe. com/products/dreamweaver/index.html**. Make sure to include the colon and the appropriate number of forward slashes.

The absolute link http://www.adobe.com/products/dreamweaver/index.html instructs the browser to find a web site named adobe.com on the World Wide Web. Then the browser looks for file named index.html inside a folder named dreamweaver inside a folder named products.

4   Choose _blank from the Target drop-down menu. Choosing the _blank option will cause the hyperlink to the Adobe web site to open in a new, blank browser window.

Set the target window for the hyperlink to open in a blank browser window or tab.

5   Press OK to close the Hyperlink dialog box. Choose File > Save, then File > Preview in Browser or press the Preview/Debug in browser button (◉) in the Document toolbar.

6   Click on the *Adobe Dreamweaver* text. Unlike the gallery and home links you created earlier, this link causes your browser to open a new tab or window.

Linking to an email address

Absolute and relative links can be used to access web pages, but it's also possible to link to an email address. Instead of opening a new web page, an email link opens up the default mail program on a visitor's computer and populates the address field with the address you specify when creating the link. As you may imagine, this kind of link can work differently depending on how your visitors have configured their computers.

In the last part of this lesson, you gave the visitor a link to some information on Dreamweaver. Now you'll link them to an email address where they can get some information on learning Dreamweaver from the folks who wrote this book.

1   On the home page, create a new line beneath the link to Adobe Dreamweaver and type **Contact info@aquent.com for classes on using Adobe Dreamweaver CS3**.

2   Highlight the text *info@aquent.com* and click the Email Link button (✉) in the Insert bar.

3   The Email Link dialog box opens with both fields automatically populated. Press OK.

The Email Link dialog box allows you to link to an email address.

Creating lists

Bulleted lists may be familiar to you if you have worked with word processing or desktop publishing applications. Lists are a helpful way to present information to a reader without the formal constraints of a paragraph. They are especially important on the Web. Studies indicate that people typically skim web pages instead of reading them from beginning to end. Creating lists will make it easier for your visitors to get the most from your web site without sifting through many paragraphs of text.

1   On the home.html page, click and drag to highlight the three lines below *Don't forget to bring:*.

2   Click the Unordered List button (≔) in the Property inspector. The highlighted text becomes indented, and a bullet point is placed at the beginning of each line.

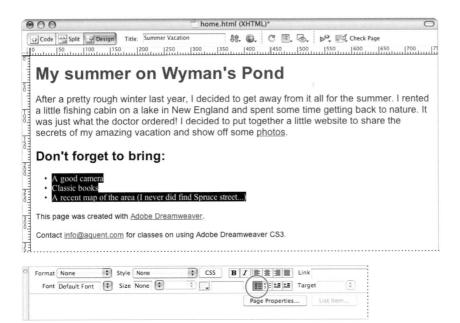

Use the Unordered list button in the Property inspector to create a bulleted list.

3   Click the Ordered List button (≔) to the right of the Unordered List button. The bullets change to sequential numbers. Like most things in Dreamweaver, additional options are available for lists.

4   Choose Text > List > Properties to open the List Properties dialog box. If it is not already selected, choose Bulleted List from the List type drop-down menu. The Numbered List and Bulleted List options in the List type drop-down menu allow you to switch between ordered and unordered lists.

5   From the Style drop-down menu, choose Square. This changes the default circular bullets to square bullets. Press OK to exit the List Properties dialog box.

Change the bullet style to square in the List Properties dialog box.

6   You may have noticed that the three lines of text in your list have lost their style. With all three lines still highlighted, select style1 from the Style drop-down menu in the Property inspector. Using the Style drop-down menu to quickly apply previously defined styles to items on the page does more than save time. It also helps ensure consistency.

7   Choose File > Save. Leave this file open for the next part of this lesson.

Using the Text Insert bar

There are a number of ways to format text in Dreamweaver. One method we haven't explored yet is the Text Insert bar. Since most of the options available in the Text Insert bar are also available in the Property inspector, you may find it more convenient to use the Property inspector for common tasks. However, you should be aware of the Character menu located in the Text Insert bar. One of the most common items in the Character menu used on the Web is the copyright symbol ©. You will now insert a copyright notification at the bottom of your Summer Vacation page.

1   Click to the left of the sentence *This page was created with Adobe Dreamweaver* and type **2007 Summer Vacation Designs**.

2   Open the Text Insert bar by clicking on the Text tab in the Insert bar.

The Text Insert bar offers many of the same options as the Property inspector for formatting text, with a few notable extras.

3 Click to the left of *2007* to place the cursor back at the beginning of the line. Click the arrow to the right of the Character button (📇) to open the Character menu, and select Copyright.

The Copyright symbol can be inserted from the Character menu.

4 Highlight the last two lines on your page, beginning with the newly inserted copyright symbol and ending with *Adobe Dreamweaver CS3*. Between the Copyright notice and the links you added earlier, these lines are becoming a bit of an eyesore. Layout considerations such as headers and footers will be discussed throughout the following lessons in this book, but for now you can use the Text Insert bar to italicize these lines to set them apart from the rest of the text on your page.

5 Click the Italic button on the left side of the Text Insert bar. Choose File > Save.

Inserting images

Images are an essential part of most web pages. Just as lists make content friendlier and more accessible, images help to give your visitors the rich, immersive experience that they've come to expect on the Web.

Image resolution

While it is possible to resize images with Dreamweaver, it's generally not a good idea. Specifying the width and height of an image in the Property inspector changes the display size of the image, but it does not resample the image the way a graphic processing application like Photoshop will. The difference may not seem immediately apparent, since a properly resized image may appear identical to an improperly resized image. Unfortunately, visitors to your web site will be the first to notice an oversight in resizing your images.

If you've ever downloaded a large file from the Web, you've probably had the experience of waiting impatiently while a progress bar inches its way across the screen like a glacier. This may be an exaggeration, but the fact is that every time you access a page on the Internet, you are downloading all of the contents of that page. Images will always significantly increase the size of an HTML file, so it's important to properly resize them before including them on your site.

Image formats

The two most common image formats on the Web are JPEG and GIF. While an exhaustive description of how each of these formats compress data is beyond the scope of this book (not to mention most people's attention span), a general overview can help you avoid some common pitfalls.

The JPEG format was created by a committee named the Joint Photographic Experts Group. Its express purpose is to compress photographic images. Specifically, it uses lossy compression to reduce the size of a file. This means that it selectively discards information. When you save a JPEG, you decide how much information you are willing to sacrifice by selecting a quality level. A high-quality image preserves more information and results in a larger file size. A low-quality image discards more information, but produces a smaller file size. The goal is to reduce file size as much as possible without creating distortion and artifacts.

Since JPEGs were designed to handle photographic images, they can significantly reduce the size of images containing gradients and soft edges, without producing noticeable degradation. However, reproducing sharp edges and solid planes of color often requires a higher quality setting.

The GIF format was created by CompuServe. GIF is an acronym for Graphics Interchange Format. Unlike the JPEG format, GIFs do not use lossy compression. Instead, GIFs rely on a maximum of 256 colors to reduce the size of images. This means that images with a limited number of colors can be reproduced without degradation. Logos, illustrations, and line drawings are well-suited to this format. Unlike JPEGs, GIFs excel at reproducing sharp edges and solid planes of color. However, since photographic elements such as gradients and soft edges require a large number of colors to appear convincing, GIF images containing these elements look choppy and posterized.

Creating a simple gallery page

Now that you have a better understanding of the types of images that are appropriate for using on your web site, it's time to build the gallery that we linked to the home page earlier in this lesson.

1   Double-click on gallery.html in the Files panel. Place your cursor after the word *Clouds* and press Enter (Windows) or Return (Mac OS) to create a new line.

2   Choose Insert > Image. The Select Image Source dialog box appears. Navigate to the dw03lessons folder that you chose as your root folder at the beginning of the lesson and open the images folder. Select clouds1.jpg and press OK (Windows) or Choose (Mac OS).

3 When the Image Tag Accessibility Attributes dialog box appears, enter **Clouds at sunset** in the Alternate text field. Press OK.

The Alternate text field in the Image Tag Accessibility Attributes dialog box corresponds to the Alt attribute of an <img> tag. Including a description of the inserted image in this field is not technically necessary, but it is good practice. It provides information about the images to visually impaired visitors using screen readers. Also, Alt text is displayed in place of images on some handheld devices and browsers with images disabled.

4 Click on the Split view button (⊞) in the Document toolbar to view the code that was written by Dreamweaver when you inserted clouds1.jpg. An <img> tag was created, with four attributes. The src attribute is a relative link to the .jpg file in your images folder. The alt attribute is the alternate text you specified in the last step. The width and height attributes are simply the width and height of the image.

Dreamweaver creates an <img> tag with a number of attributes when you insert an image.

5 Double-click on the images folder in the Files panel to reveal its contents. Click and drag clouds2.jpg to the right of the clouds1 image in the Design view. When the Image Tag Accessibility Attributes dialog box pops up, enter **Clouds over Wachusett Mountain** into the Alternate text field. Press OK. Notice that a new <img> tag appears in the Code view.

6 In the Property inspector, type **5** into the Border text field and press Enter (Windows) or Return (Mac OS). A border attribute is added to the new <img> tag in the Code view and a black, 5-pixel-wide border appears in the Design view.

7 Click on the clouds1 image in the Design view and type 5 in the Border text field in the Property inspector to give this image a matching border.

Adding a border attribute to an <img> tag with the Property inspector is a quick way to create a border, but it doesn't give you as much control or flexibility as a CSS-generated border. In Lesson 4, "Styling Your Page with CSS," you'll learn about the advantages of stylesheets.

8 Click to the right of the clouds2 image to place your cursor, and press Enter/Return to create a new line. To add the last image, you'll use the Insert bar. Collapse the Split view by clicking the Design view button in the Document toolbar. Click the Common tab in the Insert bar to access the Images drop-down menu.

9 Open the Images drop-down menu by clicking on the black arrow next to the Image button (🖻), then select Image.

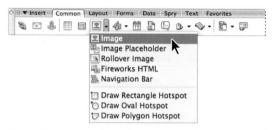

Choose Image from the Images drop-down menu in the Common tab of the Insert bar.

10 When the Select Image Source dialog box appears, navigate to the dw03lessons folder that you specified as the root for your Summer Vacation site, and select clouds3.jpg from the images folder inside. Press OK (Windows) or Choose (Mac OS). Enter **Stormy clouds** in the Alternate text field of the Image Tag Accessibility Attributes dialog box, then press OK.

11 In the Property inspector, enter **5** into the Border text field and press Enter/Return. By default everything on the page is aligned to the left. You'll learn how to build layouts using CSS and tables in the coming chapters, but for now, you can use the alignment options in the Property inspector to quickly give the page a little symmetry.

12 Choose Edit > Select All or use the keyboard shortcut Ctrl+A (Windows) or Command+A (Mac OS) to select everything on the page. In the Property inspector, click the Align Center button. Choose File > Save and leave gallery.html open for the next part of this lesson.

Linking images

Often, gallery pages on the Web contain small thumbnail images that are linked to larger, high resolution images. Like many web conventions, there are practical reasons for this format. Since all of the images on a gallery page must be downloaded by visitors in order to view the page, small images are necessary to keep the page from taking too long to load. Additionally, a user's screen isn't large enough to accommodate multiple large pictures at one time. Giving your visitor a way to preview which pictures they would like to see at a larger scale makes the page more usable and more interactive.

1 In gallery.html, click on the clouds1.jpg image to select it. In the Property inspector, type **images/clouds1_large.jpg** into the Link text field. Press Enter (Windows) or Return (Mac OS). The 5-pixel border around the image turns blue. This border indicates that the image is a link.

2 Click on the clouds2.jpg image to select it. For this image, you'll use Dreamweaver's Point to File feature to create a link. In the Property inspector, locate the Point to File icon (☉) next to the Link text field. Click and drag this icon into the Files panel. A blue arrow with a target at the end will follow your cursor. As you hover over items in the Files panel, they become highlighted. Release the mouse while hovering over the clouds2_large.jpg file.

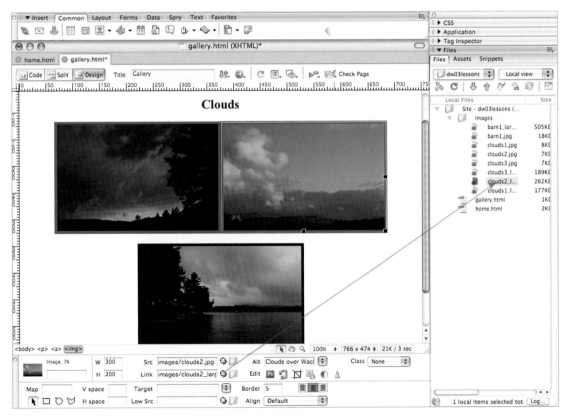

With the Point to File feature, you can simply click and drag to create a link.

3   Select the clouds3.jpg image and use the Point to File icon to link it to clouds3_large.jpg.

4   Choose File > Save and then File > Preview in Browser. Click on the thumbnails to see the large versions of each image. You'll have to use your browser's back button to get back to the gallery page, since you didn't select _blank from the target drop-down menu in the Property inspector.

Using Image Placeholders

Often, you will want to start building web pages before you have all of the final content available. This happens regularly in professional situations where different people may be responsible for preparing images, writing copy, and creating the site. Next, you'll build a second section in the gallery.html page that will eventually include a collection of barn pictures.

1   In Dreamweaver, on the gallery.html page, place your cursor to the right of the clouds3.jpg image and press Enter (Windows) or Return (Mac OS) to create a new line.

2   Type **Barns** and choose Heading 2 from the Format drop-down menu in the Property inspector. Press Enter/Return to create a line below the Barns heading.

3   Choose Insert > Image Objects > Image Placeholder. When the Image Placeholder dialog box appears, enter **barn1** in the Name text field, **300** in the Width text field, and **200** in the Height text field. Leave the Color set to the default and the Alternative text field blank. In this case, you don't know which image will eventually replace the Image Placeholder, so it's not possible to write a description. Press OK to exit the dialog box.

A gray box with the name barn1 appears. This box is simply an *<img>* tag with an empty src attribute. Now you'll insert an image into the placeholder by setting the src attribute in the Property inspector.

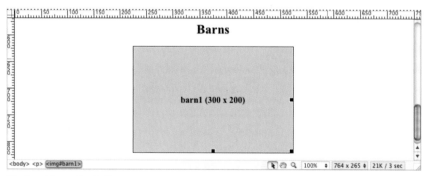

The barn1 Image Placeholder.

4   With the barn1 image placeholder selected, enter **images/barn1.jpg** into the Src text field in the Property inspector. Press Enter/Return. The barn1 JPEG replaces the gray box.

5   In the Property inspector, enter **5** into the Border text field and use the Point to File icon (☺) to link barn1.jpg to barn1_large.jpg. Choose File > Save and leave this file open for the next part of this lesson.

Editing images

Although it's best to make adjustments to your images using a professional graphics editing program like Adobe Photoshop, sometimes that's not an option. Dreamweaver offers a number of editing options, including an Edit link that allows you to quickly open a selected image in the graphics editor of your choice.

The Edit button can be customized in the File Types/Editors section of the Preferences dialog box. You can use this section to add or subtract programs from the list of available editors, and set programs as the primary choice for handling specific file extensions.

Adjusting brightness and contrast

Now you'll use Dreamweaver's Brightness and Contrast button to lighten up the clouds3 image on your gallery page.

1   Click on the clouds3.jpg image in gallery.html to select it, then click on the Brightness and Contrast button (◑) in the Property inspector.

Select the Brightness and Contrast button in the Property inspector.

A warning box appears, indicating that you are about to make permanent changes to the selected image. Press OK.

2   When the Brightness/Contrast dialog box appears, drag the Brightness slider to 20 or type **20** in the text field to the right of the slider.

3   Drag the Contrast slider to 10 or type **10** in the text field to the right of the slider. Press OK.

Resizing images

Next, you'll see how Dreamweaver allows you to quickly optimize images; you'll change the size and quality of the barn1.jpg image. But before you make any permanent changes, you'll duplicate this image in the Files panel. It's good practice to save copies of your image files before making permanent changes. Later, you'll use this backup copy to undo your changes.

1   In the Files panel, click on the barn1.jpg file to select it. From the Files panel menu, select Edit > Duplicate. A new file named Copy of barn1.jpg appears at the bottom of the list of files inside the images folder.

2   Click on the barn1.jpg image in the Document window to make sure it is selected, then click the Optimize button (🗗) in the Property inspector. The Image Preview dialog box opens; it offers many of the features included in the Adobe Photoshop CS3 Save For Web & Devices dialog box.

3   Make sure that the Options tab in the top-left corner is selected. Click on the black arrow to the right of the Quality text field and drag the slider down to 30%. The barn1.jpg image in the preview window becomes pixelated. As discussed earlier, a lower JPEG quality setting will reduce file size at the cost of image clarity.

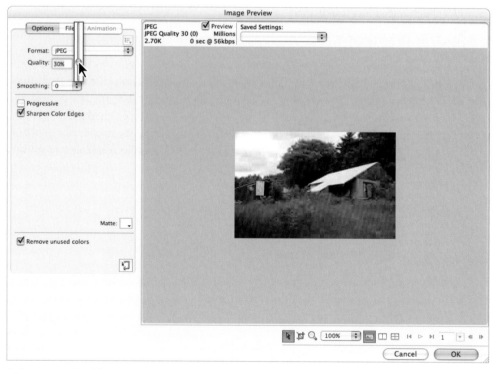

Reducing the quality of the barn1 image causes pixelation.

4   Drag the quality slider back up to 77% and click the File tab in the top-left corner of the dialog box.

5   In the Scale section, drag the % slider to 60%. The barn1.jpg image in the preview window shrinks; its new dimensions are reflected in the W and H text fields.

6   Press OK to exit the Image Preview dialog box. The barn1.jpg image is reduced to 60% of its original size.

7   Choose Edit > Undo. The W and H text fields in the Property inspector indicate that the image has been changed back to its original dimensions, but something is obviously amiss with the image.

The barn1 image has been permanently altered.

This is where careless adjustments can get you into trouble. When you use Dreamweaver's built-in image editing features, you're making permanent adjustments to the linked images. In this case, the original barn1 image was 300 pixels wide and 200 pixels high. When you used the Optimize button to adjust the size, you saved over the original file with a barn1 image that is only 180 pixels wide and 120 pixels high. Although Dreamweaver will let you display the new image at the original dimensions, the information discarded upon saving the new version cannot be retrieved.

Updating images

Since the changes made to the barn1 image cannot be undone, you'll need to use the duplicate you made earlier. To swap out the image, you'll simply change the src attribute, using the Property inspector. But first it's a good idea to rename the duplicate image to get rid of the spaces in the file name.

1 Right-click (Windows) or Ctrl+click (Mac OS) the file named Copy of barn1.jpg in the Files panel and choose Edit > Rename. Type **barn1_copy.jpg** and press Enter (Windows) or Return (Mac OS).

Although file names including spaces will usually work just fine on your home computer, many web servers aren't designed to handle them. To prevent broken links, it is common practice to use the underscore or hyphen characters in place of spaces when naming files for the Web.

2 Click on the barn1.jpg image in the Design view to select it. In the Property inspector, highlight the text that reads *images/barn1.jpg* in the Src text field.

3 Type **images/barn1_copy.jpg** and press Enter/Return. The distorted barn1.jpg image is replaced with the copy you made earlier.

4 Choose File > Save.

Self study

To practice styling text with the Property inspector, create styles for the text in gallery.html. If you're feeling bold, try copying the CSS styles from the Code view. Remember to add the appropriate class attributes to tags you wish to style.

To make the thumbnail links in gallery.html open in a new window, set their target attributes to _blank in the Property inspector.

Try adding your own photos to the gallery page. Remember to be careful when resizing them!

Review

Questions

1   Of the two most common image formats used on the Web, which is better suited for saving a logo?

2   If an inserted image is too small, can you make it larger by increasing its size in the Property inspector?

3   How do you insert a copyright © symbol in Dreamweaver?

Answers

1   Since logos usually contain a lot of hard edges and solid areas of color, the GIF format is the most appropriate choice.

2   It is possible to increase the display size of an image, but doing so will reduce image quality.

3   Use the Characters drop-down menu in the Text tab of the Insert bar.

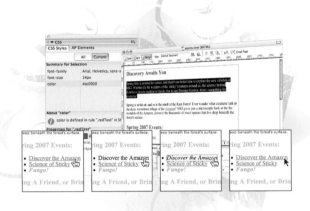

What you'll learn in this lesson:

- Introducing CSS (Cascading Style Sheets)

- Comparing CSS and *<font>* tags

- Using the CSS Styles panel

- Creating Class and Tag styles

Styling Your Pages with CSS

Many years ago, creating a beautiful web page required lots of work, using the limited capabilities of HTML tags. The introduction of CSS (Cascading Style Sheets) changed the way pages are created, giving designers an extraordinary amount of control over page formatting, as well as the ability to freely position content anywhere on a page. In this lesson, you'll learn how to take your pages further with CSS.

Starting up

Before starting, make sure that your tools and panels are consistent by resetting your workspace. See "Resetting the Dreamweaver workspace" on page 3.

You will work with several files from the dw04lessons folder in this lesson. Make sure that you have loaded the dwlessons folder onto your hard drive from the supplied DVD. See "Loading lesson files" on page 3.

Before you begin, you need to create a site definition that points to the dw04lessons folder from the included DVD that contains resources you need for these lessons. Go to Site > New Site, or, for details on creating a site definition, refer to Lesson 2, "Creating a New Site."

See Lesson 4 in action!

Use the accompanying video to gain a better understanding of how to use some of the features shown in this lesson. Open the Dynamic_Learning_DW_CS3.swf file located in the Videos folder and select Lesson 4 to view the video training file for this lesson.

What are Cascading Style Sheets (CSS)?

CSS is a simple language that works alongside HTML to apply formatting to content in web pages, such as text, images, tables, and form elements. Developed by the World Wide Web Consortium (W3C), CSS creates rules, or style instructions, that items on your page follow; you can write these rules inline (as part of a tag), directly into your page, or as an external file that can be linked to any number of HTML pages. The term cascading refers to the fact that you can apply multiple style sheets to the same web page.

A style sheet is a collection of CSS rules; typically, rules that belong to a specific project, theme, or section are grouped together, but you can group rules in any way you want. You can place style sheets directly within your page using the *<style>* tag or in an external .css file that is linked to your document with the *<link>* tag. A single page or set of pages can use several style sheets at once.

You can apply CSS rules selectively to any number of items on a page, or use them to modify the appearance of an existing HTML tag. Whenever or wherever you apply a rule, that rule remains linked to its original definition in the style sheet, so any changes you make to the rule will automatically carry over to all items to which the rule has been applied.

Each CSS rule is composed of one or more properties, such as color, style, and font size, which dictate how an item is formatted when the rule is applied. A single CSS rule can comprise several properties, just as a single style sheet can comprise multiple CSS rules. Dreamweaver's CSS Styles panel lets you easily view and modify any of these properties and change the appearance of your page in real time.

This sample rule is composed of three properties that control the color, typeface, and size of any text to which it's applied:

```
.myCoolText {
    color: red;
    font-family: Arial,Helvetica,Sans-serif;
    font-size: 12px;
}
```

Here is the result of the preceding code snippet:

This is some text that's been styled with CSS.

CSS-styled text shown in the Design view.

CSS rules can affect properties as simple as typeface, size, and color, and as complex as positioning and visibility. Dreamweaver uses CSS as the primary method of styling page text and elements, and its detailed CSS Styles panel makes it possible to create and manage styles at any point during a project.

A little bit of ancient history: when *<font>* tags roamed the Earth

Before CSS came along, you styled text on a page using the *<font>* tag; you could wrap this limited but easy-to-use tag around any paragraph, phrase, or tidbit of text to apply color, or set the font size and typeface. Although it worked well enough most of the time, the *<font>* tag was a one-shot deal. Once you applied it, that tag's job was done and you had to use a new *<font>* tag to style another piece of text somewhere else, even if the color, size, and typeface values were exactly the same.

1   In your Files panel, locate and double-click the HTML file named FontTagList.html to open it in the Document window.

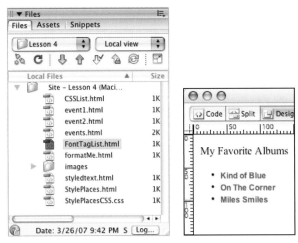

A bulleted list, formatted behind the scenes with HTML <font> tags.

2   Press the Code button (⚙) in the Document toolbar at the top of the Document window. Notice that the *<font>* tag is used to style the items in the bulleted list.

Here, a <font> tag is used to format each bullet point. If you add more bullet points, you'll need to use more <font> tags to keep the style of those bullets consistent with the others.

As you can see, there's a lot of repetition in this code.

3   Press the Design view button () on the Document toolbar. Position your cursor at the end of the last bullet, then press Enter (Windows) or Return (Mac OS) key to add a new bullet point and type **Birth of the Cool**. You'll see that the text reverts to the default typeface, size, and color. You'll have to add a new *<font>* tag with the same attributes as the others to get it to match. If you want to change any attribute for any bullet point, you'll have to adjust each tag so that the bullets match. Unfortunately, each tag exists in its own little world and HTML can't relate them to each other in any way.

You may lose the formatting between bullet points when using <font> tags.

4   Choose File > Save to save your work, then choose File > Close.

The dawn of CSS

CSS introduces a new level of control and flexibility beyond *<font>* tags, allowing for common formatting across one or all pages in a web site. One method of creating CSS rules involves creating tag- or element-based style rules. This type of rule alters the appearance of an existing HTML tag, so the tag and any content that appears within it always appear formatted in a specific way. Instead of having to add a *<font>* tag around the contents of each new bullet point in a list, it would be easier for you to tell the HTML tags used to create lists that bullet point items should always be formatted a certain way.

1   Locate and double-click the file named CSSList.html from the Files panel to open it.

2   Press the Design view button (▦) from the Document toolbar. The list that appears onscreen, unlike the one you saw in the previous example, is formatted without the use of *<font>* tags, and uses only CSS.

3   Position your cursor after the last bullet point and press the Enter (Windows) or Return (Mac OS) key to create a new bullet point. Type in **Birth of the Cool**. The new text matches the bullet points above it.

4   Press Enter/Return again to add a fifth bullet point, and type **The Columbia Years**.

No matter how many bullet points you add, the formatting is applied automatically every time.

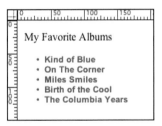

Additional bullet points are formatted like the others.

5   Select Code view at the top of the Document window so that you can see what's happening behind the scenes:

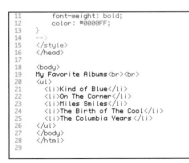

Tags are not used to format this list.

What you'll notice is the absence of any formatting tags; it's almost as though the list knows how it's supposed to format each new bullet point. That is because at the top of the page, a CSS rule is telling all list items in the page how they should appear.

6 Scroll to the top of the page and you'll see the code that makes this possible:

```
<style type="text/css">
<!--
li {font-family: Arial, Helvetica, sans-serif;
    font-size: 13px;
    font-weight: bold;
    color: #0000FF;
}
-->
</style>
```

Formatting rules for color, weight, size, and typeface are assigned directly to the *<li>* tag, which creates new bullet points in an HTML list. It's almost like a dress code for all *<li>* tags; they know that when they are used on the page, they must look a certain way. Best of all, if you need to modify their appearance, you don't have to go through every *<li>* tag in your document and modify *<font>* tags or attributes; just make your changes to that single style rule at the top of the page.

7 Choose File > Save to save your work, then choose File > Close.

How do you create CSS rules in Dreamweaver?

You create CSS rules and, in turn, style sheets, in one of three ways in Dreamweaver:

Using the CSS Styles panel: You can use Dreamweaver's CSS Styles panel to create new rules and style sheets that you can place directly within one or more pages in your site. You can easily modify rules directly from the CSS Styles panel. Furthermore, you can selectively apply rules from several places, including the Style or Class menu on the Property inspector, or the tag selector at the bottom of the Document window.

Directly from the Property inspector: Whenever you format text directly on your page using the Property inspector, Dreamweaver saves your settings as a new, named rule in your document. You can then reapply the rule as many times as you need to by using the Property inspector or tag selector. Rules that Dreamweaver creates appear in your CSS panel, where you can easily modify or rename them.

CSS styles are automatically created when you format text with the Property inspector.

In the Code view: Experienced coders can add style rules and style sheets directly in the Code view, using the *<style>* tag. You can apply rules in the Code view by using the class attribute with most HTML tags, or in the Design view, using the Property inspector or tag selector. You also can create external style sheets, or .css files, from the Welcome Screen or by choosing File > New, and editing them in the Code view in the Document window.

The first time you create a CSS rule in a page, Dreamweaver creates a new style sheet; any rules you create afterward will be added to that same style sheet.

Where are style sheets defined?

A style sheet is a collection of rules, and a single style sheet can control an entire page or an entire web site. As you create new CSS rules, or styles, they are added to an existing style sheet—if one doesn't exist, Dreamweaver creates a new one for you. You can define style sheets in three different places. To see the differences between these locations, locate and double-click the file named StylePlaces.html in the Files panel.

Although all three lines of text shown on this page appear identical, each one is formatted with a style sheet defined in a different location:

Inline: An inline style is a set of CSS properties defined directly in an HTML tag using the style attribute. These are slightly less common because you can't reuse them, which defeats the purpose of using style sheets in the first place. Look at StylePlaces.html in the Code view, and you'll notice that the style rules are written directly around the text, using the style attribute within a *<span>* tag.

Inline styles are useful when an internal or external style sheet may not be available, such as in an HTML-based email.

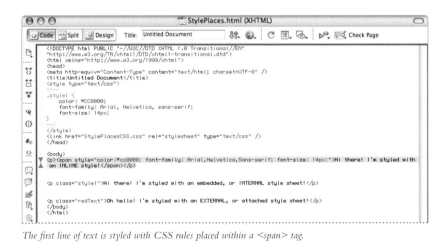

The first line of text is styled with CSS rules placed within a <span> tag.

Internal (or embedded): You create internal style sheets directly within a document, using the *<style>* tag. You define rules inside the *<style>* tag, and apply them to elements on the page using the Class or Style menus from the Property inspector. The entire style sheet is contained within the opening and closing *<style>* tags. You can add additional style sheets in the same page with more *<style>* tags.

```
<body>
<p><span style="color:#cc0000; font-family: Arial,Helvetica,Sans-serif; font-size: 14px;">Hi there! I'm styled with
an INLINE style!</span></p>

<p class="style1">Hi there! I'm styled with an embedded, or INTERNAL style sheet!</p>

<p class="redText">Oh hello! I'm styled with an EXTERNAL, or attached style sheet!</p>
</body>
</html>
```

```
StylePlaces.html (XHTML)*

Code  Split  Design   Title: Untitled Document            Check Page

<!DOCTYPE html PUBLIC "-//W3C//DTD XHTML 1.0 Transitional//EN"
"http://www.w3.org/TR/xhtml1/DTD/xhtml1-transitional.dtd">
<html xmlns="http://www.w3.org/1999/xhtml">
<head>
<meta http-equiv="Content-Type" content="text/html; charset=UTF-8" />
<title>Untitled Document</title>

<style type="text/css">
<!--
.style1 {
    color: #CC0000;
    font-family: Arial, Helvetica, sans-serif;
    font-size: 14px;
}
-->
</style>
```

The second line of text has a rule applied to it using the CLASS attribute of the <p> tag.

By default, Dreamweaver defines styles internally. You can always export styles to an external style sheet, as shown later in this lesson.

External (or attached): You can define style rules in their own document, which is saved as a .css file. You can attach .css files, or external style sheets, to any number of pages, using the CSS panel. This method is the most flexible, because you don't have to copy or redefine internal styles from page to page. Instead, all definitions remain in the external file, and changes to the rules need to only be made in that file.

```
<p class="style1">Hi there! I'm styled with an embedded, or INTERNAL style sheet!</p>

<p class="redText">Oh hello! I'm styled with an EXTERNAL, or attached style sheet!</p>
</body>
</html>
```

```
StylePlaces.html (XHTML)*

Code  Split  Design   Title: Untitled Document            Check Page

<!DOCTYPE html PUBLIC "-//W3C//DTD XHTML 1.0 Transitional//EN"
"http://www.w3.org/TR/xhtml1/DTD/xhtml1-transitional.dtd">
<html xmlns="http://www.w3.org/1999/xhtml">
<head>
<meta http-equiv="Content-Type" content="text/html; charset=UTF-8" />
<title>Untitled Document</title>

<style type="text/css">
<!--
.style1 {
    color: #CC0000;
    font-family: Arial, Helvetica, sans-serif;
    font-size: 14px;
}
-->
</style>

<link href="StylePlacesCSS.css" rel="stylesheet" type="text/css" />
</head>
```

The third line of text, like the one above it, is formatted with a rule applied via the CLASS attribute of the <p> tag.

You can make changes to an external style sheet from the CSS Styles panel with the CSS file open, or from any page to which the style sheet is attached.

You apply CSS rules to items on your page from one of four places:

The Property inspector: Use the Style or Class menu:

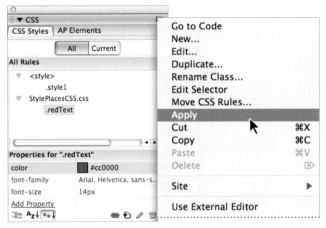

Format selected text using CSS rules directly from the Style menu on the Property inspector.

The CSS Styles panel: Choose Apply from the panel's menu:

Format a selected item in your page by selecting a style from the Rules pane and choosing Apply from the CSS Styles panel menu.

Depending on the type of page content you have selected, the Property inspector lets you apply styles using either the Style or Class menus. These menus for all intensive purposes, are identical.

The tag selector: Right-click (Windows) or Ctrl+Click (Mac OS) to launch the Tag Chooser's contextual menu on a selected tag and apply a style, using the Set Class command.

For any selected tag in the tag selector, right-click (Windows) or Ctrl+Click on (Mac OS) to apply a class to the tag.

The Text menu: Choose a style from Text > CSS Styles at the top of your screen when text is selected on the page.

Choose Text > CSS Styles to apply a class to selected text on the page.

A look at the CSS panel

The CSS Styles panel is where you create and manage all of your rules and style sheets. You can modify the properties of any CSS rule and modify them directly from the panel so that you can see your changes applied in real time as you work.

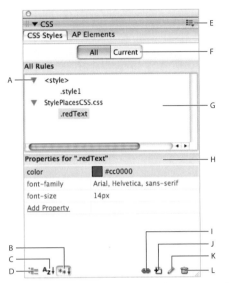

Launch the CSS panel by choosing Window > CSS Styles. A. Internal Style Sheet. B. Show only set properties. C. Show list view. D. Show category view. E. CSS panel menu. F. Switch to Current Selection Mode. G. Rules pane. H. Properties pane. I. Attach Style Sheet. J. New CSS rule. K. Edit Style Sheet. L. Delete Embedded Stylesheet.

The CSS Summary pane shows a list of rules for a selected style on your page.

The CSS Summary pane.

Creating new styles

Styling your page involves creating and applying style rules (sometimes referred to as styles) to tags and content in your page. You can create styles at any time while building a site. You can define styles in a single page, and then export them for use with other pages to maintain a consistent look across the web site. You can also create styles from the CSS Styles panel, or automatically through the Property inspector, when formatting text in your page. In the following sections, you'll explore both methods, as well as the different types of styles you can create.

Style types

There are three types of CSS rules. Each type has some key differences, and as such, you'll use them in different situations.

Tag: The purpose of a tag, or element-based style, is to alter the appearance of a specific HTML tag. Tag-based styles will alter the appearance of the tag and the content within it. You cannot selectively apply a tag, because it is in effect whenever it is used. For instance, you can create a rule definition for the *<p>* (paragraph) tag that ensures that any text within this tag always appears centered and bold. Although you cannot turn off tag-based styles at will, they are a great way to ensure consistency across multiple elements and pages where specific tags are used, such as lists, tables, and paragraphs.

Class: A custom class style can be assigned a unique name and is not associated with any specific HTML tag. Therefore, you can apply it if and when you want different types of tags and content throughout your pages. You could use the same class for a table, a paragraph, or a form field, as many times as you want. You apply a class to an HTML tag using the class attribute:

```
<p class="myText">A paragraph using a class style</p>
```

When you format text from the Property inspector, Dreamweaver automatically names and creates class styles that you can reuse on other elements. When you're looking at style sheets in the Code view, it's easy to identify the class styles because their names are always preceded by a period (.).

Advanced (IDs and pseudo-classes): An ID is a special type of rule that is unique to a single item on your page. This is typically the case when you use divs, or content boxes that you can position precisely in your document, using CSS rules. Because IDs typically contain information that is unique to a box (such as position, size, or visibility properties), a unique ID is created just for that item. Like class styles, you can assign IDs arbitrary names, but you precede them with a pound sign (#) instead of a period when you define them in a style sheet. We cover IDs in greater detail in Lesson 6, "Creating Page Layouts with CSS."

Pseudo-class selectors are rules that target a specific aspects or states of a tag or class. You'll often use pseudo-classes to control the appearance of the different states of a hyperlink—unclicked, rolled over, pressed, and visited.

Contextual selectors are rules that apply to specific combinations of tags or classes. For instance, you can have different sets of rules for a *<p>* (paragraph) and a *<b>* (bold) tag, and another set of rules for *<b>* tags inside *<p>* tags. For instance, you can designate that any text inside a *<b>* tag must be red, unless it is used within a *<p>* tag, in which case it should be blue.

Creating class styles

To begin creating your own styles, locate and open the events.html file from the Files panel. This file contains text for the McKnight Institute's Events page, and the layout has been contained within a single HTML table (we cover tables in detail in Lesson 5, "Creating Page Layouts with Tables"). You'll add style rules to this page to transform the content and explore different types of selectors.

The easiest way to create styles is to format text directly in the Property inspector. When you do, Dreamweaver automatically creates class styles from the settings you choose that you can edit, rename, and reapply to other elements.

1   If it is not already open, locate the file named events.html in the Files panel. Double-click it to open it.

2   In the Design view, select the line of text that reads *Discovery Awaits You*. This line is a header for the paragraph below it, so you'll use the Property inspector to make it more prominent by changing its color and size. Choose 24 from the Size drop-down menu on the Property inspector to increase the size of the text to 24 points. Look at the Style menu; Dreamweaver has added a new Class style named Style 1 that captures the formatting you just applied.

3   Locate the color swatch in the Property inspector, and click it to choose a color for your text from the Swatches panel that appears. Select a dark red. The color #990000 is used in this exercise. Note that the Style 1 preview in the Style menu has been updated to reflect the color you chose. Style 1 will continue to adapt to incorporate the changes you make.

As you adjust properties in the Property inspector, Dreamweaver adds them to a new class rule named Style 1.

4 Click the bold button in the Property inspector to make the text bold. This will also be added to your new style.

5 Select the line of text that reads *Spring 2007 Events*. Choose the new Style 1 class from the Style menu in the Property inspector. This will apply all of the formatting you selected for the first header in steps 1–3. Repeat this for the line that reads *Bring a Friend, or Bring Them All* so that all three paragraph headers match.

Now that all headers are using the Style 1 class, you can easily change their appearance at once by modifying this rule directly from the CSS Styles panel.

All three headers now use the same class style.

Adding styles from the Styles panel

Dreamweaver offers a Style panel, from which you can manage the styles of the different portions of text on your page. In this exercise, you'll create another style for the body text, and then apply it from the Styles panel.

1   From the CSS panel's menu, choose New. The New CSS Rule dialog box appears.

2   Click the radio button next to Class to set this as the selector type and enter **maintext** in the Name text field. Choose This document only for the Define in: option. This will add the new rule to the existing style sheet in your page. Press OK.

Choose the name, selector type, and location for your new rule.

3   The CSS Rule definition dialog box appears, featuring a series of categorized text fields and menus you can use to select properties for your new rule. Under the Type category, type **11** in the Size text field, then select pixels from the drop-down menu to the right of the Size text field. From the Font drop-down menu, choose Arial, Helvetica, sans-serif. Press the color swatch next to Color and choose a dark gray from the Swatches panel. This exercise uses color #333333. Press OK to set the properties and create the style.

Setting properties using the CSS Rule definition panel.

4 Select the entire first paragraph, which begins with *Spring time is around the corner*. From the Property inspector, locate the Style drop-down menu and choose your new style, maintext, from the menu to apply it to the paragraph.

Use the Style menu in the Property inspector on a selected piece of text on your page.

5 Follow the same method used in step 4 to apply the .maintext class to the remaining paragraphs on your page. All paragraphs in your document now share the new .maintext class.

Double-click on any word to select the entire word. Triple-click on any word to select the entire paragraph.

Creating tag styles

A tag style assigns rules directly to a specific HTML tag to alter its appearance. Unlike class styles, you can't selectively apply tag styles because they are in effect whenever the selected tag is in use. You can attach tag styles to any tag from the *<body>* tag down; as a matter of fact, the Page Properties (Modify > Page Properties) settings, such as default text formatting and background color, use a tag style assigned to the *<body>* tag.

In this lesson, you'll create tag styles for the *<strong>* (bold) and *<p>* (paragraph) tags to use throughout your page text.

1   From the CSS Panel menu, choose New to create a new rule. The New CSS Rule dialog box appears.

2   For the Selector Type, choose Tag. Select strong from the listed HTML tags in the Tag drop-down menu. Leave This document only selected, for the Define in option, then press OK.

Select the <strong> tag from the Tags menu to create a style that will apply to this tag only.

3   The CSS Rule Definition dialog box appears, and now you can specify the properties that will determine how text inside the *<strong>* tag will appear. In the Type category, choose italic from the Style drop-down menu. Press the color swatch under Color and choose a shade of red. This exercise uses color #CC0000. Press OK to create the style.

Type properties for the <strong> tag.

4 Test your new tag style by selecting a few words on your page and press the Bold button on the Property inspector to make them bold. Wherever the text appears bold, it will also follow your rule to be red and in italics.. You'll now add some rules to the *<p>* tag to redefine the look of paragraphs on your page.

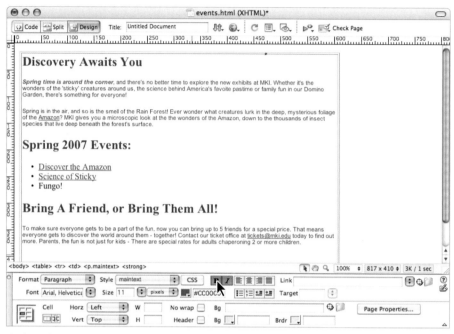

Applying the new <strong> rule is as simple as bolding text.

5 From the CSS Styles panel menu, choose New to create a new rule. When the New CSS Rule dialog box appears, set the Selector Type as Tag, and choose *p* from the list of tags. Leave This document only selected, for the Define in option, then press OK. The CSS Rule definition dialog box appears.

Select the <p> tag from the listed HTML tags. Any properties assigned will alter the appearance of this tag only.

6   In the Type category, type **16** in the Line height text field and choose pixels from the drop-down menu to the right. This increases the spacing between individual lines in a paragraph. Select the Block category from the left, and from the Block options, select Justify from the Text align drop-down menu. Press OK to create the rule.

The Block category handles the appearance of paragraphs, including alignment and justification.

The paragraphs in your document will automatically adjust, based on the rule you just created. Each paragraph was created using the *<p>* tag, so no other action was necessary. Most importantly, every paragraph added to the page from this point on will automatically follow the same rule.

You can create bold and italic text with two tags each: <b> or <strong> for bold, and <i> or <em> for italic. By default, Dreamweaver uses <strong> for bold and <em> for italic, but you can override this to use the <b> and <i> tags in the Preferences dialog box. To change this behavior, choose Edit > Preferences (Windows) or Dreamweaver > Preferences (Mac OS) and uncheck the Use <strong> and <em> in place of <b> and <i> option under General.

The Dreamweaver Preferences dialog box.

Modifying styles from the CSS panel

Once you've created style rules, you can modify them from the CSS Styles panel. When you select a rule, you can modify its existing properties or add new ones in the Properties pane at the bottom half of the panel. You can also double-click any rule to reopen the CSS Rule Definition dialog box you used to create your styles earlier. Remember that when you modify the properties of a CSS rule, all items to which the rule has been applied update; there's no need to reapply the rule. The method is the same for all selector types (class, tag, and advanced) and for rules created from the CSS Styles panel or the Property inspector.

1   At the top of the CSS Styles panel, make sure the All tab is active and locate *<style>* underneath the Rules pane; click the arrow to the left of it to expand and reveal the new rule (Style 1) that you created.

Expand the style sheet in the Rules pane and select Style 1.

2   Select Style 1; its properties will appear in the Properties pane below. Double-click the color property to edit it, and use the Swatches panel to choose an orange color. The color #FF9900 is used in this exercise. All of the headers in your page using the Style 1 class will change to the new color.

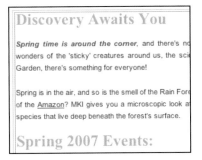

All headers using the Style 1 class automatically update to reflect the color change.

3   Double-click the font-size property to make it editable. Use the menus that appear to change the size to 18 pixels. Once again, all headers will reflect the modifications you just made.

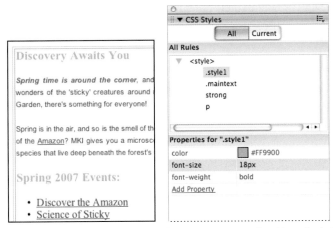

As with the color property, changes to the font-size property are reflected immediately in all headers in your page.

4   Now you'll modify the style controlling the appearance of the paragraph text on your page. Under the CSS Styles panel, double-click the .maintext rule under the Rules pane. The CSS Rule Definition dialog box will appear.

5   In the Type category, set the type size to 10 points and set the color to black, #000000. Press Apply at the bottom of the dialog box. Next, type 14 in the Line height text field and select pixels from the drop-down menu.

You should see the changes previewed on your page in the background. You may need to move the dialog box so that you can see the page.

Use the CSS Styles panel to modify properties for the maintext class.

6   Press OK to commit the changes and exit the panel.

Even though you had a line-height property of 18px set for the <p> (paragraph) tag, the line-height property you added in the .maintext class overruled it. A property in a class style will override the same property in a tag style.

To see a summary of properties for a style, select a styled item on the page and click the CSS button located on the Property inspector. The CSS Styles panel will display the Summary pane for the selected rule. Double-click any property in the summary to modify the rule in the CSS Rule Definition dialog box.

What's in a name? Naming and renaming styles

There are two types of styles (or, to be more specific, selectors), that allow you to assign a custom name: classes and IDs. As a matter of good practice, style names should be short and intuitive so that their purpose is clear: for instance, *header* instead of *style3*. Certain rules apply when you choose a style name, and certain names are not considered valid. Dreamweaver will always let you know if you try to use an invalid name.

When naming styles, the following rules apply:

- Styles names can't contain dead spaces, such as *my header*. Words must be continuous or separated only by an underscore, as in *my_header*.

- No punctuation other than an underscore is allowed.

- Style names must start with an alphabetical character; a number cannot be the first character in a style name.

You may decide to rename a style rule at some point, especially in the case of rules created automatically by Dreamweaver. There are two ways to rename a style:

- Select the style in the CSS Styles panel and choose Rename from the panel's menu.

- Choose Rename from the Style or Class menu on the Property inspector when an item using the style is selected on the page.

Class style names are always preceded by a period (.). If you don't add one when naming a new class style, Dreamweaver will do it for you. ID names are always preceded by a pound sign (#), and, just as with classes, if you don't add one, Dreamweaver will add it for you.

Creating contextual and pseudo-class selectors

Individual tags can change appearance when working in concert with one another; for example, you can have bold text appear red only when used inside a paragraph, or italic text appear bold only when part of a bulleted list. Contextual selectors apply formatting to tags and classes when they appear in a specific combination. Normally, the individual elements format as they would when used outside that combination.

To create a contextual selector:

1   Choose New from the CSS Styles panel menu to create a new rule. The New CSS Rule dialog box will appear.

2   For the Selector Type, choose Advanced (IDs, pseudo-class selectors). In the Selector text field, type **li strong**. This will set rules for the *<strong>* (bold) tag only when used within a list (the *<li>* tag adds items to a bulleted or numbered list). Choose This document only for the Define in option, then press OK.

Set the Selector Type to Advanced to create a contextual selector.

3   The CSS Rule Definition dialog box appears. Under the Type category, set the Style to italic and the color to orange, #FF6600. Press OK to create the new rule and exit the dialog box.

Set the style to italic and the color to orange under the Type category.

4   Select one of the items in the *Spring 2007 Events* list. Apply boldface to it using the B icon in the Property inspector. In addition to the text being bold, it will appear orange and italic, just as you specified in your contextual selector.

Bold type applied to any item in a list displays the new properties you created.

5   Now, try applying boldface to any word or phrase in any paragraph on your page. Bold words will appear in the same color and type style as the rest of the paragraph, unaffected by the contextual selector you created. Only items that are part of a list are affected with italic and orange text.

Because the contextual selector you created uses the newer <strong> tag instead of the <b> tag to bold text, it will not work if Dreamweaver is set to use <b> tags by default. You can change this setting under Preferences > General > Use <strong> and <em> in place of <b> and <i>. Make sure you know which tags Dreamweaver is set to use before creating a contextual selector that involves bold or italic text.

Pseudo-class selectors

A pseudo-class selector affects a part or state of a selected tag or class. A state often refers to an item's appearance in response to something happening, such as the mouse pointer rolling over it. One of the most common pseudo-class selectors is applied to the <a> tag, which is used to create hyperlinks. You'll now create a pseudo-class selector to affect the appearance of hyperlinks on the events.html page in different states:

To create a pseudo-class selector:

1 Choose New from the CSS Styles panel menu to create a new rule. The New CSS Rule dialog box appears.

2 For the Selector Type, choose Advanced (IDs, pseudo-class selectors). From the Selector drop-down menu, choose a:link. This affects the appearance of a hyperlink when it hasn't yet been visited. Choose This document only for the Define in option, then press OK.

Set the Selector type to Advanced and choose a:link from the Selector menu.

3 The CSS Rule definition dialog box appears. Under the Type category, click the color swatch next to Color and choose a brown shade from the Swatches panel that appears. This exercise uses color #996600. Press OK to create the new rule.

Set properties for a:link, or the appearance of unvisited hyperlinks.

Hyperlinks match the color set in the a:link pseudo-class selector.

4   Once again, choose New from the CSS Styles panel menu to create another rule.

5   Set the Selector Type to Advanced, and from the Selector drop-down menu, choose a:hover. Properties defined for this pseudo-class selector will determine how links appear when the mouse pointer is rolled over them. Choose This document only for the Define in option, then press OK.

Set the Selector type to Advanced and choose a:hover from the Selector menu.

6   From the Type category, click the color swatch next to Color and select the color black, #000000, from the Swatches panel. Set the Decoration to none, then press OK to create the style.

Set properties for a:hover, or the appearance of hyperlinks when the mouse pointer rolls over them.

7 To see pseudo-class selectors for hyperlinks, preview the page in a browser. Choose File > Preview in Browser and choose a browser from the list to launch it.

The link and hover states of the hyperlink that you formatted with pseudo-class selectors.

Now that you've assigned some characteristics to the hover and link states, you'll repeat the process for the remaining hyperlink states.

8 Repeat steps 1–3 for both the active and visited hyperlink states, first choosing a:active from the Selector drop-down menu and then selecting a:visited. Assign each state its own color (avoid using brown or black).

9 Choose File > Preview in Browser or press the Preview/Debug in browser button (●) on the Document toolbar to launch the page within a web browser. Experiment with the links to ensure that each state is as you formatted it.

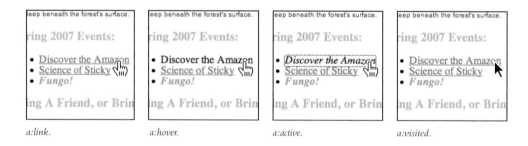

a:link.   *a:hover.*   *a:active.*   *a:visited.*

10 Choose File > Save to save your work.

When the page appears, you'll notice that the hyperlinks are formatted as you specified with the a:link selector. Move your mouse over any link, and it should change color and the underline should disappear, creating a cool rollover effect (the properties of the a:hover selector). You created pseudo-class selectors for the *<a>* tag to control formatting for different parts or different states of a hyperlink.

To modify a contextual or pseudo-class selector, use the same methods shown earlier for tag and class styles.

Internal vs. external style sheets

Now that you've seen how to modify a few items in a single page at once, you can only imagine how powerful a style sheet shared by every page in your web site can be. When you create new CSS rules, you have the opportunity to define them in the current document or in a new CSS file.

A collection of rules stored in a separate .css file is referred to as an external style sheet. You can attach external style sheets to any number of pages in a site so that they all share the same style rules.

So far, you've created internal, or embedded, styles. This means you wrote the style rules directly into the page via the *<style>* tag. Although you can format a page with an internal style sheet, this method is not very portable. To apply the same rules in another page, you have to copy and paste the internal style sheet from one page to another. This can create inconsistency among pages if the same rule is updated in one page and not the other.

To utilize the true power of style sheets, you can create an external style sheet that any and all pages on your site can share. When you change an external style, pages linked to that style sheet are updated. This is especially handy when working with sites containing many pages and sections.

You can create external style sheets in the following ways:

- Move rules from an internal style sheet into a new CSS file
- Define styles in a page in a new document via the New CSS Rule panel
- Create a new CSS document from the Start page or File menu

Now you will export internal styles into a new CSS file:

1   With the events.html document open, expand the style sheet shown in the CSS Styles panel so that you can see all of the rules you have created.

2   While holding down the Shift key, select each of the rules in the style sheet until all of them are highlighted. From the CSS Styles panel menu, choose Move CSS Rules.

Select all rules in your style sheet that you'd like to export to a new external style sheet.

3   The Move CSS Rules dialog box appears, asking if you want to move the styles to an existing or a new style sheet. Select A New Style Sheet and press OK.

4 A Save dialog box appears, asking you to choose a name and location for the new file that is about to be created. Name it **mystyles.css** and save it in the root folder of your site.

When you move the selected rules to a new style sheet, you'll be prompted to save and name a new .css file.

5 Your CSS Styles panel now shows a new style sheet: mystyles.css. The internal style sheet (shown as <style>) is still in your document, but it contains no rules. You can either remove it or add styles to it later. Click the arrow to its left to expand it and reveal all the rules it contains.

The CSS rules have been moved to a new external style sheet (.css file) and are attached to the current page.

Attaching an external style sheet to your page

Dreamweaver made the new style sheet available to the current page by attaching it. You can now apply and modify the styles in the external style sheet directly from the CSS Styles panel. To make this style sheet available to other pages, you can attach it using the Attach Style Sheet command under the CSS Styles panel menu.

1   Open the event1.html file from the Files panel. This page contains event information with no formatting applied.

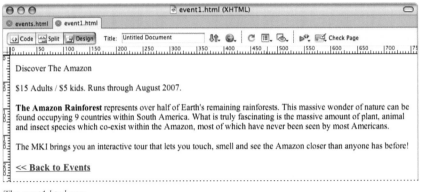

The event1.html page.

2   From the CSS Panel menu, choose Attach Style Sheet. The Attach Style Sheet panel appears.

3   Next to File/URL, press the Browse button to locate a style sheet file to attach. Select the mystyles.css file from the Select Style Sheet panel and press OK (Windows) or Choose (Mac OS).

4   On the Attach Style Sheet dialog box, leave Add as set to Link. This will attach the style sheet rather than add its contents to the page as an internal style sheet. Press OK.

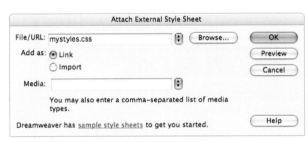

Adding an external style sheet.

The CSS Styles panel shows that mystyles.css and all of its rules are now available for use and editing.

Event1.html is now attached to mystyles.css.

Modifying attached style sheets

Because an attached style sheet appears in your CSS Styles panel, you can modify any of its rules just as you would with an internal style sheet. If you modify an external style in one page, the changes will apply across other pages that share that style sheet.

1   In the current event1.html file, select the first paragraph beginning with *The Amazon Rainforest*. Use the Style menu in the Property inspector and apply the .maintext class to it.

Apply the .maintext class to the first paragraph using the Style menu on the Property inspector.

2   In the CSS Styles panel, select the .maintext class listed under mystyles.css under the Rules pane. Double-click the font-family property in the Properties pane and change the font-family to Times New Roman, Times, serif.

3   Double-click the color property and press the color swatch to change the color to black, #000000, using the Swatches panel. Change the font-size property to 12 pixels.

Edit the .maintext class by using the CSS Properties pane.

4   If it's not already open (check the tabs at the top of the Document window), open the events.html page from the Files panel. You'll see that the paragraphs on this page have changed, reflecting the modifications you made in the event1.html file.

Because event1.html and events.html share the same style sheet (mystyles.css), changes made in one document affect items in the other that use the same style rules. In this case, paragraphs in both pages use the .maintext class, so changes to the external style sheet affect all of these paragraphs at once.

Creating a new .css file (external style sheet)

Although it's easy to export styles to a new .css file, you can also create styles in a new .css file from the get-go. The New CSS Rule dialog box gives you this option whenever you create a new rule. By creating styles in an external .css file, you can avoid the extra step of exporting them later, and make the style sheet available to other pages immediately.

1 In the Files panel, locate and open the event2.html file.

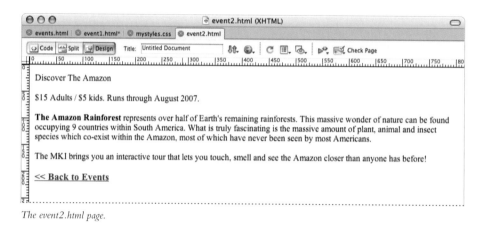

The event2.html page.

2 From the CSS Panel menu, choose New; the New CSS Rule dialog box appears.

3 Set the Selector Type as Tag, and choose body from the Tag drop-down menu. Because all visible items on your page appear inside the *<body>* tag, any rules you apply to the *<body>* tag will affect the entire page. Under Define in, choose New Style Sheet File and Press OK.

Defining a new tag style for the <body> tag in a new document.

4   You will be prompted to name and save the new .css file. Name it **morestyles.css** and save it in the root folder of your site.

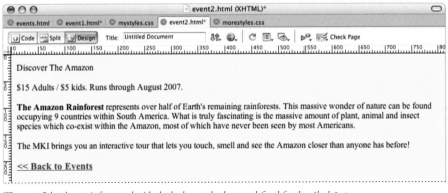

Saving the new .css file (external style sheet) in which the style will be defined.

5   When the CSS Rule Definition panel appears, choose the Background category. Set the background color to light yellow, #FFFFCC. Press OK to create the rule.

Your page's background color should be yellow, and the CSS Styles panel reflects that the style was created in a new external style sheet. Now you can attach this style sheet to any other page in your site.

The event2.html page is formatted with the background color you defined for the <body> tag.

6 Reopen the events.html file and use the methods you learned earlier to attach the new morestyles.css style sheet to it. If you're successful, the background color you applied to the event2.html page will be applied to this page as well.

CSS FYI

Inheritance

When you nest one rule inside another, the nested rule inherits properties from the rule in which it's contained. For instance, if you define a font-size and font-family for all <p> tags, it will carry over to a class style used within the paragraph that doesn't specify values for either property. It will automatically inherit the font-size and font-family from the <p> tag selector.

CSS rule weight

What happens if two classes of the same name exist in the same page? It is possible to have two identically named styles, either in the same style sheet or between internal and external style sheets used by the same page. Along the same lines, it is possible to have two rules that both apply to the same tag. If either of these cases exists, how do you know which rule will be followed?

You'll know based on two factors: weight and placement. If two selectors are the same weight (for instance, two tag selectors for the body tag), the last defined rule will take precedence.

If a rule of the same name is defined in both an internal and external style sheet in your document, the rule from the last defined style sheet will take precedence. For instance, if an external style sheet is attached to the page anywhere after the internal style sheet, the rule in the attached style sheet wins.

Self study

Create a new document and add some unique content, such as text or images, to it. Afterwards, use the CSS Styles panel to define at least one tag style, two class styles, and one contextual selector (advanced) in a new, external .css file. Create a second document and attach your new external style sheet to it, using the Attach Style Sheet command from the CSS Styles panel. Add content to this page, and style it using the style rules already available from your external style sheet. If desired, make changes to the rules from either document, and watch how both documents are affected by any modifications made to the external style sheet.

Review

Questions

1 What are the three types of selectors that can be chosen when creating a new CSS rule?

2 In what three places can styles be defined?

3 True or false: A style sheet is composed of several CSS rules and their properties.

Answers

1 Tag, Class, and Advanced (which includes contextual and pseudo-class selectors).

2 Inline (written directly into a tag), embedded (inside a specific page using the *<style>* tag) or external (inside a separate .css file).

3 True. A style sheet can contain many CSS rules and their properties. .

What you'll learn in this lesson:

- Planning designs and layouts
- Creating and modifying tables
- Comparing tables to other layout methods
- Working with layout tables and standard tables
- Importing table data

Creating Page Layouts with Tables

One of the great things about Dreamweaver is its flexibility; you have an array of tools and various creation methods at your disposal. One task for which Dreamweaver offers several different approaches is page layout. In this lesson, you will learn how to use tables on your web pages.

Starting up

Before starting, make sure that your tools and panels are consistent by resetting your workspace. See "Resetting the Dreamweaver workspace" on page 3.

You will work with several files from the dw05lessons folder in this lesson. Make sure that you have loaded the dwlessons folder onto your hard drive from the supplied DVD. See "Loading lesson files" on page 3.

Before you begin, you need to create a site definition that points to the dw05lessons folder from the included DVD that contains resources you need for these lessons. Go to Site > New Site, or, for details on creating a site definition, refer to Lesson 2, "Creating a New Site."

See Lesson 5 in action!

Use the accompanying video to gain a better understanding of how to use some of the features shown in this lesson. Open the Dynamic_Learning_DW_CS3.swf file located in the Videos folder and select Lesson 5 to view the video training file for this lesson.

Design and layout considerations

Before you use Dreamweaver, you should consider several issues regarding web layout:

Orientation is one consideration. Because you'll be designing a standard web site in this lesson, you will set up a horizontal layout. (If you were creating a web site specifically for a mobile device such as a cell phone or PDA, you might choose a vertical layout.)

Another area of concern is the overall size of your layout. The choices range, and they're based on overall computer monitor resolution in pixels (i.e., desktop size). The three most common desktop sizes are 640 x 480, 800 x 600, and 1024 x 768. (Yes, 640 x 480 is still a consideration, because believe it or not, there are still a lot of older monitors out there.) Granted, new monitors don't ship out at that resolution and haven't for quite a while. But not everyone has the latest and greatest flat-screen monitors. Average users hang onto their monitors until they see a definite need to spend the money on an upgrade. Most people use their computers to surf the Web, balance their checkbooks, and make Christmas cards, so they don't need the same amount of desktop real estate that a web designer needs. Furthermore, a web browser such as Internet Explorer or Firefox doesn't have a lot of floating windows, and doesn't need the expansive space that Dreamweaver requires.

Ultimately, the demographic you are targeting with your site will help you decide on the overall size of your layout. If you're creating a web site for a retirement community, you know your audience will primarily be older, so you might lean toward a design that will accommodate monitors set to 640 x 480 or 800 x 600. If you're targeting younger, tech-savvy users, 1024 x 768 might be a good way to go.

If you're developing an intranet site, which is an internal company site that only the employees of that company will visit, you should know how the employees' monitors are set so that you can target that specific resolution.

In this lesson, we're developing a web site for a museum; visitors to such a site will range demographically. Therefore, we will use 800 x 600 as the target size for our layout because 800 x 600 is a good overall size for accommodating different types of users with different resolution possibilities.

Remember that web standards continue to change as new technologies emerge and become more commonplace. At some point, smaller resolutions such as 640 x 480 and 800 x 600 will be phased out completely; that's already starting to happen. The bottom line is that web design and layout evolve as the technology evolves, so keep an eye out for new design trends to surface.

Tables vs. CSS

As mentioned earlier, there are different ways to approach web page layout. Each method has its advantages and disadvantages.

One advantage of tables is their flexibility and ease of use. Dreamweaver's standard and layout design modes offer several ways to manipulate tables. Another advantage of tables is that they're universal—even older browsers can recognize them.

On the downside, tables can be bulky and very restrictive when it comes to layout possibilities. Tables are an older technology that is becoming less common in terms of design trends. Another issue is that although all browsers recognize tables, they don't all treat tables in the same way. Layouts can vary from one browser to the next, depending on how the table is formatted.

With Cascading Style Sheets (CSS), you have to-the-pixel positioning, flexibility, and you can place content wherever you want fairly easily. CSS also provides you with more ways to modify page appearance in terms of formatting color, margins, borders, and so on.

The disadvantage with CSS is that since it is a newer technology, many older browsers don't support it. Even newer browsers have chosen to support CSS at different levels over the years, which can cause pages to display inconsistently from browser to browser.

Inserting a table

You will start by designing the web site's home page using tables. You'll find that you don't have to use just one table on a page; you might have multiple tables to accommodate different facets of your page layout. You can even go so far as to nest one table inside another, with each having different characteristics.

In case you're wondering why you would even use tables, have you ever tried to work without them on a blank page? You can't just drag things and place them where you want them; the code doesn't work that way. Tables are one of the elements that will allow you to get your images and text right where you want them. They're also a way to provide consistency to your layout.

To insert a table:

1 In the Files panel, double-click the index.html page to open it.

2 If your rulers aren't visible, select View > Rulers > Show.

Making rulers visible.

3 You can use guides in Dreamweaver to help establish consistent positioning in your layout. From the vertical ruler on the left side of the screen, click and drag out a guide. Because you're designing for monitors with a desktop resolution set to 800 (width) x 600 (Height) or larger, place the guide at the 750-pixel mark of the top horizontal ruler.

A ruler guide in Dreamweaver.

You didn't drag a guide out to the 800-pixel mark on the ruler because of the space that the Internet browser takes up. For instance, in Internet Explorer or Netscape, the scrollbar on the right side of the browser window absorbs some of the window's horizontal space. Some browsers also include a set of menu options on the left with different buttons for accessing bookmarks and other functions.

4 In the Title window in the Document panel, type **The McKnight Institute Home Page** as your page title. Press Enter (Windows) or Return (Mac OS).

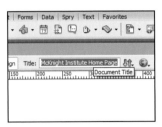

The document title area.

You'll find different ways to insert tables, including using the menus along the top of the screen, or through the Insert panel.

5 Select Insert > Table, and the Table dialog box appears. Set the number of Rows to **6** and Columns to **3**. Set the Table width to **750**, making sure that the drop-down menu is set to pixels. Next, enter **0** into the Border thickness text field. Leave the None header option selected, and the default setting in the Align caption drop-down menu.

The Table setting dialog box.

6 Choose File > Save to save your work.

Selecting tables

Selecting tables can be a little cumbersome until you get used to it. Before you add images and text, you will need to select the various table components and modify some of their basic physical attributes.

1 Place your cursor at the top of the table border; the cursor will turn into a down arrow and the column will be highlighted. Click to select a column in the table.

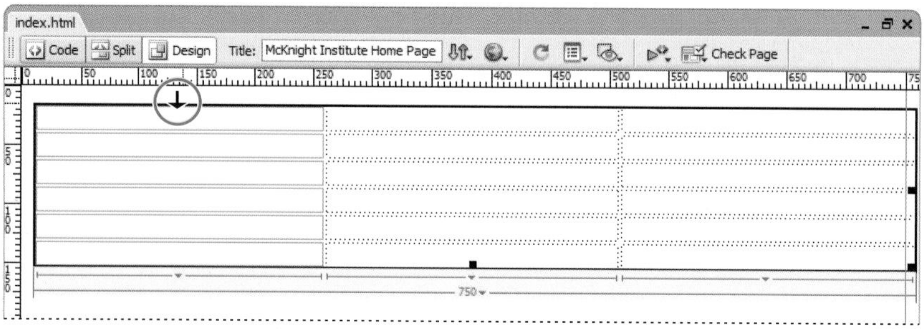

A selected column.

2 Place your cursor on the left side of the top row; this time the cursor will turn into an arrow facing to the right, with the row highlighted. Click to select the row.

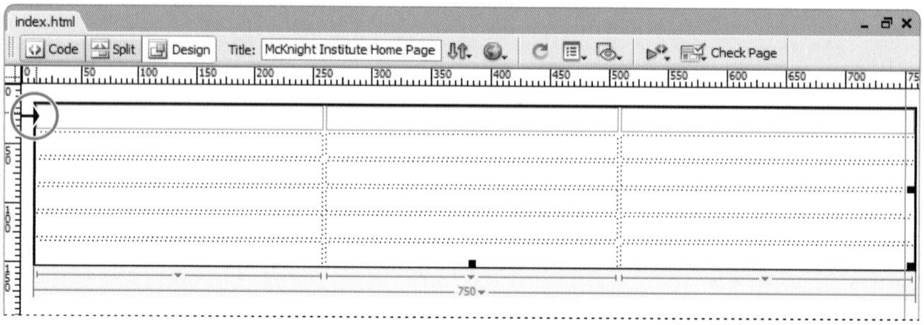

A selected row.

3 To select a column on the table itself, place your cursor at the bottom of the first column. Click on the arrow there and choose Select Column.

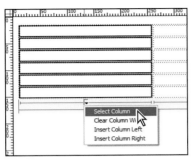

Selecting a column.

4 You can also use tags to select a table and its components. For example, click anywhere inside one of the table cells. Note the tags listed at the bottom-left corner of the page window. Select each tag—*<tr>*, *<td>*, *<table>*—and different parts of the table will be selected.

Using tags to select portions of a table.

5 To select a cell, hold down the Ctrl (Windows) or Command (Mac OS) key and click on the cell. To select multiple cells, continue to hold Ctrl/Command and click the other cells you want to simultaneously select.

6 There are many options for selecting an entire table. First click on the *<table>* tag in the lower-left corner below the Document window. This selects the entire table. Next, move your cursor to the upper-left corner of the table and click when the table icon (⬚) appears next to your cursor. You can also use the menus, click in any of the table cells, and select Modify > Table > Select Table.

Modify	Text	Commands	Site	Window

Page Properties...   Ctrl+J
Template Properties...
✔ Selection Properties
✔ CSS Styles   Shift+F11

Edit Tag...
Quick Tag Editor...   Ctrl+T

Make Link   Ctrl+L
Remove Link   Ctrl+Shift+L
Open Linked Page...
Link Target   ▶

Table   ▶   Select Table   Ctrl+A
Image   ▶   Merge Cells   Ctrl+Alt+M
Frameset   ▶   Split Cell...   Ctrl+Alt+S
Arrange   ▶

Using menu commands to select an entire table.

Modifying tables

Now that you know how to select a table, you can modify its appearance by changing several of its attributes, including, size, color, number of columns and rows, border thickness, and more.

The right side of the table extends past the guide you placed earlier at the 750-pixel mark. Now, you'll modify the table so that it aligns properly with the guide.

1 Place your cursor on the right edge of the table until it turns into a double-pronged arrow.

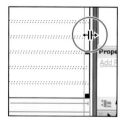

Use the double-pronged arrow to modify the width of the table.

2   Click and drag to the left to adjust the table's width. Drag your cursor so that the width matches the position of the guide. Our modified table measures 740 pixels wide. You can view your table's width by selecting the table, then checking the guide at the bottom of the table or checking the W (width) text field in the Property inspector.

Modify the tables width from the Property inspector.

You also can modify table width by typing in the value you want in the W (width) text field of the Property inspector, with the table selected.

Setting table borders

The border value also affects a table's appearance, and it determines whether the table is visible or invisible when viewed in a browser. The border value for our table is set to 0; with that value, the table will be invisible in a browser.

1   Select the table, and in the Property inspector change the border value to 1. Press Enter (Windows) or Return (Mac OS).

Adjust your table's properties in the Property inspector.

2   Preview the page in a browser by pressing the Preview/Debug in browser button (●) on the Document toolbar and you'll see the table on the page. Exit the browser and return to Dreamweaver.

3   Because you'll be using the table as a layout tool only, make it invisible again by changing the border value back to 0. We'll change other attributes, such as cell color, later, when we start to add table content.

Merging cells

The next thing to address is where the content will go and how it will fit inside the cell. Luckily, you can merge cells, divide them, and nest one table inside another, so you can customize your table in a number of ways.

In this exercise, you'll merge the cells in a table row to accommodate a graphic you'll be placing in the row.

1   Select the top row of cells, using one of the selection methods you learned earlier.

2   In the Property inspector, click the Merge selected cells button (▭) in the bottom-left corner. The three cells will merge into one big cell, with plenty of room for the graphic.

The merge button.

3   Choose File > Save to save your work.

Nesting a table inside a row

The second row is where you'll place the menu. There are seven different menu items, so you'll need a cell for each one. Because three columns are established for some of the other content that you will add later, nesting a table inside this row gives you the flexibility you need for the menu items.

1   Select the second row, then press the Merge selected cells button in the Property inspector.

2   Click inside the cell in the second row and select Insert > Table. The Table dialog box appears. Set the Number of Rows to **1** and Columns to **7**. Enter **100** into the Table width text field, and select percent from the drop-down menu. Leave the other settings as they are and press OK.

Using the Insert Table command to insert a table inside a row from another table.

Pixel-based tables are of a fixed size, so if a user resizes his browser window, the table will not resize accordingly. A table based on percentages, however, will resize based on the size of the browser window, so you'll see the table and its contents stretch as the browser is stretched. Since you nested the percentage-based table into a pixel-based table, you won't see any change if the browser is resized.

Specifying column widths

You can set up specific column widths if you want to designate a specific amount of space for column content.

1   Select the table, and then select the leftmost column by placing your cursor on the bottom of that column, clicking on the arrow, and choosing Select Column.

Selecting a column before specifying a width.

2   In the Property inspector, type **175** into the W (width) text field. Press Enter (Windows) or Return (Mac OS).

3   Repeat steps 1 and 2 for the column on the right. Don't add any values for the middle column. When you're finished, your table should look like this:

Your table, in which you'll place your menu information.

4   Create an area for the second menu at the bottom of the page by clicking in the center cell in the bottom row, then choosing Insert > Table. The settings you established for the last table are saved in the Table dialog box. Leave them as they are and press OK.

The settings used for the last table are saved in the Table dialog box.

5   Choose File > Save to save your work.

Now that you have a basic table, you're ready to start adding some content. You'll modify cells later to accommodate some of the other information you'll be adding.

Adding content to tables

You can add any content to a table the same way you add content to a page; tables just give you more control in terms of placement.

1   Click in the top cell in the top row, and choose Window > Assets to access the Assets panel.

Open the Assets panel.

2 Select the mcknight.gif file from within the images folder in the Assets panel and insert it into the cell. This image file contains the logo we'll use for our museum web site. Type **logo** when you are asked to add an alternate text tag. Press OK. You'll see the cell stretch to accommodate the size of the logo.

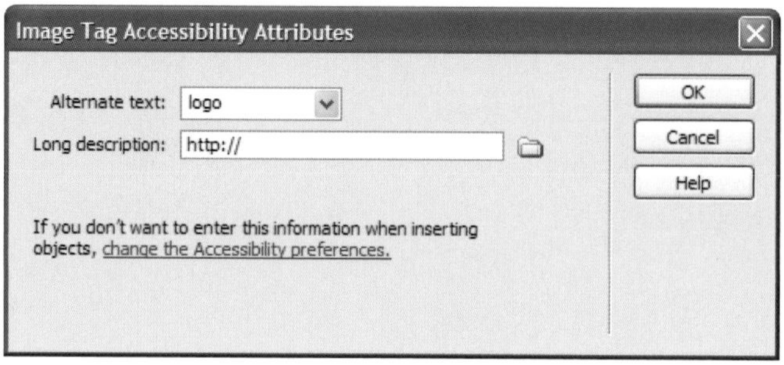

Enter logo in the Alternate text field of the Image Tag Accessibility Attributes dialog box.

3 Click in the first cell in the second row and type **Home**.

4 Click in the next cell to the right and type **Exhibits**.

5 Click in each of the remaining five cells, and type one of these headings into each cell:

Learning Center

Store

Museum Hours

Contact Us

Get a Brochure

To accommodate the content, the cells will resize as you type. When you're finished, your table should look like this:

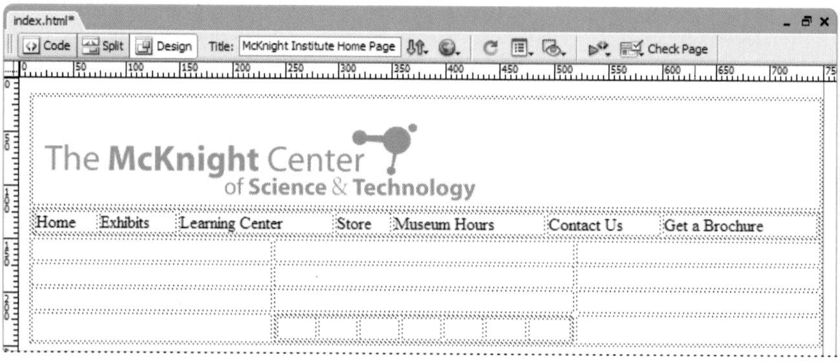

Table after adding text to the remaining cells.

Now you'll specify a width for each cell to make sure the sizing is consistent.

6 Click inside the first cell where you typed in the word *Home*. In the Property inspector, type **100** in the W (width) window. Do the same for the remaining cells in the menu.

The last cell has a number in parentheses. Even though you entered 100 in the Width window, the table is still set to match 100% of the table into which it's nested. Sometimes the table has to stretch the cells to accommodate the overall table size; the number in parentheses is the actual size of the cell.

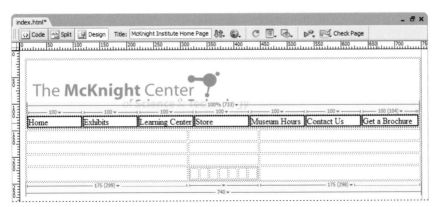

Set each cell's width to 100.

Now you need to change the text alignment to tweak the design. You can't just select the second row for this; remember, the second row actually contains a nested table. You'll need to select each cell in the nested table.

7 Select the cells by clicking the first cell of the nested table and dragging through the rest of them. Alternatively, you can hold down the Ctrl (Windows) or Command (Mac OS) key and select them one at a time.

Select all the cells in the second row by Ctrl/Command+clicking on each of them.

8 With the cells selected, go to the Property inspector and select the Align Center button (≣). As you can see, alignment works in table cells the same way it works on a page.

All of the cells are aligned to the center.

Now you'll add more text content by nesting another table and then copying and pasting text that was supplied to you as part of the exercise.

9 Click in the middle cell in the third row and choose Insert > Table. Set the number of Row to **4** and Columns to **1**. Type **375** into the Table width text field and choose pixels from the drop-down menu. Leave all other settings the same and press OK.

Adjust the settings for another nested table.

10 Click inside the cell you just nested the table into so that the cell becomes active. If this proves difficult, try clicking to the right of the table you just nested or select the *<td>* tag at the bottom of the Document window.

11 In the Property inspector, select the Vertical alignment drop-down menu and choose Top. This setting adjustment will keep the nested table at the top of the cell. This works for anything you place inside a cell, including text and images.

Adjust the cell's settings from the Property inspector.

Next, you'll copy and paste the text content for the nested table.

12 To add the text content, choose Window > Files to open the Files panel, if it's not already open.

13 Open the Assets folder, then the Text Assets folder by clicking on the plus sign (+) to the left of each folder.

14 Double-click the home_page.txt file to open it in Dreamweaver. Click and drag to select the text about halfway down the page that reads *Welcome to MKI*.

Select the text that reads Welcome to MKI.

15 Choose Edit > Copy. Click on the index.html tab in the top-left area of the page panel to return to the index.html page.

16 Click inside the top cell of the table you just pasted, then choose Edit > Paste.

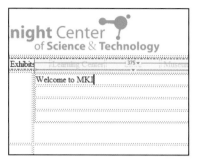

Paste the Welcome to MKI text in the top cell of your new table.

17 Click on the home_page.txt tab in the top-left corner of the page window to return to the text file you copied from earlier. Highlight the paragraph just below the *Welcome to MKI* text and copy it.

18 Return to the index.html page and paste the paragraph of text into the cell below the *Welcome to MKI* text.

Paste the paragraph from home_page.txt into index.html.

Continue this process for the next header, *Exhibits*, along with the body text that goes with it, until your table looks like this:

Copy and paste the header and body text for the Exhibits section.

19 Choose File > Save to save your work.

Adding another table

You're probably starting to get some ideas about how you can incorporate tables into your own layouts. To reinforce some of the concepts you've learned so far, let's create another nested table.

1 Click in the first cell in the third row (the cell to the immediate left of the Welcome copy) and choose Insert > Table. In the Table dialog box that appears, set the number of Row to **4** and Columns to **1**. Enter **175** in the Table width text field and select pixels from the drop-down menu. Leave the other settings as they are and press OK.

The table you inserted is in the middle of the cell; once again you'll need to establish the cell's vertical alignment.

2 To establish this cell's vertical alignment, click inside the cell so that it becomes active. In the Property inspector, click on the Vertical alignment drop-down menu and choose Top.

3 Click on the home_page.txt tab in the top-left corner of the page window to return to the text file you copied from earlier. Highlight the word *Discover*, and copy it by choosing Edit > Copy, or by using the keyboard shortcut Ctrl+C (Windows) or Command+C (Mac OS).

4   Click inside the top cell of your newly nested table and paste the text by choosing Edit > Paste, or using the shortcut Ctrl+V (Windows) or Command+V (Mac OS).

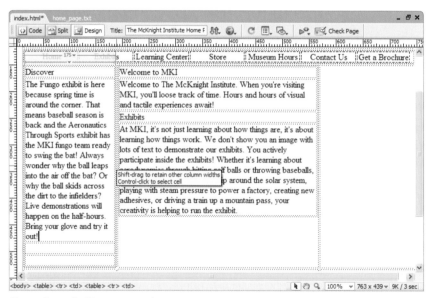

Copy and paste the other section from the home_page.txt file into your table.

5   Return to the home_page.txt file and select the paragraph below the *Discover* text you copied and pasted in step 3. Copy and paste the paragraph of text into the cell under the *Discover* text.

Copy and paste the Discover paragraph.

6 Finish the rest of the copy for the sidebar, using the *Learn* header and body copy to complete the information. When you're finished, your table should look like this:

Copy and paste the Learn *header and body copy.*

7 Choose File > Save to save your work. Preview your page in a browser by pressing the Preview/Debug in browser button at the top of the Document window.

If the text you inserted into the nested tables seems a bit crowded, you can adjust some of the table attributes to give the content more breathing room.

8 Select the nested table that contains the Discover and Learn sidebar information. An easy way to do this is to click inside the nested table and select the second table tag in the bottom-left area of the page window.

Select the second-from-left <table> tag to activate one of your nested tables.

In the Property inspector are two windows that allow you to adjust cell spacing. The CellPad window allows you to enter a value that determines how much space is inside the cell between the edge of the cell and the content. The CellSpace value determines how much space is between the cells.

9 With the sidebar table selected, enter **5** in the CellPad text field. The text in the table now has a little bit of a buffer between it and the edge of the cell.

Use the Property inspector to give your sidebar text a bit more room.

10 Select the table in the center column that contains the *Welcome to MKI* text and apply the same CellPad value of **5** for that table.

11 Choose File > Save to save your work. Preview the page again by using the Preview/Debug in browser button (●) in the Document toolbar. Note the difference in text spacing. Now you'll add another image to spice up the page a bit.

12 Click in the cell to the right of the *Welcome to MKI* text.

13 In the Assets panel, select the 3D_surface.jpg file from the Picture Assets folder within the Assets folder and insert it into the cell. Type **3D picture** as the Alternate text tag.

14 Once again, the picture shows up in the middle of the cell. Place your cursor below the inserted image and set the Vertical alignment to Top in the Property inspector.

Sometimes you'll want to modify graphics to fit table columns and rows. Do not just click and drag the images inside the cells, as this will create a stretched look. A better approach is to note the column or row width, open the graphic you want to place, and adjust its size in a program such as Photoshop or Fireworks.

Formatting tables

In addition to adjusting table and cell size, you can change other attributes, such as color, and format text content inside cells. In this exercise, you'll format table cells, and attach a style sheet to help with the process. If you're unfamiliar with styles, refer to Lesson 4, "Styling Your Pages with CSS."

1 Choose Window > CSS Styles. In the CSS Styles panel, click on the Attach Style Sheet button (●) toward the bottom-right corner of the panel.

2 Click on the Browse button, make sure you're in the dw05lessons folder, and double-click the styles.css file.

3 Make sure that the Link radio button is selected, and press OK.

Attach External Style Sheet

File/URL: styles.css ▾ Browse...	OK
Add as: ⊙ Link	Preview
○ Import	Cancel
Media: ▾	
You may also enter a comma-separated list of media types.	
Dreamweaver has sample style sheets to get you started.	Help

Select the styles.css file and press OK to attach this external style sheet.

The rightmost part of the top cell is a gray color, which doesn't match the color of the graphic and gives the cell a kind of split appearance. You can match cell colors to graphics to tie everything together.

4 Click inside the topmost cell, which contains the mcknight.gif header graphic. In the Property inspector, click the Bg color swatch (this window refers to the cell background) to bring up the Swatches panel.

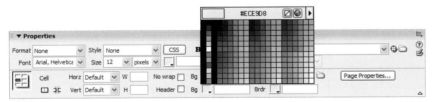

Modify the cell background color in the Property inspector.

5 Move your cursor (which should now look like an eyedropper) and click on the white portion of the mcknight.gif file to sample the color. The cell turns white.

This is a great way to blend your graphics with page colors to make everything look seamless. You can set each cell to its own color, or set multiple cell colors simultaneously.

Now you'll format the menu, sidebar, and main content cells.

6   Click in the cell containing the word *Home*. In the Property inspector, press the Bg color swatch and pick a color. This example uses color #00CC33. This cell will be different from the rest of the menu because this is the Home page.

7   Select the rest of the menu cells, from *Exhibits* to *Get a Brochure*. Choose a color from the Bg color swatch to apply it to all of the cells. This example uses color #CC9933.

8   Click inside the cell containing the word *Discover* and select a color from the Bg color swatch to assign the color to it. In this exercise, color #CCFF33 is used for the title text and #CCCC33 for the body text. Follow this procedure for each remaining text cell. For the table that contains the *Welcome to MKI* text, this example uses color #00CC33 for the headers and #00FF33 for the body copy. When you're finished, your table should look something like this:

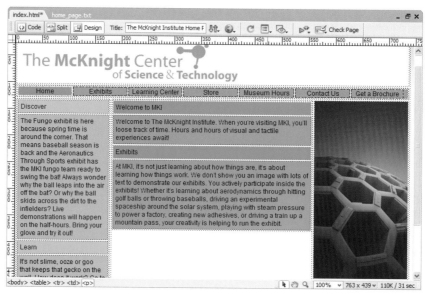

Style your tables by setting background colors for each cell.

The main cells are done, but they stick out from the rest of the page. You'll want to establish a color for the main table to tie everything together.

Working in the Expanded Tables mode

Selecting cells or content within cells can sometimes be cumbersome. This is especially true if there's no cell padding between the cells because you want to keep the table tight.

The Expanded Tables mode makes selecting cells and cell content a bit easier by temporarily adding a visible border, cell padding, and cell spacing values.

To take advantage of this feature, go to the Insert bar and select the Layout category.

The Layout category in the Insert bar.

You'll see two buttons: Standard, which is the default mode, and Expanded.

A table in Standard mode, and in Expanded Mode.

With a page that has a table within it open, click the Expanded Mode button. A dialog box appears that explains the purpose of the Expanded Mode.

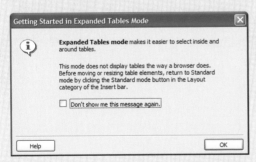

The Getting Started in Expanded Tables Mode dialog box.

Now you can see the border and cell values that have been added temporarily to make the selection process easier. Once you've made your selections and have done the work you need to do, click the Standard Mode button to return to your regular table settings.

9 Click on the cell that contains everything, the main page table. In the Bg color swatch in the Property inspector, pick an overall color for the table; this example uses color #FFCC00.

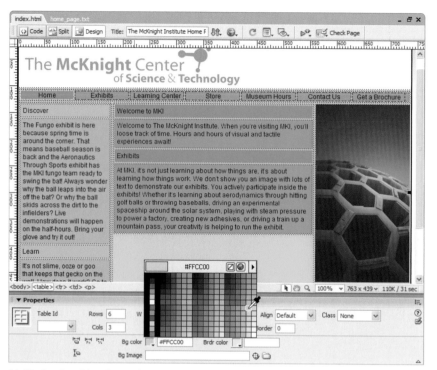

Modify the colors of the cells to make your site more appealing.

10 Choose File > Save to save your work, then preview it in a browser by selecting the Preview/Debug in browser button (⊙) at the top of the Document window. Close the web browser and return to Dreamweaver.

Now it's time to style the table cells.

11 Select the cells of the table that contain the menu items along the top of the page. Make sure you select the cells, not the table.

12 In the Style drop-down menu of the Property inspector, choose the topmenu style to apply it to the cells.

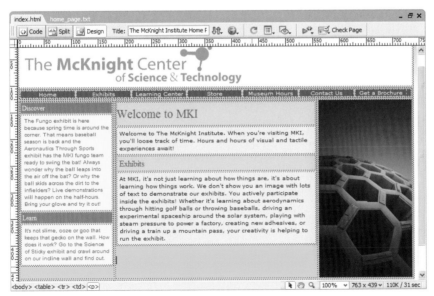

Apply the topmenu style to your menu items.

13 Continue this process with the sidebar by clicking in the cell containing the word *Discover*. In the Style drop-down menu, select the style sidebar Title.

14 Finish the process, applying the styles you think are appropriate to the remaining headers. Save your work when you're done.

One nice thing about this is that you can go back and make cell color adjustments very easily, or you can let the styles you create define everything for you!

The finished layout.

Other ways to work with tables

Now that you know the basics, it's time to move on to some other methods of creating and manipulating tables. In this section, you'll learn how to turn one cell into multiple cells, rows, and columns. You'll start by creating a blank page, with a simple one-cell table.

1   Choose File > New, select Blank Page > HTML > <none>, then press Create to create a new blank page.

Next, choose the Common tab in the Insert panel, and press the Table button (⊞).

The Insert panel.

2   In the Table dialog box, set the number of both Rows and Columns to **1**. Enter **100** in the Table width text field and select percent from the drop-down menu. Leave the other setting as they are and press OK.

3   To split the table into different rows, columns, and cells, place your cursor within a cell and, in the Property inspector, press the Split cells into rows or columns button (ᴣᴇ).

Use the Split cells into rows or columns button in the Property inspector to split table cells.

4   Choose to Split the cell into Rows, and type **4** in the Number of rows text field. Press OK.

5   Click inside the top cell and select the Split cells into rows or columns button again. This time, select the Columns radio button and set the Number of columns to **4**. Only the row you selected will split into four columns.

6 Another way to designate the number of rows and columns is to select the table and type you desired number into the Property inspector. For this exercise, set the number of columns to **8** and the number of rows to **6**.

Modify the number of columns and rows in your table.

7 Click in the first cell in the first row, and select Modify > Table > Insert Rows or Columns. In the resulting Insert Rows or Columns dialog box, you can specify the number of rows and columns and determine where you want your rows or columns to go.

Choose Modify > Table > Insert Rows or Column to exercise more control over the placement of your new rows or columns.

8 Choose the Rows radio button, set the number of rows to **1**, and direct the rows to go above the selection. The new row will take on the same characteristics as the one below it.

9 Now, say you want a header row, and a second row with columns for a menu. Select the top row and press the Merge selected cells using spans button (□) in the Property inspector.

10 Split the bottom row into more cells, for secondary navigation at the bottom of the page. Press the Split cells into rows or columns button (֏).

Modify > Table > Insert Rows or Columns doesn't work for this type of function; you need to split the cell itself.

11   Choose to Split cell into Columns, and set the Number of columns to 8.

Deleting rows and columns

Manipulating the number of rows and columns allows you to create fairly complex tables, which can be both good and bad. Nesting tables provides you with more control over each area of content that you're adding, so you'll want to use a combination of complex and nested tables to create your layouts because working with one big, complex table can be quite cumbersome. To keep your tables manageable, try deleting rows and columns:

1   Click inside the third row. Choose Modify > Table > Delete Row.

2   Click inside the first cell in the bottom row, and then choose Modify > Table > Delete Column. The number of columns changes in both the bottom row and the second row.

Importing table data

So far, you've been copying and pasting, typing in text, and inserting images. Now you'll save time and effort by importing data into your table from an external file. The import function works with .csv (comma-separated values) and comma, tab or other delimited .txt (text) files. Keep this in mind when you're preparing the content you'll be using in your web site.

1   In the Files panel, open the pages folder and double-click the hours.html file to open it.

Open the hours.html file from the Files panel.

2   Open the Assets folder in the Files panel. Open the Text Assets folder and double-click the museum_hours.txt file to open it in Dreamweaver.

The Import Tabular Data window.

To delineate the chunks of text, this text file is formatted with returns at the ends of sentences and tabs to separate certain words, such as the days of the week.

Remember this method when you're preparing content to bring into Dreamweaver. Preparing your content properly can save you a lot of time in the long run.

3   Click on the hours.html tab in the top-left area of the page window to return to the hours.html page. Click in the cell just below the menu and to the left of the test tube picture.

Next, you'll import the text file as tabular data. Dreamweaver can automatically create tables for you if you have a properly formatted file. In terms of formatting, you can separate text using tabs or commas, with each chunk of type separated by a return.

4   Choose File > Import > Tabular Data. This opens the Import Tabular Data dialog box.

5 Select the Browse button and navigate to the Assets folder located in the dw05lessons folder. Open the Assets folder, then open the Text Assets folder, and select the museum hours.txt file. You can import text files and .csv files as tabular data.

In the Import Tabular Data dialog box are options for formatting the table according to the data being imported. The word *Tab* appears in the Delimiter window; open the drop-down menu, and you'll have options for using Tabs, Commas, or other delimiters to separate text.

The Import Tabular Data window.

6 Leave the Delimiter set to Tab and everything else at the defaults. Press OK.

You can either set specific parameters for the table to be generated or let Dreamweaver construct the table automatically, based on the incoming data.

Presto! You have a table with all of the information flowed into the appropriate cells. The tabs are what create the columns, and the returns between the lines of text establish each row.

Dreamweaver sets up tables to accommodate properly formatted text files that you want to import.

The table is now ready to be formatted according to your specifications. As you can see, you can save yourself a lot of time if you think about the content you want to include in your table ahead of time. If the content is properly formatted, Dreamweaver will create a table for you with all of the data properly placed, eliminating the need for you to build a table and type or copy and paste content into each cell.

Self study

One way to learn how to take advantage of tables is to learn how other programs work in conjunction with Dreamweaver.

There's a process many web designers incorporate known as *slicing* which involves cutting up an image in Photoshop or Fireworks, using slice tools. From there, the image is dissected into separate pieces that will load more quickly than one big image. You can then export the slices as separate images, along with a web page that does the layout for you, with each image automatically placed in a table.

To learn more about this time-saving process, start to investigate Fireworks, which tightly integrates with Dreamweaver to expedite the process.

Review

Questions

1　What's the difference between a percentage-based table and a pixel-based table?

2　What setting in the Property inspector determines whether a table is visible?

3　How can you import text so that the content will flow automatically into cells and columns?

Answers

1　A percentage-based table will stretch to fit the size of the browser. A pixel-based table is fixed and will not resize.

2　The border value in the Property inspector sets a border for a selected table. If the border value is 0 (zero), the table itself will not be visible when the page is viewed in a web browser.

3　By adding tabs and returns in the document to separate the text content and then importing the file as tabular data.

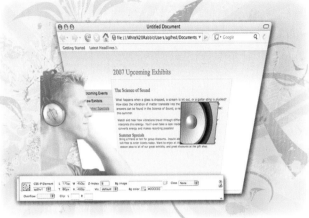

What you'll learn in this lesson:

- Understanding the CSS Box model
- Creating Divs and AP Divs
- Stacking and overlapping elements
- Styling box contents
- Using visual aids to fine-tune positioning

Creating Page Layouts with CSS

Now that you've put Cascading Style Sheets (CSS) to use, you've seen how powerful they can be for styling text, images, and tables with flexibility and ease. CSS is equally powerful as a layout tool, allowing you to freely position, flow, and overlap page content in ways not possible with HTML alone.

Starting up

Before starting, make sure that your tools and panels are consistent by resetting your workspace. See "Resetting the Dreamweaver workspace" on page 3.

You will work with several files from the dw06lessons folder in this lesson. Make sure that you have loaded the dwlessons folder onto your hard drive from the supplied DVD. See "Loading lesson files" on page 3.

Before you begin, you need to create a site definition that points to the dw06lessons folder from the included DVD that contains resources you need for these lessons. Go to Site > New Site, or, for details on creating a site definition, refer to Lesson 2, "Creating a New Site."

See Lesson 6 in action!

Use the accompanying video to gain a better understanding of how to use some of the features shown in this lesson. Open the Dynamic_Learning_DW_CS3.swf file located in the Videos folder and select Lesson 6 to view the video training file for this lesson.

The CSS Box model

CSS positions elements within a page using the Box model, which refers to rectangular virtual boxes used to hold and place content within a document. Each box can act as a container for text, images, media, and tables and takes up a certain area on the page determined by its width and height. Additionally, each box can have its own optional padding, margin, and border settings (described in detail shortly). In reference to the display of items on a page, CSS regards almost every element on a page as a box.

Although CSS regards many HTML elements as boxes, in this lesson you'll be working specifically with the *<div>* tag, which Dreamweaver uses to create new boxes when positioning content in CSS. The *<div>* tag, in conjunction with CSS rules, can be freely positioned, formatted, and even told how to interact with other boxes adjacent to it. You can also stack and overlap *<div>* containers, opening the door to flexible and creative layouts not possible with HTML alone.

If you've worked with layout applications such as InDesign CS3, the idea of creating and positioning containers for page content should be very familiar to you. Boxes created with the <div> tag can be thought of as analogous to the text and image frames you create in InDesign.

Margins, padding, and borders

The Box model allows each element on a page to have unique margin, padding, and border settings. The following figure shows the various parts of the box:

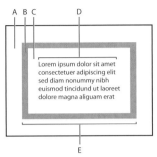

A. Margin. *B*. Border. *C*. Padding. *D*. Content width. *E*. Visible width.

Margins refer to the transparent area surrounding the box, which you set using the margin group of CSS properties. Margins can play an essential role in creating distance between a box and the content surrounding it (such as other boxes), or the boundaries of the page itself. You can set margins for all sides at once or uniquely for each side.

Padding is the distance between the inside edge of the box and its contents; by setting padding, you create space between the box and any text, images, or other contents. You set padding using the padding group of CSS properties, and, like margins, you can set them for all four sides of a box at once or for each side individually.

The **border** of a box is transparent by default, but you can add width, color, and a border style for decoration or definition around boxes. Borders sit directly between margins and padding, and define the actual boundaries of the box. You set borders using the border group of CSS properties and, like margins and padding, you can define borders for all four sides at once or for each side individually.

You can incorporate each property into any style rule and attach it to a box, similar to the way you've attached classes to paragraphs and tables in previous lessons.

The *<div>* tag

As you explore and create page layouts with CSS, you will frequently encounter the *<div>* tag. The *<div>* tag creates areas or sections within an HTML document; you can place page content such as text and images directly within sets of *<div>* tags. Dreamweaver enables you to create CSS-driven page layouts using the Insert Div Tag and Draw AP Div buttons, both of which utilize the *<div>* tag to create boxes that you can place precisely within your pages and style with CSS rules.

The CSS ID selector type

In Lesson 4, "Styling Your Page with CSS," you learned about the different selector types in CSS: classes, tags, pseudoselectors, and IDs. In this lesson, IDs become an essential part of working with CSS boxes and positioning. An ID is a special selector type created for a unique element by the same name within a page, and it's meant for one-time use only. ID rules appear within a style sheet and are preceded by a pound (#) sign.

For this reason, IDs are ideal for setting properties that need to be specific to a single element, such as positioning information. When creating layouts using the Insert Div Tag button, Dreamweaver requires you to create or assign an ID rule for each box created. When drawing boxes with the Draw AP Div button, Dreamweaver automatically creates a unique ID rule that contains positioning, width, and height information for that specific box.

Because *<div>* tags have no display attributes, they are given their properties by either an ID or a class, or both. Think of an ID as a set of instructions that give a *<div>* its unique appearance and behavior (as DNA is to a human being). An ID rule is matched to a *<div>* using the tag's ID attribute.

The Code view shows the style sheet and <div> tag that creates the container shown in the Design view below it.

Tables or boxes?

A long-standing debate has existed within the web design community about the best approach to creating page layouts. Many designers feel that tables are antiquated, and that CSS boxes need to be adopted as the primary method for positioning page content. Others assert that tables are more reliable in older browsers, and display consistently across platforms and browsers. Both sides of the discussion have some merit.

Tables are one of the oldest methods of laying out page content, and they are supported consistently by older browsers. This is an important consideration if most of your audience may not be on the latest and greatest setups.

Tables' limitations, of course, are obvious. You are restricted to the table's grid-like structure, and to achieve more complex layouts, you need to nest several levels of tables. You cannot freely position tables within the page, and they depend on the flow of other elements around them.

Boxes: The <div> tag and CSS positioning have been around for some time, but since their inception different browsers have chosen to support them at varying and often inconsistent levels. At this point, though, most CSS positioning properties and practices are supported consistently across Internet Explorer, Safari, Firefox, and Netscape. You, however, will find that testing is still necessary to expose potential inconsistencies.

The addition of the CSS Advisor and Browser Compatibility Check features to Dreamweaver CS3 is a huge benefit to designers who have chosen to embrace CSS more extensively. These tools flag and help troubleshoot any CSS-related items that may be incompatible or inconsistent in commonly used browsers. We discuss the CSS Advisor and Browser Compatibility Check in detail in Lesson 13, "Managing Your Web Site: Reports, Optimization & Maintenance."

Positioning content with AP Divs

In previous lessons, you positioned content directly within a page or using the grid-like structure of the *<table>* tag. If the limitations of these methods leave you wanting more creative flexibility, CSS gives you that intuitive drag-and-place freedom you've become accustomed to in other design applications. Boxes are created with the *<div>* tag, and their positioning information is stored within an ID rule within a style sheet. Box position is determined by the top and left CSS properties; these set the distance of the box in pixels from the top and left edges of the page (or whatever element contains it) respectively.

To get started, switch to the Layout insert panel, which contains the icons you'll need to place div and AP Div boxes within your page.

To use the Layout insert panel, make sure the Insert bar is visible (Window > Insert). The Insert panel is divided into tabs; select the Layout tab to bring the Layout insert objects forward.

If the Insert bar appears in the Menu view, choose Layout from the drop-down menu on the left-hand side of the panel.

Creating your first boxes with Draw AP Div

Now that you understand how boxes work in CSS, it's time to put that knowledge into practice. The easiest and most tactile way to place boxes is with the Draw AP Div button. An AP (Absolute Positioned) Div is placed exactly where you draw it, using the page or a containing element (such as another Div) as its point of reference. Once you've created a box, you can format it, type in it, or place images and other content into it.

1   Choose File > New. When the New Document panel appears, choose Blank Page > HTML, then press Create.

2   Choose File > Save. When the Save As dialog box appears, navigate to the dw06lessons folder. Type **layout1.html** in the Name text field and press Save.

3   On the Layout insert panel, locate and select the Draw AP Div button (🗐). Move back over the page; the cursor changes to a crosshair.

4   Click anywhere on the page and drag to draw a box in the upper left-hand corner. The box appears with a tab on the top-left edge, and handles on all sides and corners that can be used to resize the box.

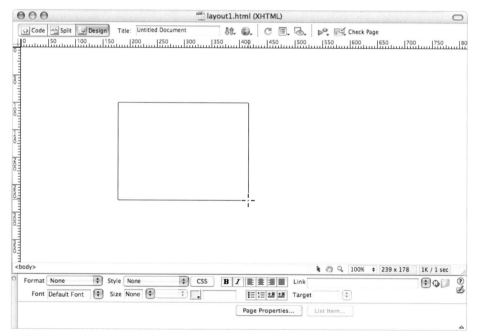

Click and drag on the stage to draw a new box.

5   Select the entire box by clicking the tab in its top-left corner; the Property inspector displays all of the options for your box, including its current width, height, and position. Press the Bg color swatch and select color #CCCCCC from the Swatches panel.

Select the entire box by clicking the tab in its upper left-hand corner.

6   Now you can add content to the box by simply typing in it. Click inside the box and type **The Science of Sound**.

Click inside the box and begin typing to add content.

7   Choose File > Save to save your work, and then preview your page by choosing File > Preview in Browser > [Default Browser] or by pressing the Preview/Debug in browser button (●) at the top of the Document window. The page launches in a new browser window; the box appears and stays where you created it in your document.

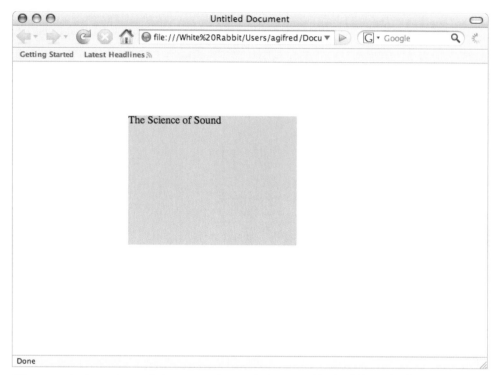

When you preview in your browser, the box you created appears in the exact position in which you placed it.

Working with the new ID rule

At the top of your Document window, switch to the Split view so that you can see both your code and design simultaneously. Scroll down in the code panel until you see the *<div>* tag that creates your box. The ID attribute of the *<div>* tag has been set to match the ID rule in the style sheet. An ID is unique to each element on a page, and, therefore, the ID rule is used for only this box.

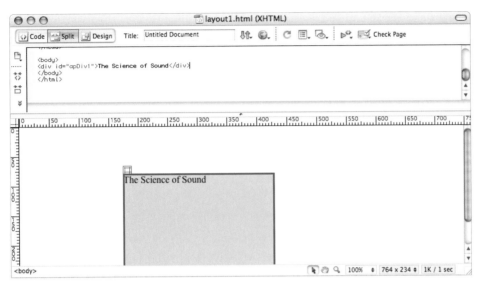

A style sheet and ID rule give the box its positioning and size information, matched by the <div> tag's ID attribute.

Under the Rules pane in your CSS Styles panel, you'll see that a new internal style sheet has been created (indicated by the *<style>* tag listed). Click the arrow to its left to expand it and you'll see the new ID rule (#apDiv1) created for your new box. Select it and look at the Properties pane—the ID rule contains all of the properties necessary to set the size and position of the *<div>* on the page.

The CSS Styles panel reveals the new ID rule
created for the new box you placed on the page.

You can toggle the Insert bar between the Tabs and Menu views at any time. When in the Tabs view, switch to the Menu view, using the Insert Panel menu in the top-right corner. When in the Menu view, choose Show as Tabs from the drop-down menu on the left.

You can toggle the Insert bar between tabbed or menu views at any time.

Now that you have the hang of it, add some more boxes on the page to form your layout:

1   Select the Draw AP Div button (▤), then click and drag to draw a new box above the one you created earlier.

Create a new box above the one you created earlier.

2   Inside the box, type **2007 Upcoming Exhibits**. Select the new text and choose Heading 2 from the Format menu on the Property inspector to increase the text size.

Add text to the new box, and assign it the Heading 2 tag from the Format menu on the Property inspector.

3   From the Insert bar above your Document window, select the Draw AP Div button. Click and drag on the page to draw a box below and to the right of the center box.

4   Click inside the box and switch to the Common tab of the Insert bar at the top.

Switch to the Common pane of the Insert bar so that you can insert an image from your site folder into the new box.

5   Select the Insert Image button (▣); Dreamweaver prompts you to choose an image from your site folder. In the images folder, select the speaker.jpg image and press OK (Windows) or Choose (Mac OS). Type **speaker** into the text field when asked to add an alternative text tag, then press OK. If the Image Tag Accessibility Attributes dialog box appears, choose Cancel. The image is placed inside the new box.

6   Save the page, and choose File > Preview in browser to see what you've done.

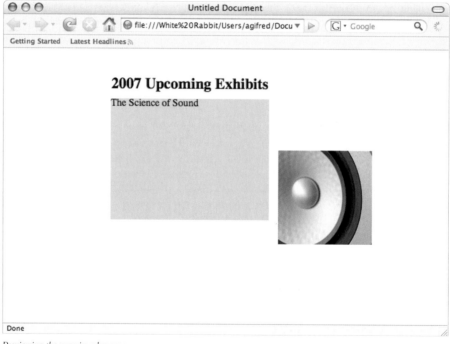

Previewing the page in a browser.

Absolute vs. relative positioning

The boxes created throughout this lesson are positioned absolutely, or at the exact pixel location you specify. AP Divs use the position CSS property and, as the name implies, the value is always set to absolute. But what does this mean, and how can different values for the position property change the way a box appears on a page?

Any element, or, in this case, any box, can have the position property applied, and one of five possible values can be set: absolute, fixed, relative, static, or inherit. The two most commonly used are absolute and relative, and although both can accept positioning properties such as top and left, they appear differently, even with identical positioning values.

Absolute: An element that is set to "absolute" strictly follows the positioning values given to it, relative only to its containing element. The containing element can be another div or the page itself. Absolutely positioned elements are pulled out of the normal flow of HTML content, and regardless of what surrounds them (e.g., text content, neighboring divs), they always appear at the exact coordinates assigned to them.

Here is an example of a div absolutely positioned within another div. The larger div (Box #1) is its containing element, so any top or left values assigned to it are relative to the boundaries of Box #1.

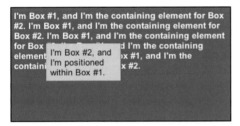

Box #2 is contained, or nested, within Box #1, and has a top value of 50 and a left value of 50.

Adding content to the containing box has no effect on the nested div. It holds firmly at its position, even if that means overlapping the other contents of Box #1.

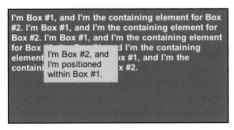

Box #2 is unaffected by the other content around it, and holds at the exact same position.

Relative: A relatively positioned element accepts values for position properties such as top and left, but also takes the normal flow of neighboring HTML content into account. Here are the boxes and values shown in the preceding two figures; the only difference here is that the position property for Box #2 has been set to relative.

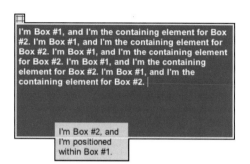

Box #2 is still offset by 50 and 50, just as before, but it's being displaced by the content before it.

Although it appears that the top and left values have changed dramatically, they haven't. Unlike absolutely positioned elements, relatively positioned elements stay within the normal flow of HTML content, which means they can be displaced by the elements (in this case, the text) surrounding them. In this example, Box #2 is still 50 pixels from the top and 50 pixels from the left, but its point of reference is the end of the preceding text content, not Box #1.

Positioning items relatively is useful when you want an item to flow in tandem with the items surrounding it. The following image shows five divs nested inside a larger div to create a menu.

MKI Gift Shoppe

Shirts & Jerseys

Hats

Tech Toys

Books & CD

CDs and DVDs

All menu items are positioned relative to one another, so they fall into place based on each other's position.

The same example is shown below, with the position set to absolute for all menu items. The result is a collapse of the menu—all of the menu items are trying to occupy the same place at the same time, without regard for their neighbors.

When set to absolute, the menu items stack on top of one another, because they all must be at the same place, regardless of the elements that surround them.

The files used for these examples are located in the dw06lessons folder, and are named absolute_relative.html and relative_menu.html. Open them in Dreamweaver and explore the code to further your knowledge.

Setting the position property to inherit instructs an element to use the same setting as its containing element. If you want a nested box to use the same value for its position property as a box it's nested within, set it to inherit. This is true of any CSS properties that can accept inherit as a value.

Modifying box properties

Like other elements in an HTML document, you can modify boxes in a variety of ways throughout the Dreamweaver workspace. Because the properties of a div (box) are controlled via CSS rules, you can use the CSS Styles panel as you have in previous lessons to modify the dimensions, appearance, and positioning of a box. You also have the flexibility of manipulating a box directly on the page with its bounding box and handles, or via the Property inspector when a box is selected. No matter which method you choose, behind the scenes Dreamweaver is rewriting the CSS properties that control it.

To make sure an entire box is selected, click the large handle on the box's top-left edge. You can also use this handle to move the box around the page.

To modify box properties:

1   Select the first box you created in the center of the stage. Using the Property inspector, set the box's width to 450 pixels and height to 400 pixels.

Select the center box and use the W (width) and H (height) fields in the Property inspector to resize it. This modifies the width and height properties within the ID controlling this box.

2   Select the box at the top of the page containing the words *2007 Upcoming Exhibits*. The left side of the Property inspector reveals the ID this box is using: apDiv2. You can use the CSS Styles panel to modify the ID rule of the same name.

3   In the Rules pane of the CSS Styles panel, select the apDiv2 rule. The Properties pane shows the properties that make up this ID.

4   Select and set the width property to 450px. Set the height property to 65px. This resizes the apDiv2 box, because this ID and its properties determine the box's appearance.

Modify the apDiv2 properties directly from the CSS Styles panel.

5   Return to the page, and select the box containing the image of the speaker. The Property inspector shows that this box's ID is apDiv3, and it will be using a CSS rule of the same name. In the CSS Styles panel, double-click the apDiv3 rule to open the CSS Rule Definition dialog box

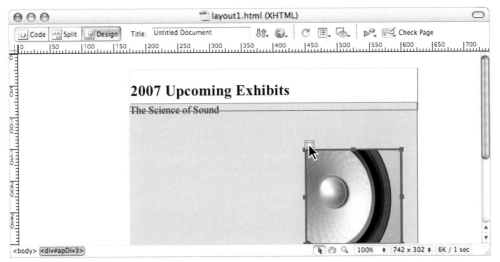

The selected box is attached to the apDiv3 ID, which you can modify from the CSS Rule Definition panel.

6   Select the Box category from the left, and set the width and the height to 150 pixels.

Under the Box category, set the width and height of apDiv3.

7   Switch to the Border category, and assign a Border Style of solid, Width of 2 pixels, and Color of #990000. Leave the Same for All checkboxes checked so that the border properties are applied equally to all four sides of the box. Press OK.

Create a border for the image.

Although you used different methods to modify the boxes, in each case Dreamweaver modified properties in each ID that corresponded to a specific box. You can choose whichever method you're comfortable with but, as you've seen, some methods afford the ability to add or modify more properties if necessary. Whereas the Property inspector allows you to modify basic width, height, and positioning properties, the CSS Styles and CSS Rule Definition panels allow you to add properties in other categories to further style the appearance of the box.

Box overlap and z-index

As you've developed this web page, you've probably seen something you didn't see when designing with tables or other HTML elements. At some point, boxes can overlap and occupy the same space on the page, which creates opportunities for creative layouts where elements can stack to create depth. Of course, when items overlap, something needs to determine the stacking order, or which elements appear on top or in back. For CSS boxes, this stacking order is determined by the z-index CSS property.

You can assign a z-index to any box; the higher the z-index, the higher its order in the stack. Items at the top of a stack appear in front, whereas anything below the box appears behind it. Every time an AP Div is drawn on the page, a z-index property is assigned to it with the next highest number available. The newer the box, the higher it appears in the stacking order. To reorder boxes in a document, simply modify its z-index. You can do this from the Property inspector, the CSS Styles panel, or the CSS Rule Definition panel.

To modify the z-index of a box:

1   Select the box containing the speaker image (apDiv3) by its handle. In the Property inspector, locate the z-index field. It shows that this box has a z-index of 3, because it was the last box created. At this point, it is positioned in front of the other boxes in the stacking order.

2   Select the large box that contains the event text (apDiv1). To bring this box forward, you'll need to increase its z-index.

3   From the Property inspector, locate the z-index text field. It reads 1; change it by clicking in the text field and typing **5**. When you deselect the box, the speaker image disappears. Although the image is not really gone (nor is the box that contains it), it is now hidden behind the larger box because its z-index is lower.

The z-index for apDiv1 from 1 to 5. Increasing this value pushes it ahead in the stacking order.

4   Save your page and preview it in a browser. The speaker image is completely hidden by the larger box that was originally behind it.

The speaker image is now hidden behind the larger box.

5   Return to the page and return the larger box to its original position; select it and use the Property inspector to switch the z-index back to 1.

In the Document window, the selected box always appears in front of other boxes. This occurs only when the box is active, and it has no effect on its actual stacking order. Be careful not to confuse an actively selected box with one that is truly at the top of the stacking order. If you are unsure, click on the page background to deselect any active boxes, or preview the page in a browser to see the true stacking order.

As you develop a layout, leave some space in the stacking order while you add boxes. You can do this by assigning z-indexes at wider intervals (such as 5, 10, 15, 20). If you need to insert a box between two others later, you'll have some numbers available to assign it a z-index in between. If the boxes always remain sequential (1, 2, 3, 4), you might end up renumbering several boxes just to fit one in between.

The Insert Div button

Another tool is available for creating boxes on your page: the Insert Div Tag button (▣). Found on the Layout pane next to the Draw AP Div button (▤), this button creates a *<div>* tag, and then requires you to attach it to an existing ID rule or create one on the spot. This way of creating boxes may seem less intuitive than just dragging and drawing on the page, but it can be useful if you either want to attach a new *<div>* to an existing rule or use the CSS Rule Definition panel to add more options to a new ID as you create it.

Insert Div Tag vs. Draw AP Div

As you've seen, Dreamweaver provides several ways to carry out most tasks. Although the result of the two Div buttons is similar, there are key differences in how Dreamweaver creates divs.

Insert Div Tag gives you the opportunity to assign a class and an existing ID at creation time. If you don't have an ID available, you can jump to the CSS Rule Definition panel to create one before the div is created. You can also determine the exact insertion point where the div will be created, which can be handy when nesting divs.

Draw AP Div is a more tactile (and designer-friendly) way to create boxes, as you can simply draw a new box right on the page. Draw AP Div eliminates the work of typing in settings by creating an ID that contains the size and position settings that reflect how you draw the box. You also can manage AP Divs from the AP Elements panel (covered later in this lesson), which can toggle off visibility for, and easily locate and select any AP Div.

To create a new box, using the Insert Div Tag button:

1   Press the Insert Div Tag button (▦) on the Layout Insert bar. The Insert Div Tag dialog box appears.

The Insert Div Tag dialog box.

2   Because you must attach each new div to an ID style, you must create a new ID rule before moving ahead. To do so, click the New CSS Style button below the ID menu.

Before you create a new div, you must create a new ID rule for it if none are available.

3   The New CSS Rule dialog box appears. Set the Selector Type to Advanced and assign the new ID the name #MenuBox in the Selector field. Select the This document only radio button. Press OK.

4   When the CSS Rule Definition dialog box appears, select the Positioning category on the left. Give your new ID a width of 180 and a height of 300. Set the Type as absolute.

5 Under Placement, enter a Top value of **100** and a Left value of **0**. Press OK to create the ID. You are returned to the Insert Div dialog box.

CSS Rule definition for #MenuBox

Category	Positioning
Type	
Background	
Block	Type: absolute
Box	Width: 180 pix...
Border	Height: 300 pix...
List	
Positioning	
Extensions	

Visibility:

Z-Index:

Overflow:

Placement

Top: 100 pix...

Right: pix...

Bottom: pix...

Left: pix...

Clip

Top: pix...

Right: pix...

Bottom: pix...

Left: pix...

Help   Apply   Cancel   OK

Set positioning and placement settings in the CSS rule definition dialog box.

6 Under ID, choose the new ID (MenuBox) you just created, then press OK.

Insert Div Tag

Insert: At insertion point

OK

Class:

Cancel

ID: MenuBox

Help

New CSS Style

The new ID appears under the ID menu, ready to be assigned to your new div.

7   A new box is created on the page with the properties you set in steps 4 and 5. Leave the default content that Dreamweaver adds; you'll change it later as you add content to your layout.

The new div appears with some default content, which you can remove or change later.

The Insert Div Tag panel does not allow you to assign an ID to a new <div> that's already in use. Even if you have several ID rules in your page, none appears in the ID menu if it is already assigned to other <div> tags on the page.

Inline vs. block boxes

How an element was created (or more specifically, by what tag) determines whether it falls into the inline or block category. You can regard elements created with *<p>*, *<div>*, or *<table>* tags as block type elements. Elements created with the *<span>* and *<strong>* tags, for instance, are considered inline elements.

The key difference between the two is how they work in the flow of your page. Block elements work like they sound, and occupy as much available space as they can, including a full-width page line before and after the element. This usually results in adjacent content being displaced. Inline elements don't push adjacent content to the next line, but rather work in the flow with the rest of the content surrounding them.

Styling boxes and adding content

Now that you've placed boxes and have the framework of a layout in place, you can add and style content with CSS classes and tag styles. You learned the ways of CSS in Lesson 4, "Styling Your Pages with CSS," and now you're armed with the styling prowess you need to make this page look great. CSS styles work hand in hand with boxes, and, even though IDs are already assigned to each box, you can apply formatting to a box and its contents, using classes and tag styles with all of the flexibility you've already discovered. You add classes to a box using the *<div>* tag's *class* attribute.

Attaching a style sheet

If you already have an external style sheet that you'd like to use, you can attach it to any page under your root folder so that page can use all of the styles you've already created. Follow these steps to add the provided style sheet to your page so that you can use styles right away:

1   From the bottom of the CSS Styles panel, click the Attach Style Sheet button (∞). When the dialog box appears, choose Browse. Select styles.css from your site's root folder, the dw06lessons folder, then press OK (Windows) or Choose (Mac OS).

The Attach Style Sheet button appears as a chain link at the bottom of your CSS Styles panel.

2 When the Attach Style Sheet dialog box reappears, press OK to attach the style sheet. The new style sheet now appears in your CSS Styles panel.

The new styles.css style sheet appears in your CSS Styles panel.

You'll see changes already applied to your page; these are the result of several tag (element) styles defined in the new style sheet.

Applying classes

You can apply classes to selected content or to an entire table, cell, div, or any containing element, using the same methods you've already learned: from the Style or Class menu on the Property inspector, from the CSS Styles panel, or from the tag selector at the bottom of the Document window.

1 Select the top box (apDiv2) on your page by clicking the tab in its upper-left corner or by selecting it in the AP Elements panel (Window > AP Elements).

2 Using the Property inspector, choose the header_main style from the Class menu. Remove the old Heading 2 from the title by selecting the text and choosing None from the Format menu (located on the Property inspector).

3 Select the large center box, and choose the bodytext_main style from the Class menu. Remove the old background color from the box by selecting No color (☑) from the Bg color swatch.

4   Now you'll add some new content to the center box; in the Files panel, locate and double-click the sound.txt file to open it. This text file contains unformatted copy that you can add to your page.

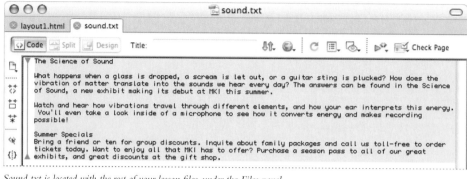

Sound.txt is located with the rest of your lesson files, under the Files panel.

5   With sound.txt open, choose Edit > Select All and then Edit > Copy to copy all the text. Switch back to your layout1.html page (click its tab at the top of the Document window), and highlight the text inside the large box. Choose Edit > Paste to paste the new text, replacing the old.

Paste the new text copied from sound.txt into the center box, replacing the old placeholder content.

6   Select the header *The Science of Sound*; use the Property inspector to apply the header2_sub style to it. Because this class is being applied at the paragraph level, it doesn't interfere with the class applied to the entire box.

Apply a style to the header, using the Property inspector.

7   Select *Summer Specials* and apply the header2_sub style to it, using the Property inspector.

8   Choose File > Save to save your work, then preview it in a browser, using File > Preview in Browser or by selecting the Preview/Debug in browser button (⊚).

Your page is starting to come together.

Setting margins, padding, and borders

As you learned earlier, each box can have unique margins, padding, and borders that you can apply for decorative or practical purposes. A look at our page reveals that you can create some breathing room in a few places between the content and the box. In addition, you can add many properties that control CSS borders to further define specific boxes and add creative flair.

1   Select the large center box that contains your page text (select it by its handle). The Property inspector reveals that this box is attached to the apDiv1 ID.

Select the center content box; you'll be applying padding and borders to style it.

2   In the CSS Styles panel, under <style>, double-click the apDiv1 rule to open the CSS Rule definition dialog box.

Double-click the apDiv1 rule shown in your CSS Styles panel to open it for editing.

3   Under the Box category, set the padding to 10 pixels. Leave the Same for All checkbox checked to make sure the setting is applied to all sides.

4   Select the Border category, and set the border Style to solid, the Width to 1 pixel, and the Color to #CCCCCC. Leave the Same for All checkboxes checked for all three border properties. Press OK to exit the dialog box.

CSS Rule definition for #apDiv1

Category   Border

Type
Background
Block   Style   Width   Color
Box
Border   ☑ Same for all   ☑ Same for all   ☑ Same for all
List
Positioning   Top: solid ⬍   1   ⬍ pix... ⬍   ▢ #cccccc
Extensions
               Right: solid ⬍   1   ⬍ pix... ⬍   ▢ #cccccc

               Bottom: solid ⬍   1   ⬍ pix... ⬍   ▢ #cccccc

               Left: solid ⬍   1   ⬍ pix... ⬍   ▢ #cccccc

               (Help)   (Apply) (Cancel) (OK)

Add a 10px padding on all sides to create space inside of the box.

5   Save your page and preview it in a browser. The overall box appears cleaner and more defined, and the text is surrounded by the right amount of space.

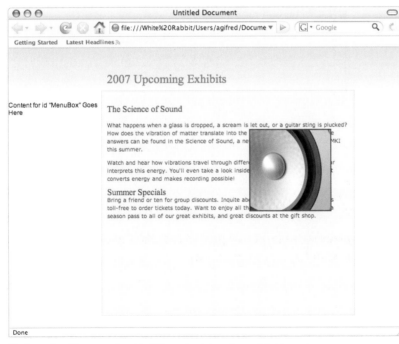

Borders and padding can make a big difference in giving a layout definition and space.

Adding margins

Just as padding plays an important role in creating space between boxes and content, margins play an important role in distancing elements from each other in a layout. You also can use margins to create space between a box and its containing element, which can be another box, or the page itself.

1   In the CSS Styles panel, double-click the ID named #MenuBox to edit it in the CSS Rule definition dialog box.

You'll be working with the lefthand box (MenuBox).

2   When the dialog box appears, select the Box category. Locate the Margin settings and uncheck the Same for All checkbox; in this case, you're going to apply a margin to only a single side of the box.

3 Under Margin, enter **15** pixels in the Left text field. Press OK to apply the margin and exit the dialog box.

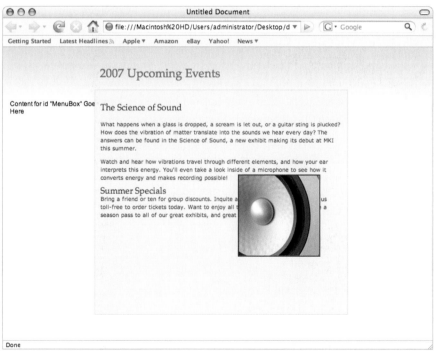

Double-click the #MenuBox ID to edit it. Add a 15-pixel margin on the left side only, under the Box category.

4 Save your page and preview it in a browser. The left side of the box now pushes itself slightly off the edge of the page to create some necessary room.

The new margin setting creates some distance between the left side of the page and the box.

Adding and formatting a list

You can add just about anything to a box, including other boxes. You can use the same elements you've become familiar with, such as images, text, tables, and lists. The Menu box on the left will feature a list that will act as a navigational aid to other areas of the McKnight Institute site.

1 Select the placeholder text inside the MenuBox *<div>* on the left and delete it. With your cursor positioned in the box, type in the following words, each separated by a return:

Upcoming Events

New Exhibits

Summer Specials

2 Select all of the words you just typed, and then click the unordered, bulleted list button (⋮≣) on the Property inspector. The words are wrapped into a new list.

Use the unordered list icon on the Property inspector
to convert the items into a bulleted list.

3 Highlight the words *Summer Special*, and locate the Link field in the Property inspector. Click the Browse for File button (📁) next to the Link field and, when the Select File dialog box appears, select the layout2.html file located under your root folder. Press OK (Windows) or Choose (Mac OS). The words *Summer Special* now link to the selected page.

4 Next, you'll create a new CSS rule to format this list. From the CSS Styles panel menu, choose New; the New CSS Rule dialog box appears. Set the Selector type as Advanced, and enter the following selector name: **#MenuBox li**. This contextual selector targets list items, but only when they appear in the MenuBox *<div>*. Select the This document only radio button, then press OK.

Create a new contextual selector that formats list items within the MenuBox <div> only.

5   On the left side of the dialog box, select the List category. In the Type drop-down menu, choose None to remove the bullet points. Select the Background category, then set the Background color to #FFFFCC, and under the Type category, set the Weight to Bold. Press OK to create the style.

6   The contextual selector you created applies to any list inside the MenuBox *<div>*, so the list is already formatted. Save and preview your page in a browser to see the results.

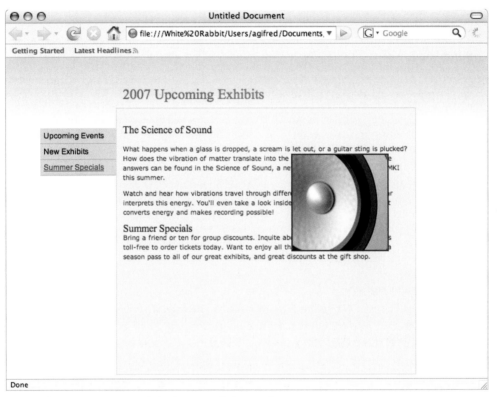

Background images can create a great look when you apply them to a box.

Exercise

Modify the #MenuBox ID to include a background-image property; use the studio.jpg image located in the images folder.

Fine-tuning layouts

To make a layout truly look professional, set aside time to properly line up, size, and coordinate elements on the page. With a layout such as this, you can use the many visual aids built into Dreamweaver to fine-tune the positioning, size, and composition of elements on a page.

Box visibility and the AP Elements panel

An advantage of using the Draw AP Div button is that any box it creates is automatically listed in the AP Elements panel, available at Window > AP Elements. The AP Elements panel serves as a simple mechanism for managing and selecting AP Divs, allowing you to easily locate an element or toggle visibility off or on for any AP Div.

Although AP Divs are automatically added to the AP Elements panel, any absolutely positioned element displays in the AP Elements panel as well. If you set a position property on an element to absolute, it becomes available in the AP Elements panel, and you can select or toggle it, just like you can AP Divs.

The visibility property

When you toggle an AP Div on or off in the AP Elements panel, Dreamweaver is actually setting a CSS property, called visibility, to one of two values—visible or hidden—for the selected element. Clicking next to any listed element under the Visibility column toggles it on or off. A closed eye indicates that the visibility property has been added and set to hidden. An open eye indicates that the visibility property has been created, but is set to visible. By default, all elements are visible, even if the visibility is not specified.

Prevent overlaps option

To prevent AP Divs from occupying the same space unintentionally, the AP Elements panel includes a Prevent overlaps option that is checked by default. To freely position or intentionally overlap AP Divs, uncheck this option.

The Prevent overlaps option.

Setting up guides

Guides are an essential part of placement and positioning, and they can ensure that elements line up properly. The freedom of CSS boxes can sometimes open the door to erratic placement of elements, so before you complete a page, it's a good idea to use guides to line up elements horizontally and vertically throughout a page.

Guides are created from the rulers that appear along the top and left edges of your Document window. Before you create guides, you'll need to make sure the document rulers are visible. If the rulers are not visible, choose View > Rulers > Show to toggle them on. To make sure you can freely place your guides, uncheck View > Guides > Guides Snap To Elements.

1   Click on the left ruler and drag toward the right to produce a new vertical guide. Release the guide at 200 pixels from the left (use the top ruler as your reference). Create a second vertical guide in the same manner at 650 pixels from the left.

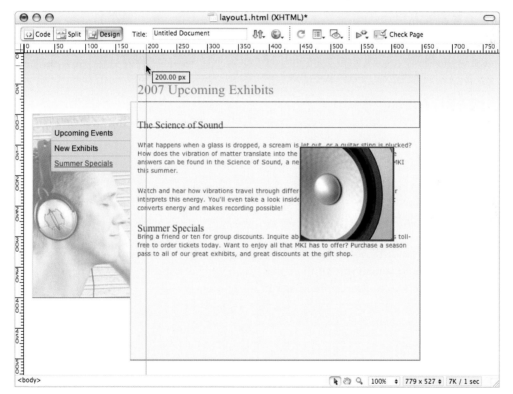

Add vertical guides at 200 and 650 pixels, using the top ruler as a reference.

2   Click on the top ruler and drag toward the bottom to produce a new horizontal guide; release it at 100 pixels from the top (use the left ruler as your reference). Create a second horizontal guide at 400 pixels from the top.

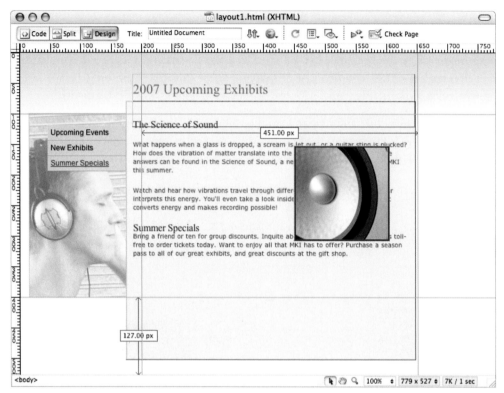

Add horizontal guides at 100 and 400 pixels from the top, using the left ruler as a guide.

3   Now you're ready to position items with the guides. Before you start, choose Window > AP Elements to launch the AP Elements panel. Uncheck the Prevent Overlaps box; you'll need the freedom to overlap items as you move them by hand.

4   On the AP Elements panel, select apDiv2; this makes the Title box at the top of the page active. Grab it by its handle and position it so that its left edge lines up with the vertical guide at 200 pixels.

Use the guides you created to slide the Title box into position.

5   On the AP Elements panel, select apDiv1; this selects the large content box in the middle of the page. Grab the box by its handle and move it so that its top edge aligns with the topmost guide (100 pixels), and its left edge aligns with the leftmost guide (at 200 pixels).

6   Slide the menu container on the left (MenuBox) down so that its top edge aligns with the topmost guide.

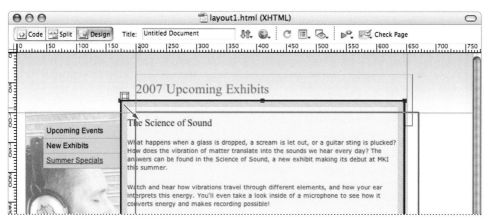

Reposition apDiv1 using the guides for reference.

7   Guides can also be useful when resizing elements to fit a layout. Click the edge of the main content box (apDiv1), and resize it by its right edge until it lines up with the guide at 650 pixels. Grab it by its bottom edge and resize it so that its bottom edge lines up with the horizontal guide at 400 pixels. The edges of the content boxes snap into place along the guides.

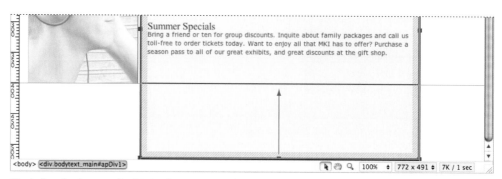

Use the bounding box around apDiv1 and resize it to match the placement of the guides.

8   Use the AP Elements panel, and select apDiv3 to highlight the box that contains the speaker photo. Grab it by its handle and reposition it as shown here.

Reposition apDiv3 to finish the layout.

9   Save your page and preview it using File > Preview in Browser.

The completed layout.

Take a moment to admire the page you've created, and congratulate yourself on a job well done. You've taken a big step toward the powerful and flexible world of CSS positioning, and away from the time-tested but limited approach of table layouts.

Self study

In a new document, create a new layout using only AP Divs, and make sure there are boxes for the following elements: a header, a footer, a left or right-side vertical menu, and a content area. Add a nested *<div>* inside your content area to contain an image of your choice. Create at least one tag style and two class styles to format your page content. Make sure to preview your work in a browser, using File > Preview in Browser or by pressing the Preview/Debug in browser button (◉).

Review

Questions

1   In what two ways can *<div>* tags be created for the purpose of layout in Dreamweaver?

2   What type of CSS rule is used to assign unique aspects to each box, such as position and size?

3   What are two ways you can select an entire AP Div in your document?

Answers

1   The Draw AP Div and Insert Div Tag buttons, located on the Layout category of the Insert bar.

2   ID styles are the best choice for styling unique elements on a page.

3   By clicking the tab in its upper left-hand corner, or selecting it in the AP Elements panel.

What you'll learn in this lesson:

- Customizing panels and panel groups
- Resizing the Document window
- Using guides and grids
- Exploring the tag selector

Fine-Tuning Your Workflow

Once you become familiar with building web pages in Dreamweaver CS3, you'll find yourself using some features more often than others. In this lesson, you'll learn how to save time by customizing the Dreamweaver environment to streamline your workflow.

Starting up

Before starting, make sure that your tools and panels are consistent by resetting your preferences. See "Resetting Adobe Dreamweaver CS3 preferences" on page 4.

You will work with several files from the dw07lessons folder in this lesson. Make sure that you have loaded the dwlessons folder onto your hard drive from the supplied DVD. See "Loading lesson files" on page 3.

Before you begin, you need to create a site definition that points to the dw07lessons folder from the included DVD that contains resources you need for these lessons. Go to Site > New Site, or, for details on creating a site definition, refer to Lesson 2, "Creating a New Site."

See Lesson 7 in action!

Use the accompanying video to gain a better understanding of how to use some of the features shown in this lesson. Open the Dynamic_Learning_DW_CS3.swf file located in the Videos folder and select Lesson 7 to view the video training file for this lesson.

Customizing panels and panel groups

Panels can be moved, grouped, and docked to help keep everything you regularly use at your fingertips. In the next part of this lesson, you'll create a custom workspace for CSS layouts. You'll start by closing the Application and Tag Inspector panel groups, then repositioning the CSS and AP Elements panels.

1   Expand the Application panel group by clicking on the black arrow to the left of its label.

Use the black arrow on the left side of the Application panel group's title bar to expand the panel.

2   Open the Application panel group's menu by clicking the button on the far right of its title bar. Choose the Close panel group option from the bottom of this context menu.

3   Expand the Tag Inspector panel group, then use its panel menu to close it as well.

If you need to reopen the Tag Inspector panel group, choose Window > Tag Inspector from the main menu. If you'd like to reopen the Application panel group, open the Window menu and choose either Databases, Bindings, Server Behaviors, or Components. Any of these options will restore the Application panel group to its default position.

4   Expand the CSS panel group by clicking on the black arrow to the left of its label. This panel group contains two panels: CSS Styles and AP Elements. To see both panels simultaneously, you'll drag the AP Elements panel out of the CSS group.

5   Click and hold the AP Elements tab. Drag this tab into your workspace to detach it from the CSS panel group. The tabs for CSS Styles and AP Elements become title bars.

Drag the AP Elements panel out of the CSS panel group.

6   To keep the AP Elements panel from interfering with your workspace, you can dock it with the other panels. Move your cursor to the left of the black arrow in the AP Elements title bar. When the four-arrow icon (✛) (Windows) or hand icon (☝) (Mac OS) appears, click and hold.

7   Drag the AP Elements panel above the title bar of the Files panel group. When a solid line appears above the title bar of the Files panel group, release the AP Elements panel to snap it into place.

8   If your Files panel group was minimized by repositioning the AP Elements panel, expand it by clicking the black arrow on the left side of its title bar. Move your cursor over the center of the AP Elements panel's title bar. When the double-sided arrow appears, drag the title bar up to make more room for the Files panel group.

9   If necessary, resize the Files panel group by dragging its title bar. When you're finished, the panels should look something like the example below. This configuration will give you quick access to the panels you'll use the most when creating a CSS-based layout.

The customized panels.

10   To save this workspace, choose Window > Workspace Layout > Save Current. When the Save Workspace Layout dialog box appears, enter **CSS Layout** into the Name text field and press OK.

11   Choose Window > Workspace Layout > Designer (Windows) or Window > Workspace Layout > Default (Mac OS) or to switch to the default workspace, then choose Window > Workspace Layout > CSS Layout to switch back to the custom workspace you just created.

Using the Favorites tab on the Insert bar

To help organize the many options available in the Insert bar, Dreamweaver groups similar items into tabs. You may have already found yourself using some items more often than others. The Favorites tab is a great way to group commonly used items into one place for quick access.

1   Double-click on the index.html file in the Files panel. In this exercise, you'll be inserting a number of Images and AP Divs to create two pages in the Sounds of Nature web site. To avoid switching between the Layout and Common tabs, you'll add these items to the Favorites tab.

2   Click on the Favorites tab in the Insert bar. Right-click (Windows) or Ctrl+click (Mac OS) in the empty gray area beneath the Insert bar tabs and choose Customize Favorites from the resulting contextual menu. The Customize Favorite Objects dialog box appears.

Right-click (Windows) or Ctrl+click (Mac OS) in the empty gray area beneath the Insert bar tabs and choose Customize Favorites.

3   On the right side of the Customize Favorite Objects dialog box, the list of Available objects is organized by the tabs indicating where each object can be found in the Insert bar. Select Image and press the Add button in the middle of the dialog box.

Select Image and press the Add button.

4   Scroll down and select Draw AP Div from the list of Available objects, then press the Add button. Press OK. The Favorites tab now features the Image and Draw AP Div buttons.

Resizing the Document window

If you're familiar with any page layout or graphics processing programs, adjusting the size of the window in which you're working is probably something that you do regularly. However, when you're working on web pages in Dreamweaver, it's a good idea to think carefully about the size of your document. Since a number of different hardware and software configurations may be used to view your content, it can be tricky to make sure your web site looks good on every user's computer. In the next part of this lesson, you'll resize the Document window to make sure the Sounds of Nature web site is being designed with the target audience in mind.

1   Index.html should still be open in your Document window. If not, open it now. Also, make sure you're in the Design view. If necessary, click the Show Design view button in the Document toolbar.

   If you're working on a Windows computer, choose Window > Cascade from the main menu. The Dreamweaver interface for Windows and Mac OS is slightly different and will be covered in the *Switching between tabs and cascading documents* exercise later in this lesson.

2   Click and drag the bottom right corner of the Document window toward the top-left corner to resize the window.

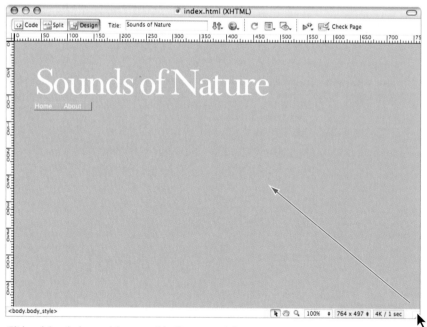

Click and drag the bottom right corner of the Document window to resize it.

If the bottom-right corner of your Document window is hidden by the Property inspector, turn off the Property inspector temporarily by choosing Window > Property inspector. Then resize the window and turn the Property inspector back on.

Resizing the Document window like this is flexible and convenient, but you may be tempted to forget about the size of your visitors' screens. An appropriate size on your new, super-deluxe, high-resolution monitor will not be an appropriate size on the ten-year-old monitor you gifted to your uncle when you upgraded.

3   To the left of the corner you used to resize the Document window in the last step, there is a Window Size drop-down menu. This menu can be used to select common monitor sizes. From the menu, choose the option that reads 760 x 420 (800 x 600, Maximized).

Choose 760 x 420 (800 x 600, Maximized) from the Window Size drop-down menu.

The options in the Window Size drop-down menu correspond to a number of common monitor sizes. In this case, an 800 x 600-pixel monitor has been chosen. The size of the page is further reduced to 760 x 420 to accommodate the menu and scrollbars of the user's browser.

Using guides

In Lesson 6, "Creating Page Layouts with CSS," you learned how AP Divs can be positioned using guides to easily create precise layouts. Guides are an invaluable tool, and Dreamweaver provides a number of features that make them even more helpful and easy to use. In the next part of this lesson, you'll add an AP Div to index.html and then place an image inside the div. First, you'll draw some guides to help you size and position the div.

1   If your rulers are hidden, choose View > Rulers > Show to turn them on.

Rulers can use inches, centimeters, or pixels in Dreamweaver. Since pixels are the most common unit of measurement on the Web, they are the default. If you prefer inches or centimeters, right-click (Windows) or Ctrl+click (Mac OS) on the rulers to access a context menu where you can choose your preferred unit. In this lesson, we'll be using pixels, so it's a good idea to stick with them for now.

2   Click inside the vertical ruler on the left side of your Document window and drag a guide into the center of the page. Double-click on this guide to open the Move Guide dialog box. From this dialog box, you can set an exact location for guides. This can be especially helpful when building a web page based on sketches or mockups.

3   Enter **38** in the Location text field and press OK. The guide is repositioned 38 pixels from the left side of the document.

4   Create another vertical guide and set its position to 494 pixels. Notice that hovering over either of these guides with the cursor produces a yellow box indicating the guide's position. Now, hold down the Ctrl (Windows) or Command (Mac OS) key and move your cursor over each guide. The blue line with arrows on either end indicates the distance between each of your guides, as well as the distance between guides and the edge of the Document window.

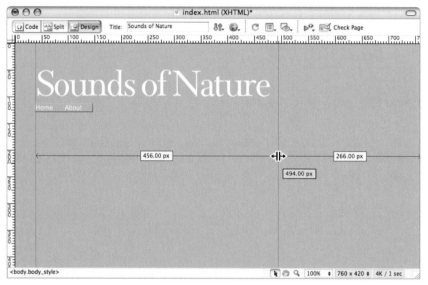

Hold down Ctrl (Windows) or Command (Mac OS) and hover over guides.

5   Drag two horizontal guides down from the ruler at the top of the Document window. Double-click on each of them, then use the Move Guide dialog box to position one of them 152 pixels from the top of the document and the other 380 pixels from the top of document.

6   Next, you'll draw an AP Div and start adding some content, but first make sure that Snap to Guides is turned on, by choosing View > Guides > Edit Guides. The Guides dialog box appears, with a number of options for customizing your guides.

If you happen to be using a color in your web page that makes the guides hard to see, you can change their color here. Also, the Lock Guides option can be a helpful way to avoid accidentally repositioning guides. For now, make sure Snap to Guides is checked and press OK.

The Guides dialog box allows you to change the color of guides and turn snapping on and off.

7   Now that your guides are set up, you're ready to add some content. With the Favorites tab selected in the Insert bar, click the Draw AP Div button you added earlier. Draw an AP Div inside the box created by your four guides.

8   If the edges of the div don't line up with the guides on your first try, select the div by clicking on its name in the AP Elements panel, then drag each edge until it snaps into place.

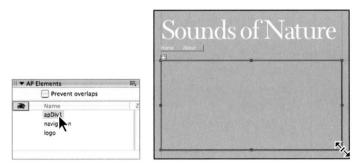

Readjust the edges of the div by selecting it in the AP Div panel and dragging its edges until they snap in place.

9   Click inside the div to place your cursor and then click the Image button in the Favorites tab of the Insert bar. In the Select Image Source dialog box, select hp_photo.jpg from the images folder inside the dw07lessons folder and press OK (Windows) or Choose (Mac OS).

10 In the Image Tag Accessibility Attributes dialog box, type **Soothing Lakefront** into the Alternate text field and press OK. The hp_photo.jpg image fits nicely inside the div you created earlier.

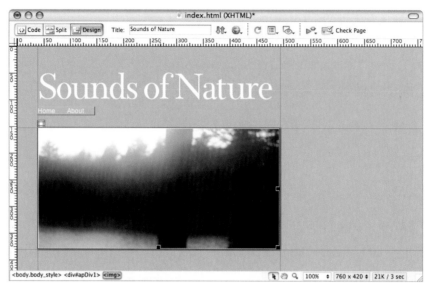

The hp_photo.jpg placed inside of the AP Div.

11 Choose File > Save and leave index.html open.

Using grids

Much like guides, grids are a great way to help keep your layout precise and uniform. In the next part of this lesson, you'll be adding AP Divs and images to the About page of the Sounds of Nature web site. Creating a custom grid will help you align and evenly distribute these new elements on the page.

1 Double-click on the about.html file in your Files panel to open the About page. You may notice that this page has a white background and uses a default typeface. Later on, you'll use the tag selector to change this.

2 Choose View > Grid > Grid Settings to open the Grid Settings dialog box. Much like the Guides dialog box, the Grid Settings dialog box can be used to specify the grid color and turn on snapping. Enter **#CCCCCC** in the Color text field and check Show Grid and Snap to Grid to turn the grid on and enable snapping.

3 For this layout, enter **38** in the Spacing text field and make sure Pixels are selected as the unit of measurement. Choosing a spacing of 38 pixels will create a series of squares which are 38 pixels high by 38 pixels wide. Press OK.

```
┌───────────────────────────────────────────┐
│              Grid Settings                 │
│                                            │
│   Color:  [▢▾] #CCCCCC      ( OK )          │
│           ☑ Show grid       ( Apply )      │
│           ☑ Snap to grid                   │
│                             ( Cancel )     │
│  Spacing: [38] [ Pixels  ▴▾]               │
│                                            │
│  Display: ◉ Lines           ( Help )       │
│           ○ Dots                           │
└───────────────────────────────────────────┘
```

The Grid Settings dialog box.

4 With the grid established, add the AP Divs that will house your images. Press the Draw AP Div button in the Favorites tab of the Insert bar. Draw a square div that is 3 grid units wide and 3 grid units high. Use the figure below for reference.

Draw a square AP Div.

5 Draw a second AP Div one grid unit below the first. Use the figure below for reference.

Draw a second AP Div one grid unit below the first.

6 Click inside the first div to place the cursor and then press the Image button in the Favorites tab of the Insert bar.

7 In the Select Image Source dialog box, select tree.jpg from the images folder in the dw07lessons folder and press OK (Windows) or Choose (Mac OS). When the Image Tag Accessibility Attributes dialog box appears, enter **tree** in the Alternate text field and press OK.

8 Repeat steps 6 and 7 to add forest.jpg to the second div. Type **forest** into the Alternate text field of the Image Tag Accessibility Attributes dialog box.

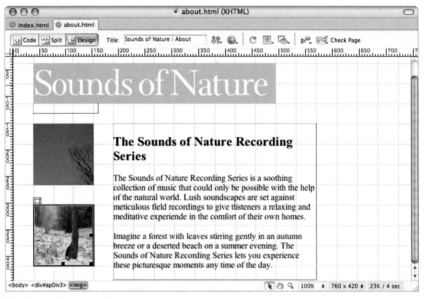

The about.html page after inserting the tree and forest images.

9 Choose File > Save and leave about.html open for the next part of this lesson.

The tag selector

In HTML, the organization of elements takes the form of a family tree. In the previous two exercises, you created AP Divs and then inserted images into them. In HTML terms, each of these images are children of the AP Divs within which they reside. It's beyond the scope of this book to explore all of the implications of these relationships, but it's important to know that they exist. The tag selector is a feature of Dreamweaver that allows you to select HTML elements based on their relationship to one another. Next, you'll explore the tag selector and then use it to apply a single style that will affect the entire about.html page.

1   With the About page open, click once on the forest image that you inserted at the end of the last exercise. At the bottom left corner of the Document window are a number of HTML tags. This is the tag selector. The *<img>* tag at the end of this line is highlighted to indicate that the forest.jpg image is selected. In addition, the Property inspector displays information and options related to this image.

With the forest image selected, the <img> tag in the tag selector is highlighted and the Property inspector displays information and options related to this image.

2   In the tag selector, click on the *<div#apDiv2>* tag to the left of the *<img>* tag. Notice that the options in the Property inspector change to reflect the selected div. In this case, you've selected the parent of the forest image.

3   To further illustrate this relationship, choose Edit > Select Child from the main menu. The *<img>* tag becomes highlighted in the tag selector, and the Property inspector changes to reflect the selected element.

4 Now, select *\<body>* on the far left side of the tag selector. The Property inspector displays options and information related to the *\<body>* tag. From the Style drop-down menu, choose body_style.

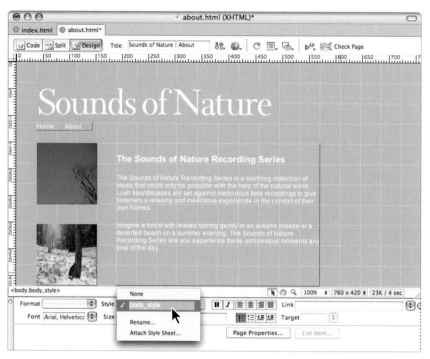

With the \<body> tag selected in the tag selector, choose body_style from the Style drop-down menu.

Since many CSS properties are inherited throughout the document, it is possible to write generalized rules that will be applied to all of the elements on a page. In this case, body_style changes the font and text color for the entire document because every element is a descendant of the body.

5 Choose File > Save and leave about.html open for the next part of this lesson.

Switching between tabs and cascading documents

By default, Dreamweaver organizes open documents with a series of tabs in the upper-right corner of the Document window. If you'd like to compare documents, or you simply prefer to use separate windows for each document, the cascade option provides an alternative for viewing open files. Next, you'll use this feature to simultaneously view the home page and the About page of the Sounds of Nature web site.

1 Both index.html and about.html should still be open. If they are not, open them now.

2 If you're working on a Windows computer, your documents is already displayed in the cascade view. If you're working on a Macintosh, choose Window > Cascade from the main menu.

The home.html and about.html documents in cascade view.

3 With each document floating in its own window, you can use the bottom-right corner to resize them as discussed earlier, or use Dreamweaver's tiling feature to display them side by side. Choose Window > Tile Vertically (Windows) or Window > Tile (Mac OS).

With the windows tiled in this fashion, it's possible to see both documents, but unless you have a very large monitor, you won't be able to see either document in its entirety. In the next part of this lesson, you'll use the Zoom tool to fit each document into its window.

Zooming

Since web sites will rarely be viewed any smaller or larger than 100% of their size by visitors on the Web, you'll probably want to use the Zoom tool sparingly. In some cases, it can be helpful for exact positioning or viewing multiple documents at once, but it's a good idea to return to 100% when you're finished. Now, you'll use the Zoom and Hand tools to navigate throughout your document, and then you'll choose a magnification setting that will allow you to see the entire About and home pages side by side.

1 At the bottom of the Document window on the about.html page, select the Zoom tool (🔍). Click twice inside the Document window to zoom to 200%.

2 With the Zoom tool still selected, hold down the Alt (Windows) or Option (Mac OS) key and click once inside the Document window. The About page zooms out to 150%.

3 At the bottom of the Document window, select the Hand tool (✋) to the left of the Zoom tool. Click and drag to the right in the Document window. The Hand tool allows you to drag a document around in its window like a piece of paper.

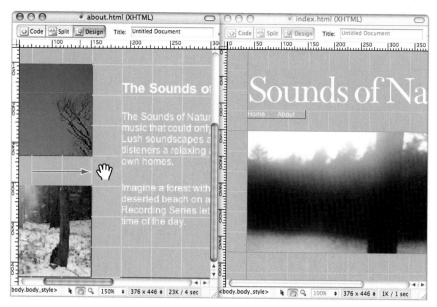

Use the Hand tool to drag a document around in its window.

4 Double-click on the Zoom tool at the bottom of the Document window to return to 100%. Now, choose 66% from the Set magnification drop-down menu to the right of the Zoom tool. Depending on the size of your monitor, this magnification level may allow you to see the entire About page. If not, use the Zoom tool or the Set magnification drop-down menu to find the appropriate size.

5   When you've found the best magnification level for your monitor, click on the title bar of index.html to make this document active. Click and drag to highlight the percentage in the Set magnification text field and enter in the magnification level you used in the about.html window. Press Enter (Windows) or Return (Mac OS) to commit the new value. When you're finished, your documents should look like the figure below.

Adjust the magnification level until both pages can be seen in their entirety.

6   To return to the tabbed view, click the Maximize button in the top-right corner of the Document window (Windows) or choose Window > Combine as Tabs (Mac OS). As mentioned earlier, you should always remember to return to 100% magnification when you're finished using the Zoom tool. Also, you'll want to make sure the Select tool is active to avoid any surprises when working on later lessons.

7   Click on the Select tool (↖) in the bottom of the Document window and choose 100% from the Set magnification drop-down menu.

Self study

In this lesson, you followed a predetermined workflow that was tailored toward producing two pages in the Sounds of Nature web site. The key to creating a streamlined workflow for yourself is planning ahead. Imagine you were creating a web site for a local bakery. Make some sketches of what the pages will look like. In Dreamweaver, spend some time setting up a workspace that would make building the bakery web site easier. Think about which elements you might use the most. Then, use the guides and the grid to help create a layout that reflects the sketches you made earlier.

Review

Questions

1   Is it possible to resize the Document window to preview how a web page will appear on different users' monitors?

2   How can you position guides on the page without dragging them?

3   Are tabs the only way to organize open documents?

Answers

1   The Window Size drop-down menu at the bottom of the Document window contains a number of preset sizes that correspond to common monitor sizes.

2   To more exactly position guides, simply double-click on any guide to open the Move Guide dialog box.

3   If you prefer to use floating windows instead of tabs, choose Window > Cascade from the main menu.

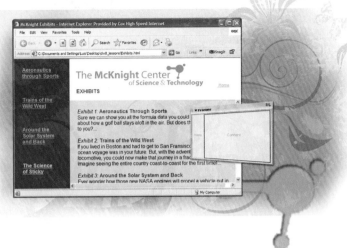

What you'll learn in this lesson:

- Creating frames and framesets
- Setting frame properties
- Using the Frames panel
- Adding and editing frame content
- Using target frames
- Adding *<noframes>* content

Working with Frames

With the frames capability in Dreamweaver, you can divide a single browser window to display several different documents at once. When you view a framed browser window, you are viewing multiple HTML documents, also known as a frameset. This lesson shows you how to create frames, and points out some helpful techniques for working with them.

Starting up

Before starting, make sure that your tools and panels are consistent by resetting your workspace. See "Resetting the Dreamweaver workspace" on page 3.

You will work with several files from the dw08lessons folder in this lesson. Make sure that you have loaded the dwlessons folder onto your hard drive from the supplied DVD. See "Loading lesson files" on page 3.

Before you begin, you need to create a site definition that points to the dw08lessons folder from the included DVD that contains resources you need for these lessons. Go to Site > New Site, or, for details on creating a site definition, refer to Lesson 2, "Creating a New Site."

See Lesson 8 in action!

Use the accompanying video to gain a better understanding of how to use some of the features shown in this lesson. Open the Dynamic_Learning_DW_CS3.swf file located in the Videos folder and select Lesson 8 to view the video training file for this lesson.

How frames work

Frames provide a way to divide a browser window into multiple regions, each capable of displaying a different HTML document.

A frameset is an HTML file that defines the layout and properties of a set of frames, including the number of frames, their size and placement, and the content that appears in each frame. When you open a frameset file, the browser also opens all relevant HTML documents and displays them in their respective frames.

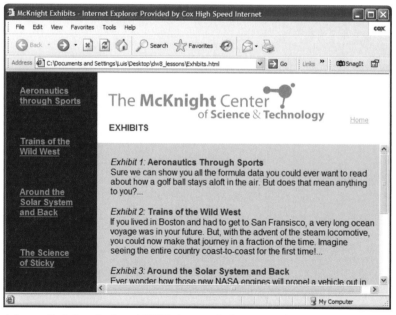

A frameset file displays all referenced HTML documents in their respective frames.

Advantages and disadvantages of frames

If you have the time (and patience), it is possible to create a page design with a framelike layout without using frames. That, however, might involve excessive steps, such as building navigation controls on every page within your site. Frames, when used correctly, can be useful for site navigation and can save you a good deal of time in the page-creation process.

Using frames is not always a good idea, however. Like many time-saving features used in web design, there are advantages and disadvantages of using frames for layout.

Here are some advantages to using frames:

- Using frames saves time and avoids repetitive work in page creation.
- The viewer's browser doesn't need to reload graphics used for navigation on every page.
- Frames enable parts of the page to stay stationary (like navigation) while other parts (like content) are able to scroll independently.

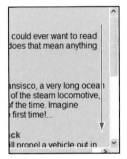

Viewers can scroll through long content in a frame using built-in scrollbars.

Here are some disadvantages of using frames:

- Aligning content precisely in different frames can be problematic.
- Viewers won't be able to bookmark individual framed pages (unless you provide specific server code).
- Testing the navigation from frame to frame can be time-consuming and many users find it difficult to navigate sites with frames.
- Framed documents are problematic for search engines.
- Documents may appear outside of the context of their frame set, such as those displayed in results from a search engine.
- Frames make it more difficult to count page or ad views.

Despite these concerns, frames are still used in many sites and are supported by Dreamweaver, so it is important to understand them. Take these advantages and disadvantages into account when deciding whether to use frames when you create pages on your own.

Common frame usage

Frames are most commonly used for navigation, with one frame displaying a document containing navigation controls, and other frames showing pages with content.

In this lesson, you'll be building an interactive Exhibits page for a museum web site. It will consist of a frameset with three frames: a narrow frame on the left with navigation controls, a short frame along the top containing the museum's logo and title, and a large frame containing the actual (and changeable) page content. Each frame will act as a container for the page it's displaying, but the page will not actually be part of the frame. When you're finished, your frameset will look like this:

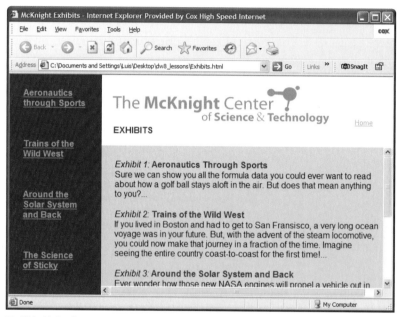

You'll build this frameset during this lesson.

Creating framesets

The best way to understand how frames and framesets work—and specifically how to work with them in Dreamweaver—is to create some.

There are two ways to create a frameset in Dreamweaver. You can choose from various predefined framesets, or you can design one from scratch. For this lesson, we'll combine both techniques, using a predefined frameset to begin, and then adding a *splitter* to customize the frameset's layout.

1 Choose File > New and click on Blank Page if necessary, then select HTML in the Page Type column and make sure *<none>* is selected in the Layout column. Press Create.

2 Make frame borders visible by choosing View > Visual Aids > Frame Borders.

Use the Frame Borders command to make your frame borders visible.

3 At the top of the Insert toolbar, click on the Layout tab.

4 On the right side of the Insert toolbar, click on the Frames button (▣·), and choose Left Frame from the top of the menu. Your page is now divided by a light gray line into two frames.

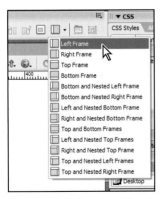

Choose a prebuilt frame layout from the Insert toolbar (Left Frame).

By default, Dreamweaver is set up to prompt you to determine the Frame Tag Accessibility Attributes. This feature allows you to tag your frames so that they are more accessible to visually impaired viewers.

5 Choose mainFrame from the Frame drop-down menu, and type **Content** into the Title text field.

6 Choose leftFrame from the Frame drop-down menu, and type **Menu** into the Title text field. You can change both titles from within the same dialog box. Press OK.

Use the Frame Tag Accessibility Attributes dialog box to tag your frames so that they're more accessible.

Changing the names of the Frame tags for Accessibility is not the same as changing the names of the frames themselves. In the next exercise, you will learn how to select frames and rename them

Selecting frames

As you view your Document window in the Design view, you can click inside each of the two frames you've created and see a blinking insertion cursor there. If you want to change a frame's properties (including borders, margins, and scrollbar access), you'll want to select each frame individually.

1 Alt+click (Windows) or Option+Shift+click (Mac OS) inside the left (leftFrame) frame in the Design view to select the frame.

2. In the Properties panel in the field for Frame name, highlight the text leftFrame and type **Menu**.

3   Alt+click/Option+Shift+click inside the main (mainFrame) frame in the Design view to select the frame.

Notice that when a frame is selected, its borders are outlined with a dotted line. You'll change your individual frames' properties later in this lesson.

Selected frames are highlighted with a dotted line border.

4   In the Properties panel, in the field for Frame name, highlight the text mainFrame and type **Content**.

Name your frames in the Property inspector.

Frame names must be one word in length, and cannot contain special characters. (Underscores are permitted.) They are also case-sensitive.

Selecting framesets

Framesets have properties too, including frame dimensions, border color, and width. To access a frameset's properties, you'll have to first select the frameset itself. Click on the internal frame border (the light gray line separating your Menu and Content frames) to select the frameset.

Click on border between your frames to select the frameset as a whole.

The Frames panel

The Frames panel allows you to see the structure of your frameset more clearly than the Document window allows. Its visual interface includes a thick border around the frameset, thin gray lines separating the frames, and a frame name clearly identifying each frame.

The Frames panel also allows you to more easily select frames and framesets than you can in the Document window, by clicking on the desired frames in the panel itself.

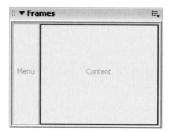

The Frames panel.

To select a frame or frameset in the Frames panel:

1 Choose Window > Frames, or press Shift+F2, to open the Frames panel.

2 To select the Content frame (which you named earlier), simply click on it in the Frames panel. Notice the selection outline that appears around the frame in the Document window, as well as in the Frames panel.

3 To select the entire frameset, click on the border around the frameset in the Frames panel. A bold, black selection outline now surrounds the entire frameset in both the Frames panel and the Document window.

Now that you have your frameset selected, you can move on to changing its properties.

Setting frameset properties

The dimensions, border width, and border color for the frames in your frameset are not set with the individual frames selected, but with the frameset itself selected. This is because your frames must always share the visible area of your page, and therefore, their sizes, borders, and so on must be relative within the frameset.

Border properties

Using the Property inspector, you can customize your frameset layout by adding borders of a particular width and/or color between your frames.

1 If necessary, click on the gray border separating your frames in order to reselect the entire frameset. The Property inspector at the bottom of your screen should now display frameset properties, including the number of rows and columns in your current frameset.

The Property inspector displays the properties of a selected frameset.

2 From the Borders drop-down menu, choose Yes to define a border between your frames. (The Default option allows the browser to determine how borders are displayed.)

3 In the Border Width field, type **6** to create a 6-pixel-wide border between your frames.

4 In the Border Color field, type the hexadecimal code of **666666** to make the border between your frames dark gray. You can also use the Color Picker to select the appropriate color swatch. Press Enter (Windows) or Return (Mac OS).

Now, you'll define the width of the frames in your frameset.

Frame dimensions

The Property inspector allows you to further customize your frameset layout by specifying the dimensions of each frame relative to the other(s).

1 Right-click (Windows) or Ctrl+click (Mac OS) on either of the rulers (horizontal or vertical) at the top and left side of your page. Choose Pixels from the context menu that appears.

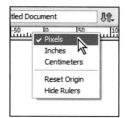

Set your ruler units to pixels whenever you're designing for the Web.

It's useful to work in pixels whenever possible in Dreamweaver, because you're designing your web pages to be viewed on a monitor, which is a pixel-based device.

2 Click the frame on the left side of the RowCol Selection area to select that frame's dimensions for editing.

Select the left side of the RowCol Selection area to edit that frame's dimensions.

3 To specify how much space a web browser should allocate to this frame, enter **175** into the (Column) Value field, and choose Pixels from the (Column) Units field. Press Enter (Windows) or Return (Mac OS).

Set the frame's width to a fixed value (175 pixels) in the Property inspector.

This sets the left frame of your frameset, where your navigation controls will appear, to a fixed width of 175 pixels. Setting a frame's width to a specific pixel value is common when you want that frame to always be the same size, as in a navigation menu.

4   Click on the frame on the right side of the RowCol Selection area to edit that frame's dimensions.

5   To specify how much space a web browser should allocate to this frame, choose Relative from the (Column) Units drop-down menu.

Set the remaining frame's width by choosing Relative from the (Column) Units drop-down menu.

This sets the right frame of your frameset, where you want your changeable content to appear, to fill the remaining space in the browser window, relative to the 175 pixels used by the left frame.

Choosing the Percent option specifies that the frame selected should be a percentage of the total width of the frameset, for example, 50% of the total width of the browser window.

You now have a frameset with two frames, one of which is set to a fixed width of 175 pixels in any browser window, the other of which is set to fill the remaining space with HTML page content of your choosing. Next, you'll change individual frame properties within your frameset.

6   Choose File > Save Frameset. When the Save As dialog box appears type **exhibits.html** into the Name text field. Navigate to the dw08lessons folder and press Save.

Saving frames and framesets

As with everything else you create in Dreamweaver, it pays to save your frames and framesets early and often. It's also true that you won't be able to preview your frameset in a browser without first saving the frameset and all of the content that appears in its frames. You can save these files individually or all at one time.

File	Edit	View	Insert	Modify	Text	Com;
New...				Ctrl+N		
Open...				Ctrl+O		
Browse in Bridge...				Ctrl+Alt+O		
Open Recent				▶		
Open in Frame...				Ctrl+Shift+O		
Close				Ctrl+W		
Close All				Ctrl+Shift+W		
Save Frameset				Ctrl+S		
Save Frameset As...				Ctrl+Shift+S		
Save All						

It's important to save your frames and framesets.

When saving a frameset, you'll have at least 3 different files that will have to be saved as a result of creating frames. There's the frameset, which is the HTML container file that houses the frames, and then there's the individual HTML files that are contained in each frame.

To save a frameset:

1   Select the frameset in the Frames panel or in the Document window.

2   Choose File > Save Frameset.

To save a frame's content:

1   Click in the frame to place an insertion cursor.

2   Choose File > Save Frame.

To save a frameset and all associated files:

1   Select the frameset.

2   Choose File > Save All.

Setting frame properties

Like frameset properties, you view and set frame properties in the Property inspector. When you set properties such as borders, margins, and the visibility of scrollbars for a specific frame, these settings override properties that you set previously for the frameset as a whole.

1 Select the right (Content) frame of your frameset by Alt+clicking (Windows) or Option+Shift+clicking (Mac OS) on it in the Document window.

2 In the Property inspector, click on the Browse button (📁) to the right of the Src text field to navigate to the source file Teaser.html. Press OK (Windows) or Choose (Mac OS). This is one way of choosing the default content of the Content frame. You'll learn other ways later in this lesson. Press Don't Save when prompted to save changes.

3 Directly beneath the Src setting, choose Yes from the Scroll drop-down menu to ensure that scrollbars appear in this frame.

Add scrollbars by choosing Yes from the Scroll drop-down.

The Default option lets each browser use its default setting to decide whether scrollbars are included. Most browsers default to Auto (which you can also choose from this drop-down menu), which makes scrollbars appear only when there isn't enough room to view the content of the frame. Choosing No from this menu prevents scrollbars from appearing.

4 Click the No resize checkbox to prevent viewers from dragging your frame borders to resize them in a browser.

Prevent viewers from resizing your frames by choosing the No Resize option.

5 From the Borders drop-down menu, choose No to hide this frame's border when viewed in a browser. This overrides the frameset's border property.

Hiding an individual frame's border overrides the frameset's border setting.

Choosing Yes from this menu shows the frame's borders, and choosing Default leaves this decision up to the browser itself. Most browsers default to showing borders, except when the frameset's border properties are set to No.

A border is hidden only when all frames that share that border are set to No.

6   In the Border Color field, enter **666666** to set all of the frame's borders to a dark gray color. Press Enter (Windows) or Return (Mac OS). This applies to all borders touching this frame, and it overrides the frameset's border color properties.

7   The Margin Width and Margin Height fields in the Property inspector set the space (in pixels) between the frame borders and the content. Set each of these to 25 pixels to give yourself some breathing room.

Setting the background color of a frame

The background color of a frame is not a property that you can set in the Property inspector. To change frame background colors, you'll need to use the Page Properties dialog box.

1   Click inside the right frame to place an insertion cursor.

2   Choose Modify > Page Properties. The Page Properties dialog box appears.

3   In the Background field, enter **d7d7d7** to set the background color of your frame to a light gray.

Set the background color of a frame (d7d7d7) in the Page Properties dialog.

4   Press OK to close the Page Properties dialog box and see the results.

Repeat these steps to change the background color of the Menu frame to #843432.

Splitting a frame

There are two ways to divide an existing frame within your frameset into discrete frames of their own. First, you can use a Split Frame command:

1   Click inside the Content frame to place an insertion cursor.

2   Choose Modify > Frameset, > Split Frame Down. A new frame is created above the Content frame.

Divide an existing frame using the Split Frame Down command.

Dragging a frame border

A second way to divide an existing frame is to drag a frame border to split the existing frame in two:

1   Choose Edit > Undo to undo the previous frame addition.

2   Alt+click (Windows) or Option+Shift+click (Mac OS) on the Content frame.

3   If necessary, choose View > Visual Aids > Frame Borders to make your frame borders visible.

4   Roll your mouse over the frame border at the top of the Content frame until you see the double-headed arrow (↕). Click and drag a frame border from that edge into the middle of the frame.

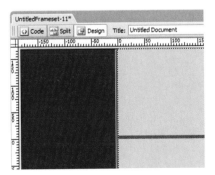

Drag a frame border to split an existing frame in two.

Once you have split a frame using either of these methods, you can reposition the border by clicking and dragging it to a new location in the frame, changing the space that is available for content:

5 Position your cursor over the border you just placed to split the frame.

6 Click and drag the border downward (or upward, depending on where you placed it) to the 100-pixel mark in the vertical ruler to the left of the Document window.

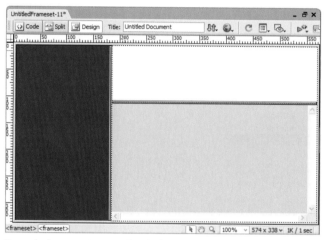

Drag a border to reposition it within the frameset.

You can use this new frame at the top of your frameset for the museum's title and logo content. The page displayed in this frame will never change as the viewer navigates the site. (You'll set the default content of this frame, using the Open in Frame command later in this lesson.)

7 Select the new frame, using the Frames panel. In the Property inspector, name it **Title**.

Now you're ready to add and edit frame content.

Specifying frame content

On your web page, you want the viewer to be able to click on a link in the navigation frame (called Menu), and have linked content appear in the main (Content) frame on the right.

The content of the Menu and Title frames, however, remains unchanged. To set the default content for each of these unchanging frames, you'll use the Open in Frame command.

1 Click in the Menu frame to place an insertion cursor.

2 Choose File > Open in Frame, or press Ctrl+O (Windows) or Shift+Command+O (Mac OS).

Choose Open in Frame to set the default content for a nonchanging frame.

3 Navigate to the dw08lessons folder on your desktop and select the HTML page Menu.html. The base content for the Menu frame has been created for you.

4 Press OK (Windows) or Choose (Mac OS) to specify the initial content of the Menu frame. Press Don't Save when prompted to save changes.

5 Repeat steps 1–4 to specify the initial content of the Title frame. Insert the Title.html file here.

6 Finally, to make these HTML pages the default content displayed when the frameset is opened in a browser, choose File > Save All.

Targeting frames

In a framed document, you must target links for them to open a document in another frame. Targeting is simply a way of specifying in which frame Dreamweaver should open the linked content.

In Lesson 3, "Adding Text and Images," you learned how to link content from one HTML page to another. For this lesson, the links from items in your menu to their corresponding pages have been made for you. Your job is to target these links to the frames you created earlier in the lesson.

To target links to previously created frames:

1   Use the Browser Preview button (⊚) to preview the Exhibits frameset in your browser. Notice that the frame pages you instructed Dreamweaver to display by default are showing in each of their respective frames.

2   Click on the first link, *Aeronautics through Sports*. Notice that the linked page doesn't appear in the Content frame as desired, but instead replaces the menu itself. This is because the link you clicked is not targeted to the Content frame.

3   Close (or minimize) your browser window and return to the Design view in Dreamweaver.

4   In the menu frame, drag your cursor over the *Aeronautics through Sports* link to select it.

5   Look at the Property inspector at the bottom of your screen. The Link field shows that this text is correctly set to link to the page Aeronautics.html when clicked. The Target field below is blank.

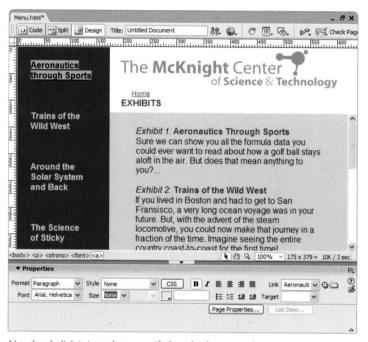

Note that the link is intact, but no specific frame has been targeted.

6   To target the Content frame when this link is clicked, click on the drop-down menu next to the Target text field and choose Content from the list. You have now ensured that this page appears in the Content frame of your frameset.

7   Use the Browser Preview button (◉) to preview the Exhibits frameset in your browser. Click on the *Aeronautics through Sports* link to see the content display in the proper frame. If you do not see the change, close the browser window and return to Dreamweaver, then preview in the browser again.

8   Repeat steps 1–7 for each link in the Menu frame, targeting the Content frame for each linked HTML page.

Multiple links can be targeted to display HTML content in different frames.

Now that you've learned to use frames at a higher level, let's look at some alternatives.

Linking to outside web pages

In the last exercise, you targeted links so that several pages from your local root folder were displayed interchangeably in the Content frame of your frameset. You're not limited, however, to linking only to local HTML pages when you target frames. You can link to outside, or remote, pages as well.

1   In the bottom-right corner of your Title frame, click and drag to highlight the word *Home*.

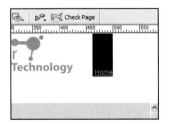

Always give the viewer a way back to your home page by creating a link back to it.

2   In the Property inspector, click in the Link field and enter **Teaser.html**.

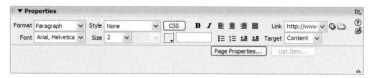

Simply linking to the home page does not automatically display it in a desired frame.

This links the *Home* text to the home page, but the page content replaces the default content in the Title frame, because you haven't yet targeted the Content frame.

3   Preview the frameset in your browser and click on the *Home* link to confirm it.

4   Return to Dreamweaver. In the Property inspector, choose Content from the Target drop-down menu to target that as the frame in which to display the page content.

5   Preview the frameset in your browser and click on the *Home* link once more to confirm that it is properly targeted.

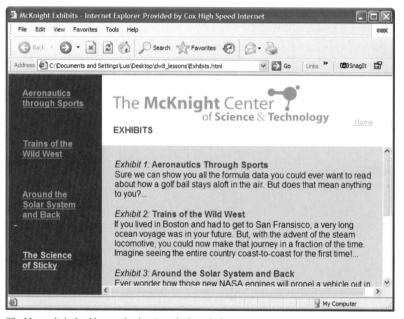

The Home *link should now take the viewer back to the home page.*

Using _top to replace a frameset

You might have noticed that other choices are available in the Target drop-down menu in the Property inspector. These choices offer other options for the frame in which a linked document should appear:

_blank opens the linked content in a new browser window (similar to a pop-up window), and leaves the current window behind it untouched.

_parent opens the linked content in the parent frameset of the frame in which the link appears. This option usually replaces the entire frameset.

_self opens the linked content in the current frame, replacing any existing content in that frame. (As you saw in the last exercise, Dreamweaver does this by default.)

_top opens the linked content in the current browser window, replacing the current frameset.

Content target using _top command replaces your current frameset in a browser window.

As you've seen, you can also select a named frame (if you've defined any) to open the linked document in that frame.

For this exercise, you'll use the _top target to open the home page in the current browser window, replacing the frameset you've just built. This is often done to ensure that the page doesn't appear to be a part of your site, while the information still gets delivered.

1   In the Title frame of your frameset, click and drag to reselect the *Home* link you targeted earlier.

2   The Property inspector should show the target of this link as the Content frame. Change this by choosing _top from the Target drop-down menu.

The _top command overrides your frameset settings.

3   Preview the frameset in your browser and click on the *Home* link to confirm that the home page opens in the browser window, not the current frame, as desired.

Adding <*noframes*> content

Some web browsers aren't capable of displaying framed pages. Dreamweaver allows you to create content to display in these older or text-based browsers by storing the content in the frameset file wrapped inside a <*noframes*> tag. Only content enclosed in a <*noframes*> tag is displayed when a user opens a framed page in a browser that doesn't support frames.

1   Choose Modify > Frameset > Edit NoFrames Content. In the Design view, a blank screen with the title *NoFrames Content* replaces your frameset.

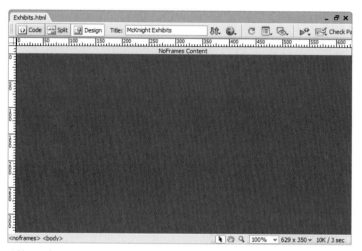

Adding noframes content ensures that everyone has access to the information on your page.

2   Enter or insert page content the same way you would normally. This content shows only when the page is opened in a browser that doesn't support viewing of your frames. The advantage of adding <*noframes*> content in this manner is that the content lives within your frameset file, and doesn't require the creation of an additional page file.

Now that you've learned how to work with framed (and non-framed) content, you can use this knowledge to inform your layout decisions as you add multimedia content in Lesson 9, "Adding Flash, Video, and Sound Content."

Self study

Try some of the following tasks to build on your experience with building and editing frames in Dreamweaver:

1　Create a new frameset and use the Bottom Frame preset to split the frameset into two frames. Add another frame, using the Split Frame Left command. Name the frames Left, Right, and Bottom, respectively.

2　Set the width of your Left frame to 30%, and the Bottom frame height to 150 pixels. Turn scrolling capability on in the Right frame. Explore the different looks that you can achieve by adding background and border colors to each of your three frames.

3　Build your own HTML page content for placement in these frames. Experiment with setting default content for these frames, and targeting different frames for this content when navigation links are clicked. For additional practice, create a *<noframes>* version of your frameset for browsers that don't support frames.

Review

Questions

1　What are the advantages and disadvantages of using frames in a web page layout?

2　When is it preferable to use the Frames panel to select frames for editing?

3　Why would you set a frame's width to a fixed value?

4　What would you do to ensure that a page shows in a specific frame by default when viewed in a browser?

5　Where does page content with a _top target display in a browser?

Answers

1　Using frames saves time and avoids repetitive work in the creation of pages. In addition, the viewer's browser doesn't need to reload graphics used for navigation on every page. Frames also allow viewers to scroll through long pages of content in a frame, using built-in scrollbars. However, aligning content precisely in different frames can be problematic. Another disadvantage is that viewers won't be able to bookmark individual framed pages (unless you provide specific server code). Testing the navigation from frame to frame can also be time-consuming.

2　The Frames panel allows you to see the structure of your frameset more clearly than the Document window allows. It also allows you to more easily select frames and framesets than in the Document window, by clicking on the desired frames in the panel itself.

3　You would set a frame's width to a specific pixel value when you want that frame to always be the same size, as in a navigation menu. A fixed-width frame displays content at the same size in any browser window, whereas other frames will resize to fill the remaining space in your frameset.

4 Saving a frameset locks HTML page content into the frame you've defined when the frameset is opened in a browser. You also can't preview your frameset in a browser without first saving the frameset and all of the content that appears in its frames.

5 When you choose _top (instead of a specific frame) as the target for your linked content, web browsers open the linked content in the current browser window, replacing the current frameset.

Lesson 9

What you'll learn in this lesson:

- Inserting Flash content
- Creating Flash buttons and Flash text within Dreamweaver
- Understanding plug-ins
- Adding video and sound files to a web page

Adding Flash, Video, and Sound Content

As connection speeds increase, people are demanding more interesting content. One way to meet that need is to add more dynamic content, instead of just plain text, to a web site. Animations, sound, and video are helping to fit the bill in terms of making web content more compelling and keeping web site visitors coming back for more.

Starting up

Before starting, make sure that your tools and panels are consistent by resetting your workspace. See "Resetting the Dreamweaver workspace" on page 3.

You will work with several files from the dw09lessons folder in this lesson. Make sure that you have loaded the dwlessons folder onto your hard drive from the supplied DVD. See "Loading lesson files" on page 3.

Before you begin, you need to create a site definition that points to the dw09lessons folder from the included DVD that contains resources you need for these lessons. Go to Site > New Site, or, for details on creating a site definition, refer to Lesson 2, "Creating a New Site."

See Lesson 9 in action!

Use the accompanying video to gain a better understanding of how to use some of the features shown in this lesson. Open the Dynamic_Learning_DW_CS3.swf file located in the Videos folder and select Lesson 9 to view the video training file for this lesson.

Making web content interesting

Adding video, sound, and animation to a web site is a surefire way to make the site more interesting and engaging. Video, for example, plays a key role in supplying interesting and varied web content, in that it gives the average person an opportunity to showcase his/her talents to a worldwide audience. Web sites such as YouTube and MySpace are prime examples of how video is impacting the Internet in this way. Video also allows companies to post commercials, speeches, and other corporate content that may not normally be available to the public.

Sound allows you to enhance web pages by supplementing visual content with music or sound effects. Sound also inspires user interaction (as you'll see later in this lesson), thereby giving the user a more interesting online experience.

Animation gives web pages a whole new life by adding movement and effects to images that still pictures just can't match. Something moving on a web page automatically draws a visitor's eye. Movement is especially effective for banner ads, buttons, and whatever else you'd like your visitors to pay attention to.

Inserting Flash movies

Adobe's Flash CS3 Professional application is primarily used to create animation and interactive projects. In terms of animation, you can use Flash to create animated web banners, buttons, splash pages, slide shows, and more. Inserting Flash animations into your web page is a great way to bring life to an otherwise static environment.

Web banners are a big part of advertising these days. And if a web banner includes moving elements, that movement will automatically draw the user's eye right to the banner. In this exercise, you will place a banner on the home page of the museum web site you've been working on in this book to help promote the museum's learning center.

1 In the Files panel, navigate to the dw09lessons folder and inside the Pages folder, double-click the banner.html page to open it.

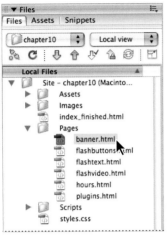

Double-click banner.html to open this file.

2 Click in the empty cell to the right of the *Welcome to MKI* text.

3 In the Assets tab of the Files panel, select the fourth button down, the Flash button (▧), to display a list of all of the Flash movies in the site.

Click the Flash button in the Assets tab of the Files panel.

Flash movies are labeled with the .swf extension. However, other programs, including After Effects and Dreamweaver, can create .swf files as well. You'll learn more about this later in this lesson.

4   Select the learningcenterbanner.swf file and drag it to the cell you clicked on in Step 2 to insert it.

5   Enter **learning center banner** in the Title text field when the Object Tag Accessibility Attributes dialog box appears, then press OK.

Name the inserted file in the Object Tag Accessibility Attributes dialog box.

As you can see, inserting a Flash movie into a web page is much like inserting an image. The width and height of the .swf are automatically established based on the file's physical size, just as they are for images such as .jpeg and .gif files.

The .swf file appears with a generic Flash icon on a gray image. You can preview the image in a number of ways.

6   Keep the image selected and go to the Property inspector. Select the Play button; the banner should appear.

Select the Play button in the Property inspector to make the banner appear.

You must have Flash Player installed to view an .swf file. If you don't have the application installed, visit http://www.adobe.com/products/flashplayer to download and install it. Also note that visitors to your web site also must have Flash Player installed to view your Flash content. A good rule of thumb when including Flash content on a web site is to let visitors know as soon as they get to your site that they'll need to have Flash Player. Be sure to include the link to the Flash Player web page (the URL provided at the beginning of this paragraph) so that visitors can download the Flash Player, if necessary.

7   After you click the Play button, it will automatically turn into a Stop button. Click on the Stop button after you've finished checking out the banner.

To see the page without the distraction of the other panels, choose File > Preview in Browser. When you're finished, go back to Dreamweaver and look at some of the buttons in the Property inspector. The Edit button, for example, automatically opens Flash if you have it installed, and then opens the .swf file in Flash. The Property inspector also includes Loop and Autoplay buttons that control the playback of the .swf.

The Property inspector contains a number of options relating to .swf files.

When designing web pages, be sure to include space in your design for .swfs if you're going to incorporate them into the page. The files can vary in size, depending on what you're using them for. To learn more about Flash, visit http://www.adobe.com/products/flash/flashpro.

Creating Flash content

As mentioned earlier, Flash isn't the only program that generates .swf files. Dreamweaver creates .swfs, too. This is good news—you don't have to learn Flash to create interesting, dynamic content for your web site.

Using Flash buttons and Flash text is a better way to make the interactive portion of a web page more entertaining for visitors than using regular text links. These features also allow you to get a bit more creative with web page design.

Flash buttons

You'll start this exercise by creating Flash buttons in Dreamweaver. This time-saving feature gives you the opportunity to work with pre-designed buttons that you modify with your own content. You have an entire library of ready-made buttons to choose from, some of which even include rollover effects.

1   Click on the Files tab in the Files panel or go to Windows > Files and, open the flashbuttons.html file in the Pages folder. Click in the first cell of the menu table just below The McKnight Center graphic.

2   Go to the Common tab in the Insert bar and choose Flash Button (🖸) from the Insert Media drop-down menu.

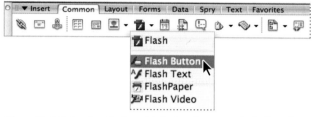

Choose Flash Button from the Insert Media drop-down menu in the Insert bar.

Before you establish how the button will look, you'll want to save and name it.

3   Go to the bottom of the Insert Flash Button dialog box and click the Browse button next to the Save As text field.

The Insert Flash Button dialog box.

4   Navigate to the dw09lessons folder > Assets > Flash Assets. Type **home.swf** into the Name text field and press Save. You're creating a new file, and this is where you'll be saving it.

Enter home.swf in the Name text field and press Save.

Now that you have the button named and saved, you're ready to establish how it will look.

5   Peruse the different buttons under the Style list to see the list of button types available. We chose Corporate-Orange for our design.

A number of button options are included in the Style list.

6   Choose a design, and type **Home** in the Button text field to designate this as the style for your Home button. Then click on the Apply button in the Insert Flash Button window. You'll see the button you're creating in the cell in which you clicked in Step 1.

7   Now, choose Georgia from the Font drop-down menu. Click Apply whenever you make a change, and you'll see the button update.

8   Some button styles, typically those that aren't perfectly rectangular or have rounded corners, have white backgrounds that cause the buttons to stick out from the pages on which they reside. To make your buttons blend in with the pages, you can simply change their background color. Click on the Bg color window and move the cursor over the flashbuttons.html page to sample the page color. The button should now blend in with the page.

Match the button's background color to the color of flashbuttons.html.

This dialog box includes a few more buttons of note:

•   The Browse button next to the Link text field is where you'll need to establish a navigational link for the button so that it takes the user to the appropriate page.

•   The Get More Styles button, which when clicked, brings you to a web page from which you can choose more button styles to download to your computer.

9   Press OK to finish placing your button and close the window.

10 Add the Home button to the Title text field of the Flash Accessibility Attributes dialog box, then press OK.

11 With the button still selected, go to the Property inspector to view the choices for the button.

12 Click the Play button and then move your cursor over the button to display its rollover effect.

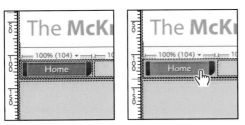

Click the Play button in the Property inspector and move your cursor over the Home button to view the rollover effect.

13 Click the Stop button once you've examined the rollover effect. If you decide to make changes to the button or if you need to add a link to it, press the Edit button in the Property inspector to return to the Insert Flash Button dialog box, where you originally created the button.

Flash Button   W 105   File ../Assets/Flash Assets/home.swf   Edit...   Class None
               H 23   Reset size

V space   Quality High   Align Default   Stop
H space   Scale Default (Show   Bg #FFCC00   Parameters...

Click the Edit button in the Property inspector to return to the Insert Flash Button dialog box and edit a button.

Practice this procedure by clicking in the next cell to the right and following the steps in this exercise again, naming the buttons **Exhibits**, **Learning Center**, **Store**, **Museum Hours**, **Contact Us**, and **Get a Brochure**. When you're finished, choose File > Save to save your work.

To practice this procedure, create buttons for the rest of the navigation bar.

Flash text

The procedure for inserting Flash text is similar to that for Flash buttons. One of the nice things about using Flash text and buttons is that because you're creating an image file, you don't have to worry what fonts to use. You can be creative and choose a font you normally wouldn't be able to because the user may not have it installed.

1 In the Pages folder in the Files panel, open the flashtext.html file. Then click in the nested table in the cell just below the *MKI Exhibits* text.

2 Go to the Insert bar and select the Insert Media button (▨). Choose Flash Text.

Select the Insert Media button and choose Flash Text.

3 Name and save the button by first clicking the Browse button at the bottom of the Insert Flash Text dialog box.

Click the Browse button at the bottom of the Insert Flash Text dialog box.

4 Name the file **aeronautics.swf**. Then, in the Assets folder, select the Flash Assets folder. You're once again creating .swf files, so you'll save them with the files you created earlier.

5 One you've saved the file, move the Insert Flash Text window to the right a little so that you can see the table into which you're inserting the files.

6 To design the Flash text, begin by typing **Aeronautics Through Sports** in the Text window.

7 Check the Show font checkbox so that you can see how the fonts look as you select them. As you're reviewing the fonts available on your computer, remember that you can pick any font style you want because you're creating an image file. Because you're creating text for a sidebar menu, you'll want to set the text size so that it's plainly visible and reasonably sized. We chose 10-point Copperplate Gothic Bold for this exercise.

Check the Show font checkbox to preview fonts.

8 Preview the text you've created by clicking on the Apply button in the Insert Flash Button dialog box.

9 Leave the text color black, but make sure to specify a Rollover color. We used #0000FF.

10 If you see a white background around your text, you can change the background so that it's the same color as your page; click on the Bg color window and then move your cursor over the flashtext.html page, so you can sample the orange page color. When you're finished, your text should blend in with the page.

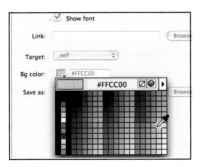

Change the background color of your text so that it blends in with the page.

11 The Browse button next to the Link text field can be used to link this button to another page. In this case, the Aeronautics through Sports page hasn't been built yet, so leave the Link field blank.

12 Press OK to finish placing your Flash text. Then add the words **Aeronautics Exhibit** to the Title portion of the Flash Accessibility Attributes window and press OK.

In the same way that you can preview a Flash button, you can also select Flash text and preview it by pressing the Play button in the Property inspector and moving your cursor over the text to see the rollover effect.

Practice this procedure by clicking in the next cell down and following the steps in this exercise, naming the Flash text items **Trains of the Wild West**, **Around the Solar System and Back**, **The Science of Sticky**, and **Water is Everywhere**.

After finishing the Aeronautics through Sports text, follow the steps in this exercise for the other cells.

13 Choose File > Save to save your work.

Adding video

Adding video to a web page is a subject for debate. You have choices regarding approaches you can take, formats from which to choose, and standards in terms of file size and video length. The choices you make depend largely on the resources you have; the format you choose is usually based on the method that gives you the best results.

Visit various web sites that offer video presented in different ways to get a feel for what works and what doesn't. Google and Yahoo! offer a lot of online video content, presented in various formats.

Flash Video

Flash Video is spreading across the Web, and is the format of choice on sites such as MySpace, YouTube, and Google. Flash Video allows users to compress video files to a reasonable size, offers smooth streaming for playback, and provides users with the ability to protect video from unauthorized copying.

Different programs create Flash Video, most notably Flash and Premiere Pro. Creating the video is an intricate process, so you'll want to do your homework and learn as much as you can about how it works in order to get the best results.

To insert Flash Video into your site:

1   In the Pages folder in the Files panel, open the flashvideo.html file. Click in the cell to the right of the *Trains of the Wild West* text.

2   Go to the Assets panel and select the Movies button to show the videos available in your site.

Select the Movies button in the Assets panel.

3   Right-click (Windows) or Ctrl+click on the trains.flv file and choose Insert from the contextual menu to open the Insert Flash Video dialog box.

4   In the Insert Flash Video dialog box, click on the Video type drop-down menu and select Progressive Download Video.

The Insert Flash Video window.

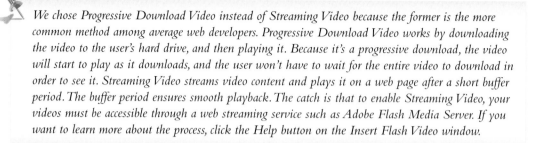

We chose Progressive Download Video instead of Streaming Video because the former is the more common method among average web developers. Progressive Download Video works by downloading the video to the user's hard drive, and then playing it. Because it's a progressive download, the video will start to play as it downloads, and the user won't have to wait for the entire video to download in order to see it. Streaming Video streams video content and plays it on a web page after a short buffer period. The buffer period ensures smooth playback. The catch is that to enable Streaming Video, your videos must be accessible through a web streaming service such as Adobe Flash Media Server. If you want to learn more about the process, click the Help button on the Insert Flash Video window.

Next, you'll want to select a skin. A skin is a control panel that shows up on top of the video, and allows the user to control video playback. In other words, this is where users can play, rewind, and fast-forward their videos.

5 Click on the Skin drop-down menu to examine your choices. You'll see a preview of the skin just below the menu. Choose any skin you like, we chose Corona Skin 3 for this example.

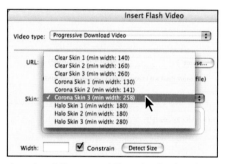

A number of skins are available in the Skin drop-down menu.

If your video is 10 seconds or longer, choose a skin that includes a slider control so that users can scroll through the video at their convenience.

6 Click on the Detect Size button so that Dreamweaver can establish the physical space the video will occupy on the page. The size is based on the size of the actual video.

You can put in your own size, too. Do not enter a size that's bigger than the original video, because the video will stretch and pixelate. 320 x 240 is the average size of a web video. Full-screen video (720 x 480) is not a good idea because a video that size is a big file that will take a long time to download and play properly, even with a broadband connection.

Auto play and Auto rewind can be annoying to the user, as they can take away the user's sense of control. Use those features sparingly.

7 Press OK to insert the video.

You won't be able to see the video in Dreamweaver, so choose File > Preview in Browser to preview it in a web browser.

Insert the Flash video into your web page.

8 Choose File > Save to save your work.

QuickTime video and Windows Media

QuickTime and Windows Media are also common video formats used on the Web. They're somewhat similar to each other, but there are some advantages of QuickTime over Windows Media, namely in that QuickTime offers more compression options for better quality and optimal file size management.

To see a QuickTime video, you need to have QuickTime installed. You can download QuickTime from *http://www.apple.com/quicktime/download*. To view Windows Media files you need Windows Media Player, which you can download at *http://www.microsoft.com/windows/windowsmedia/download*.

QuickTime and Windows Media video are inserted into a page the same way as Flash Video. The difference between the video formats is that users create QuickTime and Windows Media video using different software applications, including Adobe Premiere Pro and Apple Final Cut Pro.

To insert QuickTime and Windows Media video:

1 In the Files panel, open the quicktime.html file in the Pages folder. Click in the cell to the right of the *Trains of the Wild West* text.

2 Go to the Assets panel and select the Movies button to show the videos available in your site.

3 Right-click (Windows) or Ctrl+click (Mac OS) on the trainsorenson.mov file and choose
Insert from the contextual menu to insert it into the cell. You'll see a plug-in icon () on
the page, indicating that a plug-in is required to see the file.

The Plug-in icon.

4 When you insert a plug-in file, you need to manually establish the size of the file. In the
Property inspector, type **320** in the W (width) window and **260** in the H (height) window.

The video itself is 320 x 240. You are using 260 for the height to allow space for the
controller. QuickTime and Windows Media files already have a controller built in with
the plug-in. You will need to allow a little extra space for the video controls when you're
entering a size manually.

5 To preview the file, click the Play button in the Property inspector or preview the
page in a web browser by pressing the Preview/Debug in browser button (⊙) on the
Document toolbar.

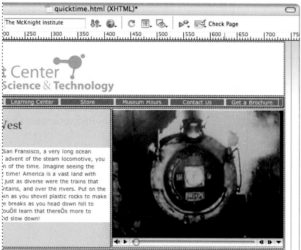

Preview the video file.

This file is named trainsorenson.mov because of the type of compression used on it. The
Sorenson codec is a common form of web video compression. Choosing the right codec is
a bit of an art form.

You should use a codec that's universal and not exclusive to the software that's generating it so that the average user visiting your site will be able to see the video. Various programs specialize in compression, among them the Adobe Media Encoder through Premiere Pro, Apple's Compressor, and Autodesk's Cleaner. To learn more about compression, type the word **codec** into the Google or Yahoo search field.

Other web video considerations

In addition to size, consider the following when you're preparing video for the Web:

Length: Unless you'll be offering video through a streaming video service, keep the video length down to keep the file size manageable and the progressive playback smooth.

Audio: Although stereo is nice, using stereo files on the Web is a little iffy, as many home users don't have stereo speakers hooked up to their computers. Stereo creates a larger file size and doesn't add that much to the quality of the sound unless you're doing some tricks with the balance between the speakers, which people without speakers won't hear anyway. Keep your video sound set to mono to help manage the file size a bit more effectively.

Lots of movement, animated graphics, and effects: These things make a video look nice, but increasing the file size can interrupt playback.

Copywritten material: Be careful when choosing material for your video, especially when it comes to music. Pirating is a big issue today. Unless you have the rights to the music or you have permission from the music publisher and are paying royalties, you can't use music for promotional or commercial purposes when it comes to publishing material on the Web.

Inserting sound

Sound is another element you can use to enhance your web site. Sound has the same considerations as video: it can take a while to download and it requires a plug-in, such as QuickTime or Windows Media Player, to hear it.

You can incorporate different types of sound files into a web page. Pick a format that will run on any computer, whether the user is on the Windows or Mac OS platform. Three formats are common: .aif, .wav, and .mp3.

Files in the .aif or .wav format are similar. The main difference is where they originate. Windows is generally linked to the .wav format and Mac OS is associated with the .aif format. The Windows and Mac OS platforms can read both formats. In addition, these files sound similar to one another: both are dynamic and result in full-sounding, high-quality files.

You can also play .mp3 format files on both the Windows and Mac OS platforms. The big advantage to using an .mp3 file is that it's typically smaller in size than an .aif or .wav file. The .mp3 format may not reproduce full CD-quality sound, but it downloads faster and takes up less hard drive space. MP3 players, such as Apple's iPod, have become very popular since you can tote around literally thousands of songs on them.

1   To insert sound, in the Files panel, double-click the sound.html file located in the Pages folder. Click in the left cell just below the *Can you identify the train by its sound?* text.

2   In the Common tab of the Insert panel, select the Media drop-down menu, and choose Plugin.

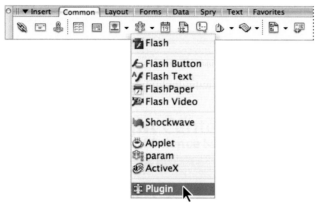

Choose Plugin from the Media drop-down menu.

3   In the Select File dialog box, go to the Assets folder located in the dw09lessons root folder. Choose the Audio Assets folder and select the Train Pass 1.mp3 file.

Select the Train Pass 1.mp3 file located in the Audio Assets folder.

A plugin icon (▦) will appear in the table, indicating that a plugin is required to hear the sound.

4   Preview the page in a browser by pressing the Preview/Debug in browser button (●). The sound plays automatically.

Because you'll be inserting more than one sound in this exercise, you need to change the parameters of the sound so that the user has to click the sound in order to hear it; otherwise, all three sounds play at the same time. You also do this because users generally want to control the media and be able to play video and sound at their convenience.

5   After previewing the page in the browser, return to Dreamweaver.

6   Keep the plugin selected and click the Parameters button in the Property inspector.

Define the plugin's parameters by clicking the Parameters button in the Property inspector.

7 In the Parameters dialog box, type **autoplay** in the Parameter column and **false** in the Value column. Press OK.

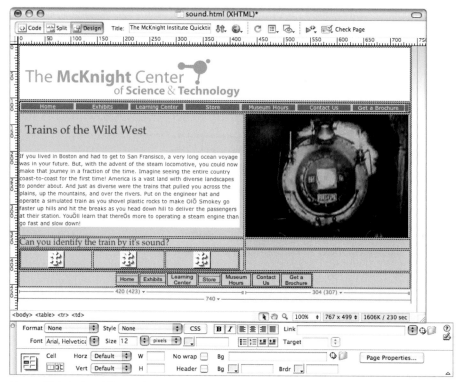

The Parameters dialog box.

8 Preview the page in a browser again, and note that you need to press the Play button in the plugin application in order to hear the sound.

9 Return to Dreamweaver when you finish previewing the page. Click in the cell next to the plug-in and follow the same procedure to insert the Train Pass 2.mp3 file. Finish with the last cell and the Train Pass 3.mp3 file. Don't forget to set the parameters for each file.

Your modified plugin and Property inspector.

Preparing audio for the Web

Audio has the same considerations as any other digital file type. You need to pay attention to file size while trying to maintain quality.

Various programs offer audio editing and format capabilities. This includes programs such as Adobe Soundbooth, Apple Soundtrack Pro, and Audacity (which is available as a free download on the Web).

Once you've edited a sound to your liking, you'll need to set up certain technical specifications for the final file. This includes the type of file you'll output (.mp3, .aif, etc.), whether the sound is in stereo or mono, and a sample rate. For the Web, a good sample rate is in the 22KHz–32KHz range; 22KHz is at the low end of acceptable quality, and anything higher than 32KHz will start to weigh down the file size.

Stereo is nice, but unnecessary, unless you're moving sound from the left speaker to the right speaker and vice versa. You can save a significant amount of file space by keeping the sound file set to mono.

There are a number of compression choices when it comes to audio. Your best bet is to experiment and see what gives you the results you want. Creating audio files is very much like creating video for the Web—there are no definite answers; you need to experiment to find the best balance between file size and quality.

Self study

The best way to learn more about video for the Web is to experiment. Try inserting and compressing videos using different codecs and file types. You'll find that the results will vary, depending on the file type and codec you choose, and also on the type of video content.

Review

Questions

1   When inserting Flash Text, what type of file is inserted into the web page?

2   What plug-in is needed to view an .flv file?

3   What is a *skin* when referring to a Flash Video file?

Answers

1   When Flash Text is inserted into a page in Dreamweaver, a .swf file is used.

2   In order to view an .flv file, a user must have the Flash Player plug-in installed on their computer.

3   A set of controls on top of the video that control video playback.

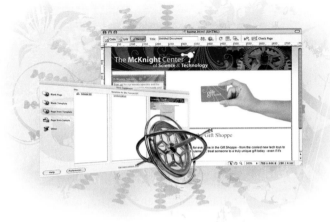

What you'll learn in this lesson:

- Inserting and adding snippets
- Using library items to reuse common items
- Creating and modifying page templates
- Repeating and creating editable regions

Getting Modular with Reusable Items

Dreamweaver site definitions allow you to take advantage of extensive management and maintenance tools, including the ability to reuse, repeat, and maintain common items such as menus, logos, code, and even entire page layouts. Dreamweaver's unique snippets, library items, and page templates are indispensable for maintaining a consistent appearance and making site-wide updates a snap.

Starting up

Before starting, make sure that your tools and panels are consistent by resetting your workspace. See "Resetting the Dreamweaver workspace" on page 3.

You will work with several files from the dw10lessons folder in this lesson. Make sure that you have loaded the dwlessons folder onto your hard drive from the supplied DVD. See "Loading lesson files" on page 3.

Before you begin, you need to create a site definition that points to the dw10lessons folder from the included DVD that contains resources you need for these lessons. Go to Site > New Site, or, for details on creating a site definition, refer to Lesson 2, "Creating a New Site."

See Lesson 10 in action!

Use the accompanying video to gain a better understanding of how to use some of the features shown in this lesson. Open the Dynamic_Learning_DW_CS3.swf file located in the Videos folder and select Lesson 10 to view the video training file for this lesson.

Creating reusable page elements

You may have heard the term *modular* before; whether referring to a prebuilt house that you can cart away and place on your property, or a well-built, scalable web site, modular refers to anything you can break down into standardized, reusable components.

Most web sites contain common elements such as headers, footers, and menus that appear consistently across each page. The ability to convert these elements into reusable items is essential for maintaining a consistent look and feel across your pages. Add the ability to make components manageable from a single place and to make sitewide updates, and editing becomes a breeze.

Dreamweaver provides three modular features: snippets, library items, and templates. Each feature offers a different level of reusability, from simple code tidbits to entire pages, complete with navigation, content, and styling.

Introducing snippets

As you build pages and web sites, you'll find yourself creating many similar items several times over. Whether you're creating a two-column layout table or a contact form, snippets make it possible to add any piece of code to a common library, where you can reuse it by simply dragging and dropping it into the page. You can store virtually any item on a page as a snippet.

Dreamweaver comes with an extensive library of common navigation bars, form elements, tables, and even JavaScripts, which are available at any time from the Snippets panel. Snippets are stored as part of the Dreamweaver application, and they are not specific to any Dreamweaver site. You can add your own snippets directly within Dreamweaver, and they will be available for you to use at any time on any site.

The Snippets panel is like a super clipboard, and using a snippet is similar to copying and pasting an element onto your page. Changes to a snippet in the Snippet panel will not update snippets you've already used in your pages. For this reason, snippets are a great way to store and place any common page elements that you don't need to manage globally.

The Snippets panel

The Snippets panel displays all available Dreamweaver snippets, broken down by category. You can add and edit snippets and categories directly from the Snippets panel. Using a snippet from the Snippets panel is as simple as locating it and dragging it from the panel to the page. Choose Window > Snippets to launch the Snippets panel and take a detailed look.

The Snippets panel contains dozens of ready-to-use snippets.

To use a snippet, simply drag it from the Snippets panel onto your page.

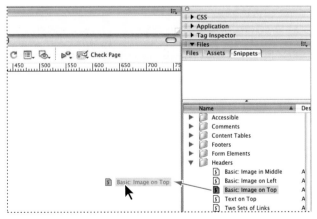

To use a snippet, drag it from the Snippets panel and drop it onto the page.

Built-in snippets

Dreamweaver provides many ready-to-use snippets that serve as great starting points for forms, lists, and navigation bars (to name a few); many of these require little more than text changes and some basic styling. In the following lesson, you will use some of these snippets to quickly build existing pages for an online store.

Before you get started, open the file home.html, located in the Files panel (Window > Files, or the F8 shortcut key on both Windows and Mac OS). This page is the storefront for the McKnight Institute Online Gift Shoppe. Eager shoppers can purchase MKI items in five categories: Clothing, DVDs, Tech Toys, Books & CDs, and Gift Certificates. Your goal is to create the storefront, a category page, and multiple item pages from reusable page elements. This will make the web site faster to build and easier to maintain, and it will keep the pages' look and feel uniform at all times.

The home.html page serves as the storefront for the online Gift Shoppe.

To use snippets in your layouts:

1   With home.html open, choose Window > Snippets to launch the Snippets panel. In the category list, locate and expand the Navigation folder, and then click to expand the folder named Vertical beneath it. You'll use one of the snippets in this category to create a menu for this page.

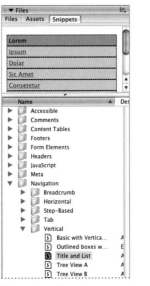

Browse the ready-made menus under
Navigation > Vertical in the Snippets panel.

2   Inside the Vertical folder, locate and drag the *Title and List* snippet from the panel into the leftmost column of your page above E-Weekly Specials.

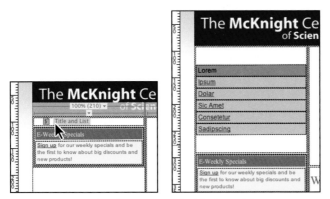

Drag-and-drop the Title and List snippet to the left column of the page.

3 A new menu is placed that you can now modify and style. Modify the title to read Products, and modify the five links below the title to read **Clothing**, **Cool Toys**, **Books & CDs**, **DVDs**, and **Gift Certificates**.

Modify the Title and List menu for the Gift Shoppe product categories.

4 From the Files panel, locate and open the category.html page. You will use this page to display products in each category, with links to details and pricing for each one. You'll use another snippet from the Dreamweaver library to create a breadcrumb-style menu that shows users where they are within the store.

5 From the Snippets panel, go to Navigation > Breadcrumb and expand the folder. Drag the snippet named *Angle bracket denotes path* to the {breadcrumb} table cell. Delete the {breadcrumb} placeholder text.

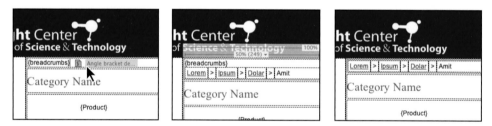

On the category.html page, add a breadcrumb-style menu from the Snippets panel to the top row of the table.

6 Click and drag to select the cells between Lorem and Amit, and choose Edit > Cut to remove them from the navigation. Replace the word *Lorem* with **Home** and the word *Amit* with **Category Name**. For now, you'll leave the actual category name unknown until you develop this page further.

Select and delete any unneeded cells in the new menu.

In a few easy steps, you saved a lot of time by using snippets instead of creating these two navigation menus from scratch. You'll find that Dreamweaver provides many excellent snippets that are a great basis for just about any page element.

A finished menu, created in half the time, thanks to snippets.

It's not Latin or pig Latin; it's Lorem Ipsum, a dummy language that the printing industry has used for centuries. Created by a typesetter, this jumble of letters and words is used as a placeholder for real text so that you can see how a layout appears when it is full. If you ever need some Lorem Ipsum, use the free, online Lipsum Generator at http://www.lipsum.com. It can create as much text as you need to fill space until the real text is available.

Creating new snippets

When you can't find what you need, or if you've created something on a page that's like nothing else in the Snippets panel, you can save it as a brand-new snippet for use in the future. You can create new snippets directly from the Snippets panel, and from any selected element(s) on a page.

In this section, you'll create a table that displays each product in a category, along with an image and its price. By converting the table and its contents to a new snippet, you can easily place the snippet from the Snippets panel anytime you need to add a new product to a category.

1   Make sure the category.html page is open in the Document window. In the middle of the category.html page, locate the top-left cell in the middle table that reads {Product}. Delete the {Product} placeholder text, and insert a new table in the cell, using the Table button (▦) on the Insert bar above your Document window.

Before adding a table to your layout, you'll first remove the {Product} placeholder text.

2   Using the Table dialog box that appears, type **3** into the Rows text field and **1** into the Columns text field. In the Table width text field, type **100** and select percent from the drop-down menu. Type **0** into the Border thickness text field, then press OK.

Set the properties of the new table.

3 In the new table, type **Product Name** in the first row and a temporary price of **$0.00** in the last row. You need to insert a placeholder in the middle row for any product image that will appear here.

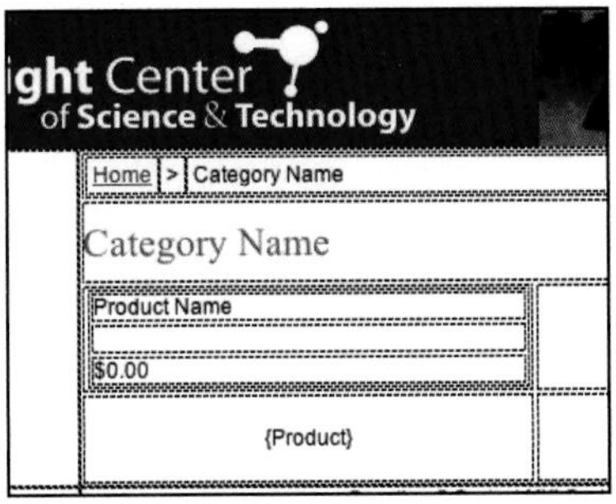

You will be converting this product display table to a snippet shortly.

4 Because snippets are global (not specific to a site definition), using an image that's specific to this site is not a good idea. Instead, you'll use an image placeholder that doesn't reference any actual image file, but creates the space and tag necessary to add a new image when the time is right. Click inside the middle row and choose Image Placeholder, under the Image button (🖻) menu from the Common Insert bar.

5 When the dialog box appears, assign the image a name of **product** and a size of 150 pixels by 150 pixels. Enter **#3366FF** in the Color text field. For now, type the word **product** in the Alternative text field. Press OK to insert the new placeholder.

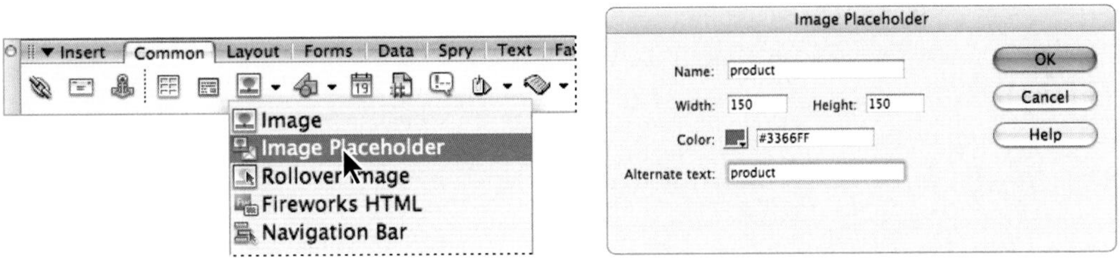

Add an image placeholder instead of an actual file to save room for an image later.

6   Choose File > Save to save your work.

7   Now you're ready to save this product display table as a new snippet. Select the table, and make sure that none of the categories in the Snippets panel are highlighted. Choose the New Snippet button (⊟) at the bottom of the Snippets panel.

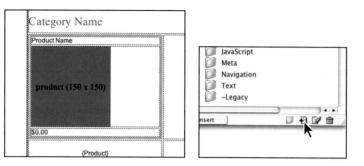

First select the finished table, then click on the New Snippet button at the bottom of the Snippets panel.

8   In the Snippets panel, you can assign a Name and Description to the new snippet. Assign the name **Product Display** and press OK. The new snippet now appears in your Snippets panel, along with the category folders.

The new snippet is now in your Snippets panel.

Because style sheets are defined in the head of a page, they are not copied over with items that you add to the Snippets panel. Items will appear unformatted in the Snippets panel, and each item will only format properly when placed if the styles it references are available.

9   To use your new snippet, drag a copy of it to each of the remaining three cells marked {Product}. Make sure you remove the placeholder text from each cell first.

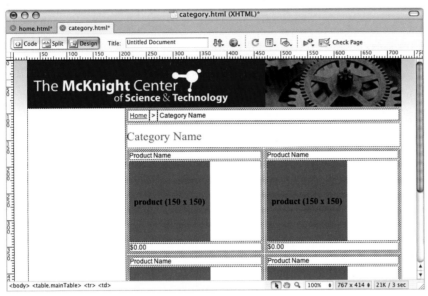

In just seconds, you've created a place for four products, using your new snippet.

Organizing your snippets

As you add your own snippets, you can use folders inside the Snippets panel to categorize and sort them by project, by type, or however you choose.

1   At the bottom of the Snippets panel, select the New Snippets Folder icon (⬚) to create a new folder. By default, a folder is created inside any selected folder, or at the top level, if none is selected.

2   Name the new folder McKnight, as this is where snippets related to this project will go.

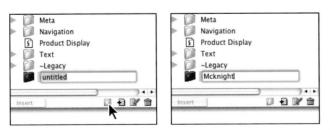

Your new folder is added to the selected folder; if no folder is selected, it will be created in the top level.

3 Drag the Product Display snippet into the new folder; it will be moved and appear indented below the folder.

Drag a snippet to a folder to move it.

4 Because your McKnight web site has many sections, you can sort snippets even further, into section-specific folders. With the McKnight folder selected, choose the New Snippet Folder icon to create a folder one level down. Name the new subfolder **Store**.

5 Drag the Product Display snippet into the new subfolder.

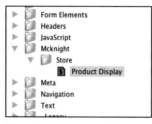

Move the new snippet into the Store subfolder.
You can create other subfolders later for other site sections.

> *To rename a selected folder or snippet, select it and choose Rename from the Snippets panel menu.*

Editing snippets

Because snippets are not specific to any Dreamweaver site, you can edit a snippet at any time from within Dreamweaver. Remember, editing a snippet will not change any copies of it that are already used in a site. It will simply modify the snippet for future use.

1   In the Snippets panel, select the Product Display snippet you created (remember, it's now under McKnight > Store).

2   Click the Edit Snippet button at the bottom of the panel. The Snippet panel appears, and displays the code that makes up your snippet.

Edit Snippet dialog box.

3   Locate the *<img>* tag: this creates the placeholder image that this snippet contains. Inside the *<img>* tag, find the attribute that reads *background-color*. This sets the background color you chose earlier for the image placeholder.

4 Modify the attribute to read **background-color: #CC0000**. This will change the placeholder color to a dark red. Press OK.

```
pe: ⊙ Wrap selection          ○ Insert block
re: <table width="100%" border="0" cellpadding="
        <tr>
          <td>Product Name</td>
        </tr>
        <tr>
          <td><img src="" alt="product" name="
width="150" height="150" id="product"
style="background-color: #3366FF" /></td>

ter:
```

```
pe: ⊙ Wrap selection          ○ Insert block
re: <table width="100%" border="0" cellpadding="
        <tr>
          <td>Product Name</td>
        </tr>
        <tr>
          <td><img src="" alt="product" name="
width="150" height="150" id="product"
style="background-color: #CC0000" /></td>

ter:
```

Change the background color of the image placeholder to #CC0000 (dark red).

The snippet preview now reflects the color change.

![Files panel showing Snippets tab with Product Name placeholder preview in dark red, labeled product (150 x 150)]

The next time you place this snippet, it will appear just as the preview window shows here.

The Snippet panel lets you modify a snippet only via its HTML code. Here's a shortcut; you can modify a snippet by dragging it into a new document, making any changes in the Design view, or recreating the snippet by choosing New Snippet from the Snippets panel. If you select the folder containing the original snippet and save it under the same name, you will be prompted to replace it.

Introducing library items

When an item repeats across several pages (such as a menu, company slogan, or footer), updating it requires opening each page that uses it and performing the same edit over and over. This means a lot of retyping or copy-and-paste work, which can lead to mistakes or inconsistencies.

With Dreamweaver's library items, you can save any common element and manage it from a master copy in your site folder. When you place a library item on a page, the item remains attached to its master; any changes you make to the master will automatically update any instances of the item placed throughout your site. Dreamweaver makes sure that any instances of a library item remain in sync regardless of where and how frequently they appear in a site.

Library items (unlike snippets) are specific to each Dreamweaver site, and they are stored as separate .lbi files in your site's Library folder. To manage your library items, launch the Assets panel (Window > Assets), and select the Library button (📖) from the left.

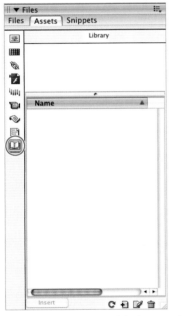

The Library Items category of the Assets panel.

You can add, edit, and manage all library items in your site directly from this panel. You're now ready to identify and convert elements on your store pages to library items so that you can manage and update them easily.

To create and place a new library item:

1   Click on the home.html tab in the top of the Document window to open the home page. Select the table that contains the left side navigation menu. Hint: click on any border inside the table to select it.

2   In the Assets Panel, click the Library button (📖), then from the panel menu, choose New Library Item. The selected menu is added as a new library item; name it **Main Menu**. If you're prompted to update links, choose Update. This ensures that any hyperlinks or references to image files are preserved.

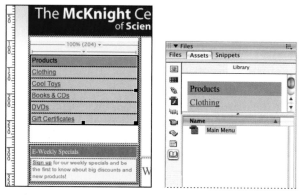

Use the Assets Panel menu to create a new library item from a selection.

3   The menu on the page is now attached to the new library item you created. Note that library items on a page appear highlighted in yellow. Now you're ready to add this library item to other pages.

Library items on the page appear highlighted in yellow.

4 Open the category.html page, locate the new Main Menu library item in the Assets panel, and drag it into the left column of the page. An instance of the Main Menu is placed.

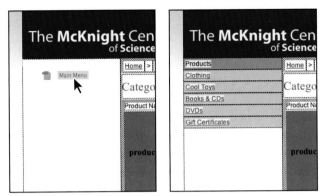

Adding a library item to a page is as simple as dragging it from the Library Items list and dropping it on the page.

5 Open the product_detail.html page from the Files panel. As you did in step 4, drag a copy of the Main Menu library item from the Assets panel to the leftmost column of the page. Just as before, an instance of the Main Menu is placed.

6 Switch back to the category.html page in your Document window. Now you're ready to create another library item from the footer that appears on each page. Select the entire footer at the bottom of the page. You'll be converting this to a new library item that you can repeat across the other pages.

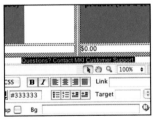

Select the footer of the category.html page.

7   Use the New Library Item button (⊞) at the bottom of the Assets panel to create a new library item from the selected footer. Name it **Footer** when prompted.

Select and convert the footer text to a new library item.

8   Switch back to the home.html page in your Document window. Select and delete the old footer at the bottom of the page, and drag the new Footer library item from the Assets panel in its place.

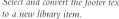

Replace the "static" footer with the new library item. Any changes to the footer will now automatically reflect on this page.

You've now unified the main menu and the footer on all three pages by converting them to library items. When you make changes to the original library items, all instances across all three pages will automatically update.

Exercise

Following the same method outlined in step 8, replace the old footer on the product_detail.html page with the new Footer library item.

Modifying and updating library items

The convenience and power of library items are apparent when you need to update a common item across several pages. Because all instances of a library item remain attached to a master copy, when the master item is edited from the library item list, every instance mirrors these changes.

Now that you're taking advantage of library items in the pages that make up the Gift Shoppe, you can easily make updates across several pages at once. You can edit library items from the Assets panel or by choosing the Open button from the Property inspector when a library item instance is selected on the page.

| Library item | Src /Library/Main menu.lbi | Open | Detach from original |
| | | | Recreate |

Use the Open button on the Property inspector to edit a selected library item.

1   From the Library Items list in the Assets panel, double-click the Main Menu library item to open it for editing. It will appear in the Document window.

Double-click an item in the Library Items list to open it for editing.

2   Where it currently reads *Products*, select the text, then type **Shop For:**.

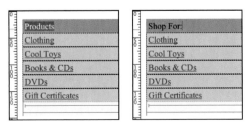

Modify the menu header in the original library item.

3   Click and drag from the second cell to the bottom cell to select all five cells. Change the cells' background color to orange (#FFCC33), using the Bg Color swatch. Choose File > Save to save the changes to the library item.

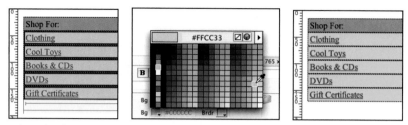

Select and apply a background color to multiple table cells at once in your menu.

4   A dialog box appears, letting you know where the item is used. You now can update the item across all pages. Choose Update to have Dreamweaver change the menu on the remaining pages.

Choose Update, and Dreamweaver will update the library item in all pages that use it.

5 When the update process is complete, click the Close button to exit the Update panel.

Open home.html, category.html, and product_detail.html, and you'll see that all instances of the menu have been updated in all three pages.

All pages that make use of your library item are now up to date.

Because style sheets are defined in the head of a page, they are not copied over with page elements that you add to the Library or Snippets panels. Items will appear unformatted in the Library Items preview panes. If a library item references a specific style, the style sheet in which it's defined will need to be available on the page for you to see the correct formatting.

Introducing templates

If you are creating several pages that need to share the same look and layout, Dreamweaver templates are for you. A Dreamweaver template is a master document from which other pages can be created; these pages inherit all of the elements from the original template, but you can modify each page to include unique content and elements. As with library items, when you edit a template, all pages based on that template will update to reflect your changes.

When you create a template, you specify editable regions, or areas of the page that you can modify. By default, all elements of a page created from a template are locked for editing; you can make changes only from the original master template. You can set sections of a page as editable so that you can add or modify content without accidentally (or intentionally) disturbing the original layout.

Templates are also a great mechanism for controlling access to pages on a site. If you need to provide editing ability to others, you can lock out important page elements and give users access to only certain sections of the page.

Templates are site-specific and are stored in a Templates folder under your site's root folder. You open, edit, or create templates from the Templates list in the Assets panel.

Dreamweaver templates work with Contribute CS3, a basic but powerful web content management tool. You can design and manage templates that can be modified and published by Contribute users.

Creating a new template

For the MKI Gift Shoppe section, you need to duplicate category and product detail pages for a number of product types and items. To do this, you'll set up templates for each page so that new pages can be easily spawned but will remain consistent with the master layout in look and layout.

Before you start, make sure the Assets panel is open and visible (choose Window > Assets). Select the Templates list button (📄) from the Assets panel on the left side.

Select the Templates list button in the Asset panel.

1   In the Files panel (Window > Files), locate and the double-click the product_detail.html page to open it for editing.

2   Save the product_detail.html page as a template by choosing File > Save As Template. The Save As Templates dialog box appears.

Name the new template, and choose Save to save the template.

3   Leave the current site selected at the top, and name the new template product_detail. Choose Save to save the template. If prompted, allow Dreamweaver to update any links by choosing Yes from the dialog box.

The new template is now listed in the Assets panel.

The template now appears in the Templates list in your Assets panel.

Working with editable regions

Next, you will need to define editable regions, or areas that you can modify on any pages created from this template. For this, you'll use the Templates group of buttons from the Common category of the Insert bar.

The Templates group of buttons located on the Common Insert bar.

1   Select the placeholder text in the product_detail template that reads *Product Title*. On the Insert bar, locate the Template objects group and expand it by clicking the arrow on its right side. Select Editable Region. The New Editable Region dialog box appears.

2   Name the new editable region **Product Title**, and press OK. The placeholder text now appears inside a blue box with a tab at the top. This portion of the page and the content within it will be editable in any pages created from this template.

Use the Editable Region button to create a new editable region from an empty space or existing content.

3   Click in the righthand table cell, below the cell that contains the Product Title, and click the Editable Region button on the Insert bar above your document. In the New Editable Region dialog box, name the new region **Product Info**, and choose OK. This sets aside room to add a product description.

Create a new editable region below the product title where the product description will go.

4   Click in the table cell to the left of *Product Info*; this is where a product image will go. To set aside the right amount of room, create an image placeholder by selecting the Image Placeholder button (🖼) located under the Images group of the Insert bar above your document.

5   When the Image Placeholder dialog box appears, set the size to 300 x 300, enter **#FFCC00** into the color text field, and enter **product_image** into the Name and Alternate text fields. Note that image names can't contain spaces or punctuation. Press OK to create the image placeholder.

Create a new image placeholder where the product image will go. You'll add this to a new editable region.

6 Click the image placeholder to select it, and then click the Editable Region button located under the Templates group of the Insert bar above your document. Name the new editable region Product Image, and press OK. The finished template now contains three editable regions—one each for product title, description, and image.

The finished template.

7 Choose File > Save to save the template.

At this point, you can create any number of pages and manage them from this template. The editable regions you created will allow you to add content to any new pages based on this template, but will protect the main layout and page elements from unintended changes.

Creating new pages from templates

Now you're ready to add a detail page for several products in the Gift Shoppe. Each product detail page will be based on the new template you have built.

You can create new pages from a template in two ways:

- from the Templates list in the Assets panel
- by choosing File > New > Page from Template

Don't see that new library item or template you just added? Sometimes the Assets panel needs a little help catching up. If you're sure you added a library item or template, but you don't see it listed, click the Refresh button (C) at the bottom of the Assets panel. This will update the list.

To create a new page from an existing template:

1 In the Templates list, select the new product_detail template. From the Assets Panel menu, choose New from Template. This opens a new, untitled document based on the template.

Select a template in the Template list and choose New from Template to create a new page.

If you try to click in different areas of the page, you'll notice that you can't modify or select any area of the page other than the editable regions.

2 Choose File > Save and save the document as toys_gyroscope.html in your site's root folder.

3 From your Files panel, open gyroscope.txt, located in the text folder. This file contains information for a gyroscope available in the store.

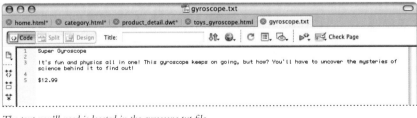

The text you'll need is located in the gyroscope.txt file.

4   Copy and paste the product title (Super Gyroscope) from gyroscope.txt into the editable region marked Product Title. Copy and paste the remaining product information into the Product Info editable region.

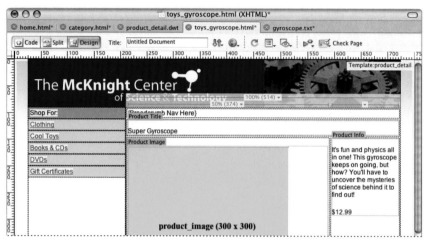

Copy the text into the appropriate regions.

5   Double-click the image placeholder to select a new image. When prompted, choose the gyroscope_lg.jpg file, located in the images folder. The placeholder will be replaced with the image of the gyroscope.

6   Now that you've placed all of your content, save the page. Preview it in a browser by choosing File > Preview in browser and selecting a browser from the menu.

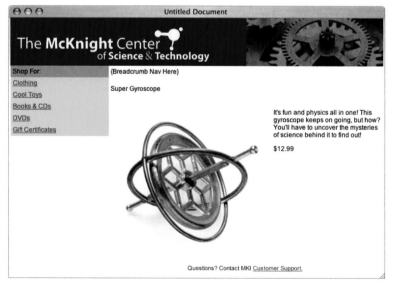

Save your page and preview it in a browser to see your work.

7 After viewing your page, close the browser and return to Dreamweaver. You can leave the page open, or close it by selecting File > Close.

Reusing templates

Now you'll create another new page from the same template. This time, however, you'll use the File menu instead of the Assets panel, demonstrating a different method of starting a new page from a template.

1 Choose File > New, and choose Page from Template from the New Document panel that appears. You should see the current site, and the single template available under it: *product_detail*. Select it and press Create.

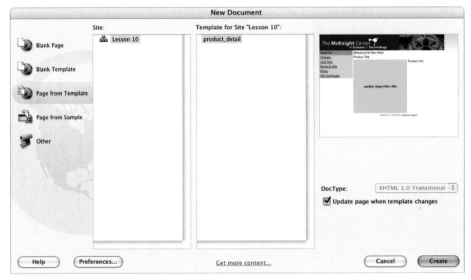

Select a template from the current site definition to create a new page from it.

2 Save the new untitled document in your site's root folder as toys_microscope.html.

3 Use the Files panel to open microscope.txt, located under the text folder. This file contains a description for the toy microscope you'll place on this page.

4   Just as you did with the gyroscope, paste the product title *Mega Microscope* into the Product Title editable region, and the product information and price into the Product Info editable region.

5   Replace the image placeholder with the microscope_lg.jpg file in the images folder. Save the page and preview it in a browser to see it without the editable region flags.

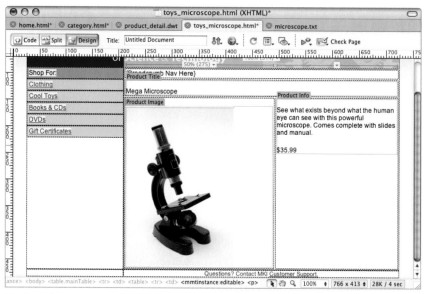

The finished microscope product page.

To hide the flags and bounding boxes for editable regions, deselect View > Visual Aides > Invisible Elements. Be careful, however; this may turn off some visual aids you actually want to see.

Exercise

Using the methods you just learned, create two new pages for the Robot and Newton's Cradle toys from the product_detail template. Name them **toys_robot.html** and **toys_cradle.html**, respectively. Use the following resources to fill up the pages: robot.txt and cradle.txt (under the text folder), and robot_lg.jpg and cradle_lg.jpg (under the images folder).

Modifying templates

To make changes to the four new product pages you built, you'll need to open the original template on which they're based.

1 In the Templates list in the Assets panel, double-click the product_detail template to open it for editing.

2 Select the table cell that holds the *Product Title* placeholder text. Using the Property inspector, apply the header_main class from the Style drop-down menu to the table cell.

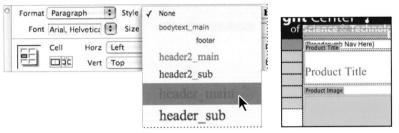

Select the table cell surrounding the product title and apply the header_main class to it.

3 Choose Window > Snippets to open the Snippets panel. Locate the *Angle bracket denotes path* snippet under Navigation > Breadcrumb.

4 Drag-and-drop a copy of the snippet in the cell that reads *{Breadcrumb Nav Here}*. Delete the placeholder text so that only the snippet is left.

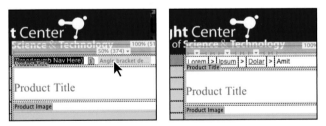

Add a breadcrumb nav snippet to the cell above the product title.

5   Modify the snippet as shown in the following figure so that the links read **Home > Cool Toys**. Set the width of the snippet's table to 200 pixels, using the Property inspector. This breadcrumb menu will enable users to return to the Cool Toys category page or the main store page from any product detail page. You can leave the default links for now.

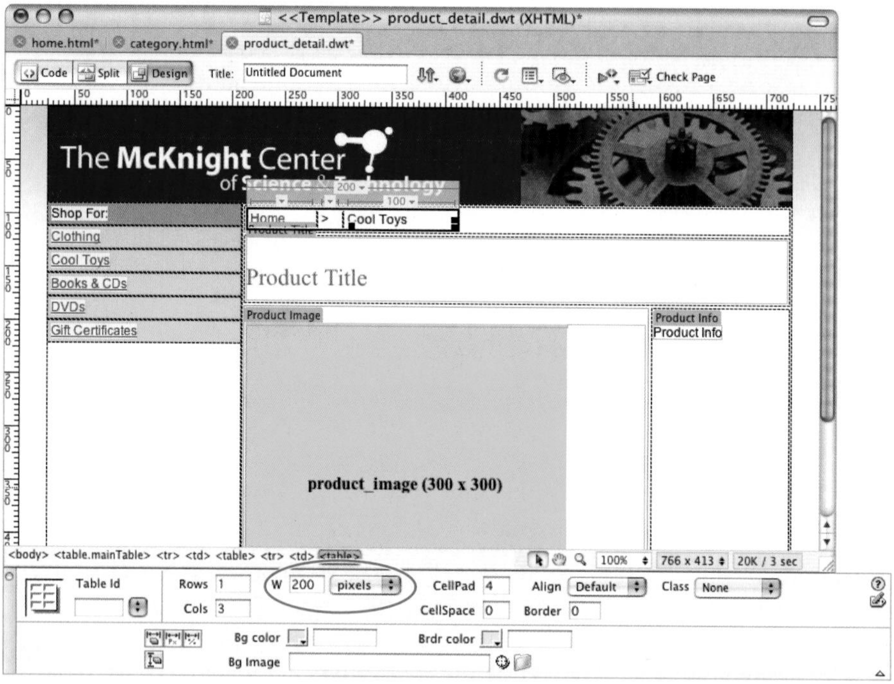

Modify the snippet and set it to 200 pixels wide. Leave the default links (which currently uses the pound sign [#] as a placeholder).

6   Choose File > Save. The Update Template Files dialog box appears; choose Update to update all of the pages shown.

7   Choose File > Close to close the template, and, from the Files panel, open any of the four product pages you have created so far. The new menu and title styles have been applied to all four.

Repeating regions

A single region may not be the best way to display the content you add to a template-based page. You may require a template that can handle a number of items, such as a table that displays products in a category. If you need to build a flexible template that can hold any number of uniform items, you can add a repeating region to it.

Repeating regions allow you to define an element on a template as repeatable, when you create a page based on that template, you can increase, or repeat, the number of regions to accommodate the information. You'll also be able to reorder these repeated regions at any time without having to move the content. You can set elements such as a table row, paragraph, or small display table as a repeating region, and then duplicate as many as you need to fit the content at hand.

A repeating region is not automatically editable. You'll need to set editable regions inside any repeating element in order to add to or edit its content.

In the following steps, you'll add a repeating region to your category.html page and convert it to a template so that you can use it to display any number of products in a specific category.

Tag selector

The tag selector can be a valuable tool when trying to select parts of complex page layouts that contain nested tables. The tag selector is located in the bottom-left corner of your Document window, and displays your current location on the page as a chain of tags.

Click anywhere within the part of the page you're targeting, then use the tag selector to click on the tag you're trying to select.

1   Open the category.html page from the Files panel.

2   The table in the center contains two rows with two display tables each. Click inside either of the small tables in the first row.

3   To select the entire row, use the tag selector in the bottom-left corner of the Document window, and work your way up the tags from right to left until the entire row is selected. Choose Edit > Cut to remove it.

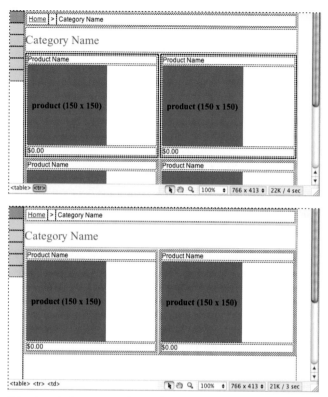

Select the entire first row using the tag selector and remove it.

4   Select the entire remaining row; you'll use this row as a repeating region so that you can add the rows you need to hold products.

5 From the Template button group (📄▾) on the Common Insert bar, choose Repeating Region. Because you haven't saved this page as a template yet, a dialog box will appear, letting you know that you need to convert the page to a template before you add regions. Press OK.

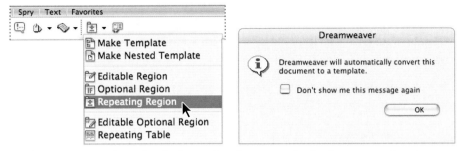

Use the Repeating Region button from the Common Insert bar to convert the selected row to a repeating region.

6 When the Repeating Region dialog box appears, assign the new region the name **Products**, and press OK.

The row is now a repeating region, which you can duplicate in any page created from this template.

7 Choose File > Save As Template, and save the new template as **category_display**.

8 In the left display table, highlight the Product Name placeholder text. From the Template group on the Common Insert bar, choose Editable Region. Name the new region **Product Name**, and press OK.

9 Select the placeholder image below the new editable region, and click the Editable Region button; name the new region **Product Image**, and press OK. Now select the price below the Product image, and again choose Editable Region from the Common Insert bar. Name the new editable region **Product Price**, and press OK.

10 Use the methods in steps 6 and 7 to set editable regions for the product name, image, and price on the righthand display table. Assign the names Product 2 Name, Product 2 Image, and Product 2 Price to these editable regions.

11 Choose File > Save to save this template.

Templates can't contain duplicate region names. If you try to set two editable regions with the same name, Dreamweaver will give you an error message.

Putting repeating regions into action

You're now ready to create a page from the new category_display template and see how repeating regions work.

1 Launch the Assets panel and select the Templates category on the left. Then select the category_display template, and choose New from Template from the Assets panel menu.

Select the new template and create a new page from it using the Assets panel menu.

2   Save the new document as **category_toys.html** in your site's root folder. You'll notice the new repeating region in the middle of the page—its tab features four buttons that allow you to add, remove, and shift repeating regions up or down in the stacking order.

Use the button set at the top of the repeating region to add a new row with two more product display tables.

3   Click the plus sign button (**+**) on the top of the repeating region; a new table row with two more product display tables appears. In the next step, you'll fill in these four product tables with information to complete your page.

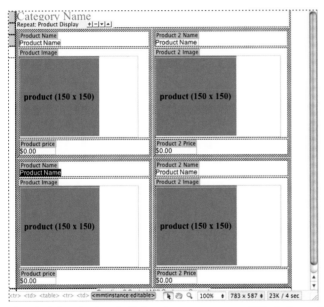

Copy the information from the file located at text > toys.txt to fill in the four product slots in the page.

4 From the Files panel, open the toys.txt file located in the text folder. This contains the names and prices of the four products you'll add. In each of the four product tables, fill in the information for the products shown here. Double-click each image placeholder and replace it with the appropriate image that matches the product description.

Use the cradle_sm.jpg, gyroscope_sm.jpg, microscope_sm.jpg, and robot_sm.jpg files located in the images folder.

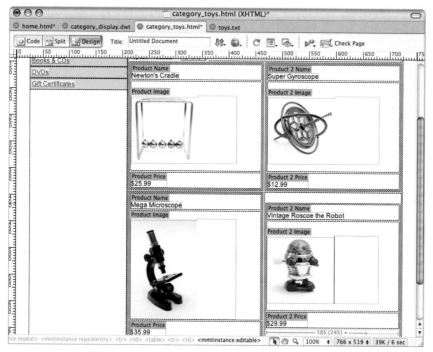

Add the product information to each of the four product tables.

5 The four products now appear in the category page, and you can use the up-and-down arrow buttons above the repeating region to reorder the rows. Bring the bottom row that contains the microscope and robot above the top row by clicking in either toy's table and using the up-arrow button.

Reorder the rows using the up and down arrow buttons at the top of the repeating region.

Detach from Template command

If you want to modify a template-based page beyond what the editable regions allow, you can use Modify > Templates > Detach from Template command, which breaks the current page away from the master template, allowing you to edit it freely. Keep in mind that a page detached from a template will no longer be updated if you make any changes to the original template.

Self study

Open one of the four product detail pages you created, and use Detach from Template to break it away from the product_display template. You'll then be able to freely edit other elements on the page that you did not include in the original editable regions. Create some variations on the newly detached page by trying a new layout, modifying product and picture positioning, or applying a new style to the product title, price, or description. Use the Templates section of the Assets panel to create a new template from the page.

Review

Questions

1 What are two key differences between snippets and library items?

2 How do you add a new snippet to Dreamweaver?

3 Where are library items and page templates stored? Which panel do you use to manage them?

4 What happens to pages based on a template when you modify the original template?

5 True or false: Repeating regions are automatically editable in pages that use them.

Answers

1 Snippets are stored as part of the Dreamweaver application, and are available regardless of which site or document you're working on; library items are specific to a site definition. Copies of a snippet never update when the original snippet is edited; a library item will update all instances of itself throughout a local site when a change is applied to it.

2 You can drag a snippet from the Snippets panel onto the page, or position your cursor in the page and double-click the snippet in the Snippets panel.

3 Library items and page templates are stored in the Library and Templates folders (respectively) under your local site. You can manage both, using their specific categories on the Assets panel.

4 Dreamweaver will update all pages based on that template to reflect any changes made to the original template.

5 False: You must first set editable regions within a repeating region to add content.

What you'll learn in this lesson:

- Using the Code and Design views
- Taking advantage of the Coding toolbar
- Validating your code
- Formatting your code

Under the Hood: Editing in the Code View

Dreamweaver provides exceptional code-editing support to complement its powerful visual layout tools and application development features. You can adapt the coding environment so that it fits the way you work, changing the way you view code, reformatting your markup, or importing and using your favorite tag library.

Starting up

Before starting, make sure that your tools and panels are consistent by resetting your workspace. See "Resetting the Dreamweaver workspace" on page 3.

You will work with several files from the dw11lessons folder in this lesson. Make sure that you have loaded the dwlessons folder onto your hard drive from the supplied DVD. See "Loading lesson files" on page 3.

Before you begin, you need to create a site definition that points to the dw11lessons folder from the included DVD that contains resources you need for these lessons. Go to Site > New Site, or, for details on creating a site definition, refer to Lesson 2, "Creating a New Site."

Getting to your code

You can view the source code for Dreamweaver documents in several ways. You can display it in the Document window by switching to the Code view, you can split the Document window to display both the visual page and its related code in Split view, or you can work in the Code inspector, a separate coding window. The Code inspector works like a detachable version of the Code view for the current page.

1 From the dw11lessons folder, open the file knowcode.html.

2 Choose View > Code to view the code for this page in the Document window.

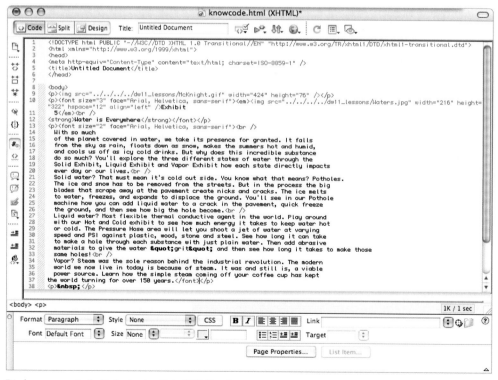

Display your page in the Code view to edit the HTML code.

3 Choose View > Code and Design allows you to code and visually edit the page in the Document window at the same time. The code appears in the top pane and the page appears in the bottom pane.

4 From the Document toolbar, click on the View Options button (▤.), and choose Design View on Top from the drop-down menu to display the page on top.

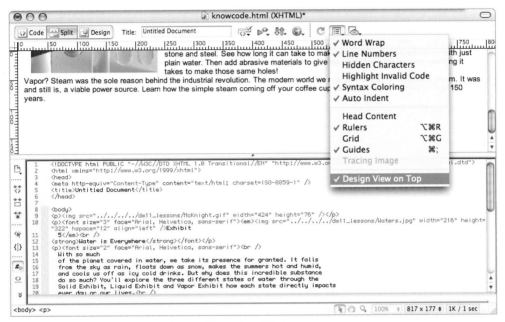

Choose Design View on Top to switch the location of the Code and Design views.

5 Drag the splitter bar, located between the two panes, to adjust the size of the panes in the Document window. Remember, the Code view is updated automatically when you make changes in the Design view, but you have to refresh the document in the Design view by clicking in the Design view or pressing F5 after making changes in the Code view.

6   Choose Window > Code Inspector to view your code in the separate Code inspector window. Working in the Code Inspector is just like working in the Code View except it is in a separate window. This might be useful, depending on how you choose to manage your workspace. Click on the close button to close the Code Inspector for now.

```
1   <!DOCTYPE html PUBLIC "-//W3C//DTD XHTML 1.0 Transitional//EN"
    "http://www.w3.org/TR/xhtml1/DTD/xhtml1-transitional.dtd">
2   <html xmlns="http://www.w3.org/1999/xhtml">
3   <head>
4   <meta http-equiv="Content-Type" content="text/html;
    charset=ISO-8859-1" />
5   <title>Untitled Document</title>
6   </head>
7
8   <body>
9   <p><img src="../../../../dw11_lessons/McKnight.gif" width="424"
    height="76" /></p>
10  <p><font size="3" face="Arial, Helvetica, sans-serif"><em><img
    src="../../../../dw11_lessons/Waters.jpg" width="216" height=
    "322" hspace="12" align="left" />Exhibit
11      5</em><br />
12  <strong>Water is Everywhere</strong></font></p>
13  <p><font size="2" face="Arial, Helvetica, sans-serif"><br />
14      With so much
15      of the planet covered in water, we take its presence for
        granted. It falls
```

You also can view your HTML code in the Code Inspector window.

Accessing code with the tag selector

You can use the tag selector to select, edit, or remove tags without ever having to exit the Design view. The tag selector, situated in the status bar at the bottom of the Document window, displays a series of tags that correspond to elements on your page. In this exercise, you will use the Quick Tag editor to remove a *<font>* tag from your code. The *<font>* tag is an older method of changing the way fonts are displayed on your screen. These days, designers are using CSS to style their text; however, before you can use CSS, you should remove the older font tag. This is often a tedious process that involves locating both the open and close tags and deleting them by hand in the Code view. The Quick Tag Editor allows you to easily remove both open and close tags with a single click.

Use the tag selector to select, edit, or remove tags while in the Design view.

To use the Quick Tag Editor:

1   Switch back to the Design view and click in the main paragraph of your page in the Document window. The *<body>* tag, as well as the *<p>* and *<font>* tags that follow it, appear in the tag selector.

2   Click the *<body>* tag in the tag selector. The entire body of the page is highlighted.

3   Right-click (Windows) or Ctrl+click (Mac OS) on the *<body>* tag in the tag selector. A contextual menu appears.

4   Choose Quick Tag Editor from the menu. The Quick Tag Editor appears, allowing you to edit the body tag if you chose. The Quick Tag Editor is designed to speed up workflow while working in the Design view. Instead of switching to the Code view to make changes, you can make changes directly in the status bar of the Design view. You will not be making any changes to the body tag right now.

5   Press the Enter (Windows) or Return (Mac OS) key to close the Quick Tag Editor.

Next, you'll remove a font tag, using the Quick Tag Editor.

6   Click in the main paragraph of your document again. The same tags appear in the tag selector.

7   Right-click (Windows) or Ctrl+click (Mac OS) on the *<font>* tag in the tag selector.

8   In the contextual menu that appears, choose Remove Tag.

9   Because you've removed the font styling from your body text, the font reverts to its default unstyled appearance. You could now choose to style this paragraph with CSS.

Editing an HTML tag with the Quick Tag Editor

You can also use the Quick Tag Editor to edit an HTML tag in your document. For example, in this exercise, you will change the background color of your page by adding an additional attribute to the *<body>* tag.

Use the Quick Tag Editor to simplify code editing.

1   Select the *<body>* tag from the tag selector at the bottom of the Document window.

2   This time, press Ctrl+T (Windows) or Command+T (Mac OS), instead of using the drop-down menu options described earlier. The Quick Tag Editor opens at the top of your screen.

3   Type a new attribute into the *<body>* tag so that it reads *<body bgcolor="d7d7d7">*. Press the Enter (Windows) or Return (Mac OS) key to accept the change and turn the background color of your page to a light gray.

Inserting tags with the Tag Chooser

You can use the Tag Chooser to insert any tag in the Dreamweaver tag libraries (which include Macromedia ColdFusion and ASP.NET tag libraries) into your page.

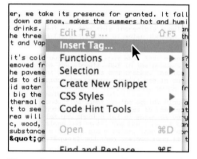

You can insert an assortment of HTML tags from Dreamweaver's tag libraries with the Tag Chooser.

1   Switch to Code view by choosing View > Code or by pressing the Code view button (⊡) on the Document toolbar.

2   Click to place an insertion point in line 17 of your code, just before the words *But why does this incredible substance do so much?*.

3   Right-click (Windows) or Ctrl+click (Mac OS) and select Insert Tag. The Tag Chooser appears. The left pane contains a list of supported tag libraries, and the right pane shows the individual tags in the selected library.

4   Select the *HTML tags* library on the left, and the *br* (line break) tag on the right.

5   Click the Insert button to add the tag to your code. The Tag Editor for the <br> tag appears. Press OK, and close the Tag Chooser by clicking the Close button.

6   Switch back to the Design view by choosing View > Design or by pressing the Design view button (⊡) on the Document toolbar, and note that a new line break has been added before the text *But why does this incredible substance do so much?*.

Now let's look at some other features of Dreamweaver CS3 that allow you to work with HTML code.

Inserting and editing comments

Comments are descriptive text that you insert in HTML code to explain the code or provide other information. By default, the text of the comment appears only in the Code view and is not displayed in a browser. You can also modify existing comments. In this exercise, you'll add your own comment to the HTML code, and edit a comment already in the code.

1   Make sure you're still in the Design view. Click to place an insertion cursor in the line below your last line of text.

2   Select Insert > Comment.

3   Dreamweaver displays the Comment dialog box. Type **Add links here** as your comment and press OK.

4   A box appears warning that you will not be able to see comment markers in the Design view unless you select View > Visual Aids > Invisible Elements. Press OK. You will now enable the preference to view Invisible Elements.

5   Choose Edit > Preferences (Windows) or Dreamweaver > Preferences (Mac OS) and click on the Invisible Elements category. Check the box for Comments, and press OK. You will now see a small icon with an exclamation point—this is the visual representation of your comment.

6   Switch back to the Code view by choosing View > Code or by pressing the Code view button ( ) on the Document toolbar. Comments are very useful when viewing a file in Code view; they can serve as instructions to be followed at a later date (as they are here) or may simply be used to identify sections of a page.

In the line that corresponds to the location of your comment, Dreamweaver has inserted a comment tag (in gray, by default) that looks like this:

Comments inserted into your code can provide
any information about the page that you choose.

7   Return to the Design view by choosing View > Design or by pressing the Design view button on the Document toolbar ( ). Click on the Comment marker to select it, then edit the comment's text in the Property inspector to read **Add links here by Friday**.

8   Choose File > Save to save your work.

Working in the Code view

As we've seen, the Code view is a hand–coding environment for writing and editing HTML, JavaScript, and scripting languages such as PHP and ColdFusion, among others. In addition to its writing and editing capabilities, Dreamweaver also allows you to change the way HTML is displayed in the Code view.

Change the way HTML is displayed in the Code view with Code View Options.

View options

You can set word wrapping, display line numbers for the code, highlight invalid code, set syntax coloring for code elements, set indenting, and show hidden characters from the View > Code View Options menu.

Choose from the options listed in the Code View Options menu.

- **Word Wrap** wraps the code so you can view it without scrolling horizontally. This option doesn't insert line breaks; it just makes the code easier to view.

- **Line Numbers** displays line numbers along the side of the code.

- **Hidden Characters** displays special characters in place of white space. For example, a dot replaces each space, a double chevron replaces each tab, and a paragraph marker replaces each line break.

- **Highlight Invalid Code** causes Dreamweaver to highlight in yellow all HTML code that isn't valid. When you select an invalid tag, the Property inspector displays information on how to correct the error.

- **Syntax Coloring** enables or disables code coloring.

- **Auto Indent** makes your code indent automatically when you press Enter while writing code. The new line of code indents to the same level as the previous line.

The Coding toolbar

The Coding toolbar contains buttons that let you perform many standard coding operations, such as collapsing and expanding code selections, highlighting invalid code, applying and removing comments, indenting code, and inserting recently used code snippets. The Coding toolbar is visible only in the Code view and appears vertically on the left side of the Document window. To see what each button does, position the cursor over it until a tool tip appears.

ICON	TOOL NAME	USE
	Open Documents	Lists the documents that are open. When you select a document, it is displayed in the Document window.
	Collapse Full Tag	Collapses the content between a set of opening and closing tags (for example, the content between \<body\> and \</body\>). You must place the insertion point in the opening or closing tag and then click to collapse it.
	Collapse Selection	Collapses the selected code.
	Expand All	Restores all collapsed code.
	Select Parent Tag	Selects the content and surrounding opening and closing tags of the line in which you've placed the insertion point. If you repeatedly click this button, and your tags are balanced, Dreamweaver will eventually select the outermost \<html\> and \</html\> tags.
	Balance Braces	Selects the content and surrounding parentheses, braces, or square brackets of the line in which you've placed the insertion point. If you repeatedly click this button, and your surrounding symbols are balanced, Dreamweaver will eventually select the outermost braces, parentheses, or brackets in the document.
	Line Numbers	Hides or shows numbers at the beginning of each line of code.
	Highlight Invalid Code	Highlights invalid code in yellow.
	Apply Comment	Wraps comment tags around selected code, or opens new comment tags.
	Remove Comment	Removes comment tags from the selected code. If a selection includes nested comments, only the outer comment tags are removed.

ICON	TOOL NAME	USE
✏	Wrap Tag	Wraps selected code with the selected tag from the Quick Tag Editor.
🗋	Recent Snippets	Inserts a recently used code snippet from the Snippets panel.
⊘	Remove or Convert CSS	Lets you move CSS to another location, or convert inline CSS to CSS rules.
⇥	Indent Code	Shifts the selection to the right.
⇤	Outdent Code	Shifts the selection to the left.
◈	Format Source Code	Applies previously specified code formats to selected code or to the entire page if no code is selected. You can also quickly set code formatting preferences by selecting Code Formatting Settings from the Format Source Code button, or edit tag libraries by selecting Edit Tag Libraries.

The number of buttons available in the Coding toolbar varies depending on the size of the Code view in the Document window. To see all of the available buttons, resize the Code view window or click the Show More arrow (⹁) at the bottom of the Coding toolbar.

Collapsing and expanding tags and code blocks

Dreamweaver lets you collapse and expand code fragments so you can view different sections of your document without having to use the scroll bar. When you select code, Dreamweaver adds a set of collapse buttons next to the selection (minus symbols in Windows; vertical triangles in the Mac OS). Although you can select code fragments by making selections in the Design view or the Code view, you can collapse code only in the Code view.

At times, Dreamweaver may not collapse the exact fragment of code that you selected. Dreamweaver uses smart collapse to collapse the most common and visually pleasing selection. For example, if you selected an indented tag and then selected the indented spaces before the tag as well, Dreamweaver would not collapse the indented spaces, because most users would expect their indentations to be preserved. If you want to disable smart collapse and force Dreamweaver to collapse exactly what you selected, you can do so by holding down the Ctrl/Command key before collapsing your code. Additionally, Dreamweaver places a warning icon on collapsed code fragments if a fragment contains errors or code that is unsupported by certain browsers.

1   To collapse code, make sure you are in the Code view by pressing the Code view button (⊡) on the Document toolbar. Click and drag to select the code enclosed between the *<body>* and *</body>* tags.

2   Select Edit > Code Collapse > Collapse Selection, or click one of the collapse buttons next to the selection. The *<body>* fragment is collapsed to make viewing your code easier.

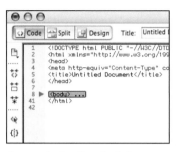

An example of a collapsed code fragment.

3   Next, you will collapse the code outside a selection. Select the collapsed *<body>* fragment by clicking on it.

4   Select Edit > Code Collapse > Collapse Outside Selection. All other code is now collapsed.

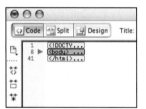

You can also collapse code outside a selection.

5   Reverse the collapse by double-clicking the collapsed *<body>* fragment. Alternatively, you can select Edit > Code Collapse > Expand Selection. The *<body>* code is restored to its original view.

Select Edit > Code Collapse > Expand All. All of your code fragments are now restored to their original view at once. To save time, you can also select the code to be collapsed by simply clicking in the tag that encloses it.

6   Now you'll try these out with tags: in the Code view, place the insertion point inside an opening or closing tag (for example, inside the *<body>* or *</body>* tag).

7   Select Edit > Code Collapse > Collapse Full Tag. This collapses the tag and all of the content it encloses.

8   Try collapsing the code outside a full tag by placing the insertion point inside an opening or closing tag—for example, inside the *<body>* or *</body>* tag—then selecting Edit > Code Collapse > Collapse Outside Full Tag.

9   Now that you know how to collapse tags and code blocks, select Edit > Code Collapse > Expand All to restore your code to its original (expanded) configuration so you can move on to the next exercise.

Edit	View	Insert	Modify	
Undo			⌘Z	
Redo			⌘Y	
Repeating Entries			▶	
Code Collapse			▶	Collapse Selection ⇧⌘C
				Collapse Outside Selection ⌥⌘C
Edit with BBEdit				Expand Selection ⇧⌘E
				Collapse Full Tag ⇧⌘J
Tag Libraries...				Collapse Outside Full Tag ⌥⌘J
				Expand All ⌥⌘E

You can expand all code to restore it to its original configuration.

Validating your code

In addition to the many options available for formatting your code, you can also use Dreamweaver to find out if your code has tag or syntax errors. Dreamweaver can validate documents in many languages, including HTML, XHTML, ColdFusion Markup Language (CFML), JavaServer Pages (JSP), Wireless Markup Language (WML), and XML. You can validate the current document or a selected tag.

Highlighting and correcting invalid code

As mentioned earlier in this lesson, you can set Dreamweaver to highlight invalid code (in yellow) in both the Design and Code views. When you select a highlighted section, the Property inspector offers information on how to correct the error.

1   Use the File > Open command to open the file knowcode_bad.html from your dw11lessons folder. This page has an intentional error built in which is immediately visible as the yellow highlight font tag.

2   Switch to the Code view. Invalid code will not be highlighted by default in Code view. In order to view the invalid code, you must enable this option in the View menu.

3   Select View > Code View Options. Alternatively, you can click the View Options button in the toolbar at the top of the Code view or the Code inspector.

4   Turn on the Highlight Invalid Code option by selecting it from the menu.

5 The line that contains your invalid code is highlighted in yellow. Now the code is highlighted in both views.

Invalid code is highlighted in yellow in both the Design and Code views.

6 In the Code view, click once on the highlighted (invalid) code. In the Property inspector, a highlighted question mark appears, along with a comment that the tag is incorrectly formatted.

The Property inspector identifies the invalid code and suggests how to correct it.

As the Property inspector suggests, you cannot correct invalid code in the Design view.

7 Correct the error by clicking after the word font in line 10. Type the word **size** (which is the correct tag <fontsize>) and the highlighting disappears.

8 Choose File > Revert to undo the correction you just made. We'll look at some other validation methods in the next exercise.

Using the Check Page menu

The options available in the Check Page menu analyze your documents for accessibility issues, broken and orphaned links, and browser compatibility, as well as for potential markup (code) problems. Because this lesson is primarily concerned with code editing, you'll focus here on the Validate Markup option.

The Validate Markup option

The Validate Markup option lets you validate the current document or a selected tag.

1 Select File > Validate > Markup. The Validation tab of the Results panel lists the syntax errors it found.

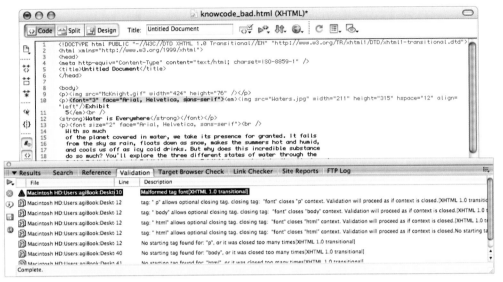

The Validation tab of the Results panel lists any syntax errors found during validation.

2 Double-click the first error message which is the Malformed tag font. This is the same error you viewed in the last exercise.

3 As you did in the last exercise, change *font="3"* in line 10 to **fontsize="3"**. Choose File > Validate > Markup again, and note that the error is gone.

4 To save the report as an XML file, click the Save Report button (▣) on the left side of the Results panel.

5 To view the report in your primary browser (which lets you print the report), click the Browse Report button (◉).

Using the Validator section of the Preferences dialog box, you can specify the tag-based languages against which the Validator should check, the specific problems that the Validator should check for, and the types of errors that the Validator should report.

Formatting code

Once you've validated your code, you can further change its look by specifying formatting preferences such as indentation, line length, and the case of tag and attribute names.

1 Select Edit > Preferences (Windows) or Dreamweaver > Preferences (Mac OS).

2 When the Preferences dialog box appears, select Code Format from the Category list on the left. The Code Format preferences appear on the right.

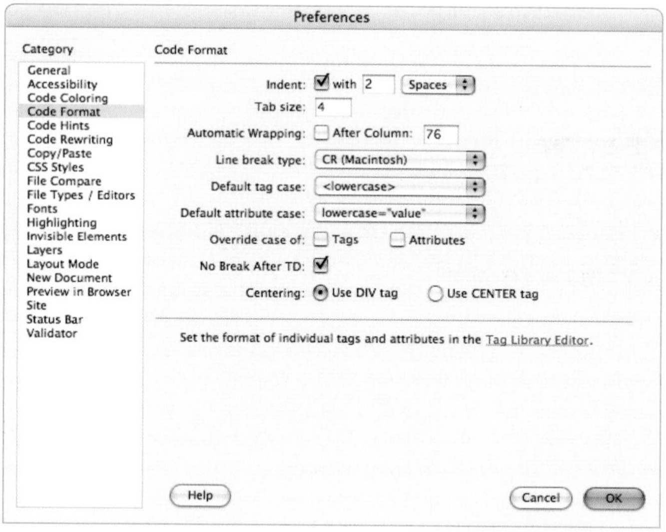

Choose from the Code Format preferences to further change the look of your code.

3 The Code Format preferences allow you to change the way code is written in Dreamweaver. For example, when you press the Tab key, your cursor will indent 4 spaces. Using this preference window, you could increase or decrease the amount of the indent. Press Cancel; you will not be changing any preferences at this point.

Apply Source Formatting

If you make changes in the Code Format preferences, those options are automatically applied only to new files created in Dreamweaver. To apply new formatting preferences to an existing file, first open Knowcode.html located in the dw11lessons folder, then select Commands > Apply Source Formatting.

Use the Apply Source Formatting command to apply new formatting preferences to existing documents.

Indenting

Dreamweaver also offers indentation options for you as you write and edit code in the Code view or the Code inspector. You can change the indentation level of a selected block or line of code, shifting it to the right or left by one tab.

1   Select any block of code and press the Tab key. Alternatively, you can select Edit > Indent Code.

Indent your code as you write (or edit) it for better organization and easier searching.

2   To unindent the selected block of code, press Shift+Tab, or you can select Edit > Outdent Code.

3   Choose File > Save to save your work, then close the file by choosing File > Close.

Congratulations! You've finished the lesson.

Self study

Using your new familiarity with editing HTML code in Dreamweaver, try some of the following tasks to build on your experience.

1   Open the knowcode.html file from the dw11lessons folder on your desktop. Switch to the Code view, and, using the tag selector and the Quick Tag Editor, change the font size of the headline *Exhibit 5: Water is Everywhere* from 3 to 5. Return to the Design view to see the results, and then experiment further with editing tag attributes, using the Quick Tag Editor.

2   Switch back to the Code view and, using the Coding toolbar, collapse the code fragment for the *<head>* section of the knowcode.html document. Apply a comment following the collapsed *<head>* fragment, and edit it, using the Property inspector. Try out some of the other formatting options available in the Coding toolbar.

3   Open the knowcode_bad.html file from the dw11lessons folder on your desktop. Activate the Highlight Invalid Code option, and run Validate Markup on your document. Double-click on any listed errors to highlight them in your code. Then save an XML report of the validation, and view that report in your web browser.

Review

Questions

1   What is the significance of working in the Code view in Dreamweaver?

2   Why does Dreamweaver not always collapse the exact fragment of code you've selected?

3   When are the code formatting options that you specify in Code Format preferences applied?

4   What advantages are there in using the tag selector to select, edit, and/or remove HTML code?

5   How do you know where invalid code exists in your document and how to fix it?

Answers

1   The Code view is a hand-coding environment for writing and editing HTML, JavaScript, server-language code such as PHP and ColdFusion, and any other kind of code.

2   Dreamweaver uses smart collapse to collapse the most common and visually pleasing selection. For example, if you selected an indented tag and then selected the indented spaces before the tag as well, Dreamweaver would not collapse the indented spaces, because most users would expect their indentations to be preserved.

3   The code formatting options that you specify in Code Format preferences are automatically applied only to new documents that you subsequently create with Dreamweaver. However, you can apply new formatting preferences to existing documents using the Apply Source Formatting command.

4   You can use the tag selector to select, edit, or remove tags without exiting the Design view. The tag selector, situated in the status bar at the bottom of the Document window, displays a series of tags that correspond to elements on your page.

5   With the Highlight Invalid Code option selected, Dreamweaver highlights invalid code in yellow in both the Design and Code views. When you select a highlighted section, the Property inspector offers information on how to correct the error.

What you'll learn in this lesson:

- Creating forms
- Working with the *<form>* tag
- Adding form elements
- Styling forms with CSS
- Choosing processing options
- Validating forms

Building Web Forms

HTML forms allow you to gather information from visitors to your web site. In this lesson, you'll learn how to add form elements such as text boxes and radio buttons to make your site more interactive.

Starting up

Before starting, make sure that your tools and panels are consistent by resetting your workspace. See "Resetting the Dreamweaver workspace" on page 3.

You will work with several files from the dw12lessons folder in this lesson. Make sure that you have loaded the dwlessons folder onto your hard drive from the supplied DVD. See "Loading lesson files" on page 3.

Before you begin, you need to create a site definition that points to the dw12lessons folder from the included DVD that contains resources you need for these lessons. Go to Site > New Site, or, for details on creating a site definition, refer to Lesson 2, "Creating a New Site."

See Lesson 12 in action!

Use the accompanying video to gain a better understanding of how to use some of the features shown in this lesson. Open the Dynamic_Learning_DW_CS3.swf file located in the Videos folder and select Lesson 12 to view the video training file for this lesson.

Forms in everyday (web) life

HTML forms are commonly used for questionnaires, hotel reservations, order forms, data entry, and a variety of other applications. Users provide information by entering text, selecting menu items, and so on, and then submit that information to you via a server.

Here's an example of a simple form that includes labels, radio buttons, and push buttons (used to reset the form or submit it):

Forms are a great choice when you want to gather information from your audience.

How forms work

An HTML form is a section of a document containing normal content, markup, special elements called controls (checkboxes, radio buttons, and menus, for example), and labels on those controls. The form is completed when a user modifies its controls (by entering text and selecting menu items), and submits the form to an agent for processing.

You can add these controls, commonly called fields, to a page in Dreamweaver, but when the user clicks the Submit button, his browser won't know what to do with the information he's entered. To identify this information as part of a package, and to specify the route that information should take when submitted, you need to create a Dreamweaver form.

Building a contact form

In this lesson, you'll build a contact form for the McKnight Institute. This form allows users to define the exhibits and events that they are most interested in receiving more information about, and it provides you with that data so you know which users want what information. The best forms allow users to interact with you and your site while providing you with information about them.

Inserting the *<form>* tag

The first step in building a form in Dreamweaver is to add a form element, which serves as a container for the form fields you'll be adding to it. In hand-coded HTML, you do this by inserting the *<form>* tag into your code. In the Design view, you can add a form element using the Form button.

1   Choose File > Open. When the Open dialog box appears, navigate to the dw12lessons folder. Select the formbase.html file and press Open.

2   Place an insertion cursor where you want your form to appear. Because this is an existing page, click with your mouse in the white area underneath the *Let us know where to send additional information about the museum* text.

Insert your cursor under the Tell Me More! header.

3   In the Insert toolbar, choose the Forms tab to display options for adding form elements to a page.

Options for adding form elements to a page are found in the Forms tab of the Insert toolbar.

4   From the Forms tab of the Insert toolbar, click on the Form button (▢).

5   You should now see a dotted red outline on your page. This is how a form is displayed in the Design view. If you don't see this outline, choose View > Visual Aids > Invisible Elements to turn on the form element's visibility.

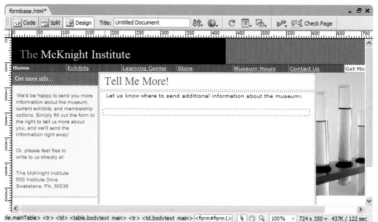

A dotted red outline on your page indicates a placed form element.

Now you'll take a look at the code generated by the steps you just completed in the Design view.

6   In the Document toolbar just above your Document window, click on the Code button (▣) to switch to your page's HTML code view.

7   In line 59 of your code, you should see the newly added *<form>* tag. If not, go back to the Design view and click on the form element. When you return to the Code view, it is highlighted in the HTML code for the page.

In HTML code, a form element is added using the <form> tag.

Setting form properties

Notice that the *<form>* tag includes four different attributes, or descriptors. These attributes are listed as *id*, *name*, *method*, and *action*, and they represent the HTML form element's properties. Rather than type the values for these attributes into the code, you'll switch back to the Design view and add them using the Property inspector.

1   In the Document toolbar, click on the Design view button (▣) to return to the visual representation of your page.

2   Make sure the form element you added in the previous exercise is selected by clicking on the edge of its red outline. A form field element must be selected before you modify its properties.

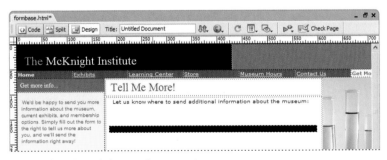

Select the form element before you edit its properties.

3   In the Property inspector at the bottom of your Document window, notice the fields for each form property inside the *<form>* tag.

The fields in the Property inspector reflect properties found inside the <form> tag in HTML code.

Adding a unique name in the Form Name field makes it possible to identify and/or control the form with a script, such as a JavaScript or a VBScript. It is also very important for form validation, which we discuss later in this lesson.

The name you chose in the Form Name field is duplicated in the code for the id attribute, which adds accessibility and scripting access to your form.

4   In the Form Name field, enter the name **Contact**.

The Action field allows you to specify the program, or Common Gateway Interface (CGI) script, that processes the user's form data. You can type in the path to this program, or use the Browse button to navigate to the desired file. In most cases, you'll need to get this information from your system administrator or hosting provider.

5   Because we have not yet defined the processing method for this form, leave the Action field blank.

The Method menu

The Method drop-down menu is where you'll choose the method used to transmit the data to a server. The Method drop-down menu includes the following choices:

Default uses the browser's default setting to submit the form data to a server. Most browsers use the GET method by default.

GET includes the form data as part of the URL of the request to the server. GET has a length limitation of 8,192 characters in the URL and is less commonly used to send long forms than the POST method.

POST is similar to GET, but it embeds the form data in the header of the server request instead of in the URL. Although the POST method is the most commonly used, be aware that pages sent by this method cannot be bookmarked and are not encrypted for security purposes.

6   Choose the POST method for this exercise.

7   Choose application/x-www-form-urlencoded from the Enctype drop-down menu. The Enctype field defines the encoding type of the data being submitted to a server.

Application/x-www-form-urlencoded is used in most situations, unless you're asking the user to upload a file, in which case you'd choose multipart/form-data.

The optional Target property specifies the window or frame in which to display the data returned. The target value is included in the <form> tag only when you choose to specify it. For more information on target values, see Lesson 8, "Working with Frames."

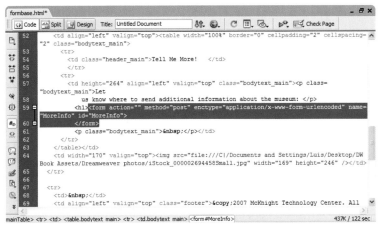

Form properties are set in the Property inspector.

8 Switch to the Code view to see how Dreamweaver creates HTML code for the properties you just defined.

Setting form properties in Design view saves you the effort of writing all this HTML code.

9 Return to the Design view to continue with this lesson.

Now that you've defined the properties of the form, you'll use options in the Insert toolbar's Forms tab to add elements to the form.

Adding form elements

A Dreamweaver form is not a form until you add the elements, or fields, that allow the user to provide information to you. Thankfully, the Forms tab of the Insert toolbar contains everything you need to insert any kind of form field into your page.

The Forms tab in the Insert toolbar contains everything you need to add interactive fields to your form.

Common form elements

Of the 11 form elements you can add using the Insert toolbar, these are most commonly used:

- **Text fields** accept alphanumeric text entries, in single- or multiple-line formats, or in a password (bulleted) format.

- **Checkboxes** allow users to make as many choices as they want from a list of options.

- **Radio buttons** allow only mutually exclusive choices, in that selecting one radio button deselects all others in the group.

- **List menus** permit the selection of single or multiple items from a scrolling list, whereas Jump menus allow you to set each option from a scrolling list to link to a document or file.

- **Buttons** perform actions when clicked. You can assign the default Submit or Reset action to buttons, or define other processing tasks in a script.

A good way to understand all of the options available in Dreamweaver for adding elements to a form is to add them to the form you created earlier.

Adding text fields

The simplest and most common type of form field is the text field. Users can enter anything, from their name to their credit card number to their dog's name, into a text field. You control the formatting of their responses using the Property inspector.

1   Click inside the red outline of your form to specify where you want your text field to appear. For this exercise, it appears at the top of the form.

2   Click on the Text Field button (▭) in the Insert toolbar. The Image Tag Accessibility Attributes dialog box opens, allowing you to set attributes to make your form field more accessible.

Make your form more accessible by changing your setting here.

3 In the Image Tag Accessibility Attributes dialog box, specify the following:

- Enter **Name** in the Label field to place this label on your field. (Labeling your field is not the same as naming your field, described later in this exercise.)

- In the Style section, leave the default setting of Wrap with label tag selected. The other options make your field more or less accessible when viewed in a browser, but Wrap with label tag works best when you're building your form in the Design view.

- Choose Before form item in the Position section to make the label for your text field precede the field itself. (Radio buttons usually have their labels after the button.)

4 Press OK. A new, labeled text field appears within the form outline on your page.

The settings you entered define the look of the Name field as it's added to your form.

5 If it's not already selected, click to select the text field, and notice the options that become available in the Property inspector.

6 In the Text Field box on the left side of the Property inspector, enter **Name** to make this field accessible for scripting and validation.

7 Enter **65** in the Char Width field to set the text input area to a width of 65 characters.

8 Enter **30** in the Max Chars field to set the maximum number of characters that can be entered. For example, if this was a telephone number field, you probably would have limited it to 10 characters.

9 Choose Single Line from the Type options. Choosing Password would cause the user's entry to appear as black dots, even though the correct value would be submitted to the server. We discuss the Multi-line option later, in the *Adding a text area* section.

10 Repeat steps 1–9 to add Address and City/State/Zip text fields beneath the Name field. Press Return to move one line down after each field and expand the depth of the form.

11 Choose File > Save As. In the Save As dialog box, navigate to the dw12lessons folder and type **McKnightform.html** into the Name text field. Press Save.

Now, preview the open page in a browser by pressing the Preview/Debug in browser button (◉) on the Document toolbar. Your form should look like this:

This is what your form should look like with text fields added.

Adding checkboxes

You'll probably want to have several checkboxes in your forms. They're valuable when you want to get specific responses from your users, and you don't want to give them the opportunity to enter incorrect information into text fields. Again, you control the formatting of their responses using the Property inspector.

To add checkboxes to the form:

1 Press the Return key after your City/State/Zip field to specify where you want your checkbox to appear.

2 Click on the Checkbox button (☑) in the Insert toolbar. The Input Tag Accessibility Attributes dialog box opens.

3 In the Input Tag Accessibility Attributes dialog box, type **Exhibits** in the Label field to place this label on your checkbox.

4 Leave the rest of the sections in this dialog box set to their defaults and press OK. A new, labeled checkbox appears within the form outline on your page.

5 If it's not already selected, click to select the checkbox itself, and notice the options that become available in the Property inspector.

Settings specific to the checkbox you've just added to your form appear in the Property inspector.

6 In the Checkbox Name field on the left side of the Property inspector, type **Exhibits** to make this field accessible for scripting and validation.

7 Type **Exhibits** in the Checked Value field to define the data that's passed to the server when the user checks this checkbox.

8 Choose Unchecked in the Initial State section. This setting defines how the checkbox appears when the page is first loaded.

9 The Class drop-down menu allows you to apply a Cascading Style Sheet (CSS) to style this form field. (We discuss using CSS to style form fields in more detail later in this lesson.)

10 Repeat steps 1–9 to add Membership and Donations checkboxes beneath the Exhibits field.

Now, preview the open page in a browser. Your form should look like this:

Your form, with checkboxes inserted, should look like this.

Adding radio buttons

When you add radio buttons to your form, you encounter the same settings in the Property inspector as you do when you add checkboxes. The only difference between checkboxes and radio buttons is that from a group of radio buttons, only a single option can be selected. Checkboxes allow the selection of multiple options.

To make two or more individual radio buttons mutually exclusive, you select two or more radio buttons and give them the same name in the Property inspector.

Creating a group of radio buttons by adding buttons one by one is more time-consuming than it's worth. Thankfully, Dreamweaver offers a more efficient method for creating a list of mutually exclusive options: the radio group.

Adding radio groups

The Radio Group button (▣) in the Insert toolbar provides a quick and easy way to add a list of radio buttons to your form. The same rules regarding naming and values apply, but the Radio Group dialog box allows you to include several entries in a group at once.

1   Press the Return key after your Donations field to specify where you want your radio buttons to appear.

2   Click on the Radio Group button in the Insert toolbar. The Radio Group dialog box opens, and offers several property options.

Set properties for your radio group in the Radio Group dialog box.

3   In the Name field of the Radio Group dialog box, type **Membership Status** to give the group a name that associates all of the radio buttons together.

4   In the Label column of the Radio buttons section, assign a label to each button. Click on the first entry in this column and label it **Member**.

5   In the Value column of the Radio buttons section, you assign a value to each button to be passed back to the server. Click on the first entry in this column and type **Member**. This returns a value of Member when the user clicks on the Member radio button.

6   Select the Line breaks radio button in the layout using section to specify how you want Dreamweaver to express the radio group in the HTML markup. Because radio buttons are usually aligned vertically, this choice is selected by default.

7   Repeat steps 1–6 to add VIP Level and Patron radio buttons beneath the Member button. Click the + button when you want to add a new radio button to the group.

8   Press OK. Choose File > Save, then preview the open page in a browser. Your form should look like this:

After adding the radio group, your form should look like this.

Adding lists and menus

Lists and menus show choices within a list that permits users to choose single or multiple options. The List option displays as a scrolling list, and the Menu option displays as a drop-down menu. As is the case with most form fields, you set the properties for lists and menus in the Property inspector.

1   Press the Return key after your radio group to specify where you want your list/menu to appear.

2   Click on the List/Menu button (▤) in the Insert toolbar. The Input Tag Accessibility Attributes dialog box opens.

3   In the Input Tag Accessibility Attributes dialog box, type **Language** in the Label field to place this label on your list/menu. Leave all other sections in this dialog box as they were set in the previous exercise.

4   Press OK. A new, labeled list/menu appears within the form outline on your page.

5   If it's not already selected, click to select the list/menu itself, and notice the options now available in the Property inspector.

Enter the settings for your newly added list/menu in the Property inspector.

6   In the List/Menu Name field on the left side of the Property inspector, type **Language** to define the field name that's passed to the server when it processes the form.

7   The Type options let you define whether the field is displayed as a scrolling list or a drop-down menu. Click on the List radio button to choose this option. Notice that more settings become available on the right side of the Property inspector.

8   Enter **3** in the Height field to set the number of items to be visible at any given time in the scrolling list.

9   Click in the checkbox to the right of the Selections option to allow multiple selections. With this feature activated, users can choose more than one option from your list at a time.

10   Click on the List Values button to enter items for your scrolling list. The structure of the List Values dialog box is identical to that of the Radio Group dialog box. Enter **English** as your first Item Label, and **en** for the first value to be returned.

Now you will add two more items to the list, French and Spanish.

11 Click the plus button in the left corner of the List Values window and enter **French** as the second Item Label. Then click under the en value and type **fr**. Click the plus button again. Enter **Spanish** as the third Item Label, and, finally, click under the value fr and enter **sp**. Press OK.

12 Choose File > Save to save your work

Now, preview the open page in a browser. Your form should look like this:

Now the user can choose in which language they want their additional information delivered.

Adding a text area

Sometimes within a Dreamweaver form, you want to have a field that simply provides an open area into which users can enter text. For this form, you'll add a Textarea element to provide a region for users to type in their comments about the museum.

1 Press the Return key after your Language list to specify where you want your text area to appear.

2 Click on the Textarea button (▢) in the Insert toolbar. The Input Tag Accessibility Attributes dialog box opens.

3 Enter **Comments** in the Label field to place this label on your text area. Leave all other sections in the dialog box at their previous settings.

4 Press OK. A new, labeled, text area appears within the form outline on your page.

5 Click to select the text area, and notice the options now available in the Property inspector.

The Property inspector contains formatting options for your text area.

6 In the TextField name field on the left side of the Property inspector, enter **Comments** to define the field name that's passed to the server when it processes the form.

7 Enter **40** in the Char width text field to set the text input area to a width of 40 characters.

8 Leave the Num lines text field set to 5, and leave Type set to Multi line.

9 The Wrap drop-down menu defines how the text wraps from line to line within the text area. Because most of these choices aren't consistent across different browser versions, choose Default from this menu to let the browser choose the wrap method.

10 Leave the Init Val and Class settings at their defaults and choose File > Save, then preview the open page in a browser.

The form so far, as rendered by Internet Explorer.

Adding a File Upload field

If you want users to be able to upload a file to your server—for example, a photo for ID purposes—you'll want to add a File Upload field.

1 Press the Enter (Windows) or Return (Mac OS) key after your Comments field to specify where you want your file field to appear.

2 Click on the File Field button (🗋) in the Insert toolbar. The Input Tag Accessibility Attributes dialog box opens.

3 In the Input Tag Accessibility Attributes dialog box, enter **Upload** in the Label field to place this label on your file field. Leave all other settings as they are.

4 Press OK. A new, labeled, file field, with the Browse button included, appears within the form outline on your page.

5   If it's not already selected, click to select the file field, and notice the options that become available in the Property inspector.

Set the properties for your File Upload field in the Property inspector.

6   In the FileField Name field on the left side of the Property inspector, enter **Upload** to define the field name that's passed to the server when it processes the form.

7   Enter **30** in the Char width text field to set the text input area to a width of 30 characters.

8   Enter **30** in the Max chars text field to set the maximum number of filename characters that can be entered.

9   The Class drop-down menu allows you to apply a CSS to style this form field. (We discuss using CSS to style form fields in more detail later in this lesson.)

10 You are now finished with the file field section of your form. Users can now either enter the desired filename or click Browse to navigate to it.

For the file field element to actually upload a user's file to your server, you'll need to ask your server administrator how the server is configured to accept files.

Choose File > Save, then preview the open page in a browser. Your form should look like this:

You're almost finished adding form fields to your form.

Creating Submit and Reset buttons

As you might expect, none of the field elements you've been adding to your form do any good if the user doesn't have a way to send the information to you. Buttons provide the means for the user to either submit form data, or to reset the fields and start over.

1 Place your cursor after the Upload field, then press Enter (Windows) or Return (Mac OS) to specify where you want your button(s) to appear.

2 Click on the Button icon (⬚) in the Forms tab of the Insert toolbar. The Input Tag Accessibility Attributes dialog box opens.

3 In the dialog box, specify the following:

- Leave the Label field blank, as the button is labeled by default by its function.

- In the Style section, leave the default setting of Wrap with label tag selected.

- Choose a Position is irrelevant here, as the button will be labeled with its function. Leave this setting at its default.

4 Press OK. A new button, labeled *Submit* by default, appears within the form outline on your page.

5 If it's not already selected, click to select the button, and notice the options now available in the Property inspector.

Button properties are set in the Property inspector.

6 In the Button Name field on the left side of the Property inspector, enter **Submit** to make this field accessible for scripting and validation.

7 Enter **Submit** in the Value field as well. This is the label that appears on the button. For future reference, you can type any message you think the user will understand here.

8 The three options in the Action section specify the action carried out when the user clicks this button. Submit and Reset are self-explanatory, but the None option builds a generic button that you can set to trigger a JavaScript behavior, which we'll discuss later in this lesson.

9 The Class drop-down menu allows you to apply CSS to style this form field, another technique covered later in the lesson.

10 Repeat steps 1–9 to add Reset and Validate buttons next to the Submit button. Choose Reset from the Action section in the Property inspector for the Reset button, and None for the Validate button.

Preview the open page in a browser. Your form should look like this:

Your form should now look like this... all substance, but very little style.

Now that you've finished adding the necessary form fields to your Contact Form page, you'll add style to the form and its elements, using CSS.

Styling forms with CSS

In Lesson 4, "Styling Your Pages with CSS," you explored the many ways you can use CSS to format text and position content on an HTML page in Dreamweaver. The usefulness of CSS is not limited to static page content, however. Dynamic content, such as form fields, can also be successfully and creatively styled using CSS.

The CSS Styles panel

Attaching external styles

Because you're already familiar with the available CSS options, we focus on applying them to the form elements you've added in this lesson. The styles you apply have been created for you, but you must attach them to your form page in order to access them.

1   With your form page open, open the CSS Styles panel by choosing Window > CSS Styles.

2   In the CSS Styles panel, click on the Attach Style Sheet button (●) in the lower-right corner of the panel. The Attach External Style Sheet dialog box opens.

Select the CSS file you want to attach using The Attach External Style Sheet dialog box.

3   Next to the File/URL field, click the Browse button and select formstyles.css from the dw12lessons folder. Press OK (Windows) or Choose (Mac OS) to exit the Select Style Sheet File dialog box.

4   In the Attach External Style Sheet dialog box, click the Link radio button to create a link *<href>* tag in the code for this page, and reference the location of the published style sheet. Most major web browsers support the link method.

5   In the Media drop-down menu, you can define the target medium for your style sheet. For this exercise, leave this setting at its default.

For more information on media-dependent style sheets, see the World Wide Web Consortium (W3C) website at http://www.w3.org/TR/CSS21/media.html.

6   Press OK to attach the style sheet to this document.

Setting a background color

Once the formstyles CSS is attached, the backgrounds of your form fields change to a light blue color. This happens because formstyles.css contains a tag selector rule, which instructs the *<form>* tag you added earlier in the lesson to include a background color. The rule redefines the *<form>* tag, so the color is applied only to the background of the form fields themselves, and not to the entire body of the page.

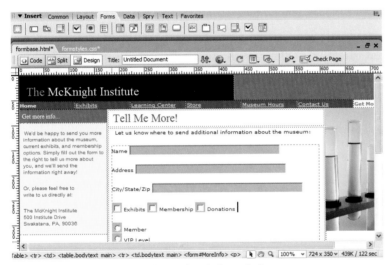

The formstyles CSS contains a rule that specifies a background color.

A major benefit of using CSS is that once you complete the initial styling, you can revisit the CSS file and change the included style rules. Because the blue background doesn't fit in with the color scheme of your museum site, you'll edit the form rule to change the background to a light gray.

1   If it's not already visible, open the CSS Styles panel by choosing Window > CSS Styles.

2   Click on the All button to show all styles attached to this document (as opposed to those applied to a Current selection). Locate formstyles.css in the list of All Rules, and expand it by clicking on the + (Windows) or triangle (Mac OS) button to its left.

3   From the list of style rules included within formstyles.css, click on the input rule to select it for editing.

CSS can be redefined on the fly.

4   Click on the Edit Style button at the bottom of the CSS Styles panel. The CSS Rule Definition dialog box opens.

5   Select the Background category to the left, and, in the Background color field to the right, type the hexadecimal code **d7d7d7**, to replace the current color.

6   To preview the change to the background color, click Apply. Press OK to accept the change.

You've successfully changed the background color of your form fields by editing an attached CSS.

You've just used a tag selector CSS rule to change the background color of your form. Next, you'll use a class style to change the appearance of the labels on your form fields.

Styling form elements

You probably noticed another CSS rule included in formstyles.css along with the *<form>* definition. It's a class style called *.labels*, and it contains properties that change the font, color, and weight of your form field labels.

The .labels rule can also be edited in the CSS Styles panel.

1   In the CSS Styles panel, click on the *.labels* CSS rule to select it, then click on the Edit Style button to open its CSS Rule Definition dialog.

2   Select Type from the Category list on the left and notice that the following properties have been defined for this rule:

 •   The Font list has been changed to Arial, Helvetica, sans-serif.

 •   The Weight has been edited to make it bolder.

 •   The Color has been set to a hexadecimal notation of 843432, maroon.

Change the type style of your form field labels in the CSS Rule Definition dialog box.

3   Press OK to accept these properties.

Applying the .label style

The .labels class style will change the font, color, and weight of your form field labels, but you'll have to apply this style to the appropriate text first.

1　In the Document window, place your cursor in the Name label, which precedes the first text field in your form. Click to place an insertion cursor there.

2　In the Property inspector, click on the Style drop-down menu to see a list of available class styles.

3　Choose labels from this list to apply the class style.

Class styles are applied manually using the Property inspector.

The .label style will apply to the rest of the labels.

Applying the .label style to all of the labels in the form.

These are just a few of the ways you can use CSS to style form elements. Experiment further with different properties to make your form more visually pleasing.

Form processing and validation

As attractive as CSS styling can make your form in Dreamweaver, you can't collect form data without using a server-side script or application (i.e., CGI, JSP, ASP) to process the data.

CGI scripts are the most popular form of server-side scripting mechanism to process form data. Several web sites offer free CGI scripts that you can use. The hosting company which hosts your web site may also provide CGI scripts that perform many common tasks, such as collecting email addresses or allowing visitors to send you comments through a web form.

It's also worth noting that form validation, a method for ensuring that the user has entered the correct type of data in the form's fields, also requires scripting to work correctly. Thankfully, Dreamweaver is capable of adding JavaScript code that checks the contents of specified text fields. This code is added through the use of the Validate Form behavior.

Adding form validation

The Validate Form behavior provides checks and balances for users when they complete forms on your site. You can make certain fields required, make sure a user has entered a value in a required field, or make sure a user has entered the correct type of information in a field. You can run validation on all fields in a form, or on individual fields contained in that form.

The first step, however, is to get to know the Behaviors panel.

A look at the Behaviors panel

Generally speaking, the Behaviors panel provides a means for you to add JavaScript code to your page without actually having to type in the code. The code it inserts adds interactivity to your site, and is usually triggered by some user action. For example, when the user clicks on or hovers over a link, the behavior performs a task. Behaviors are hardly limited to use with forms, as they're commonly used to add rollovers, open new windows, check for plug-ins, and add navigation elements, among other functions.

Specifically, you use the Behaviors panel to add, modify, and remove behaviors. Because you can apply multiple behaviors to the same object, you can also reorder them in the Behaviors panel.

To set behaviors:

1   Access the Behaviors panel by choosing Window > Behaviors. It docks with the Tag panel on the right side of your screen. If necessary, expand the panel grouping and click on the Behaviors tab to bring it to the front.

The Behaviors panel.

2   In the Document window, select the Validate button you created earlier.

3   Click the plus button (+) at the top of the Behaviors panel to see the list of available objects for the selected object. In this case, the menu displays options associated with a button element. If an option is grayed out, that action is not available for the selected object.

The behaviors displayed are only those associated with a button element.

4   Select Popup Message action. The Popup Message dialog box appears.

5   Type **Validate this form!** into the Message text field, and press OK.

Enter text into the Popup Message window to have it appear on the screen.

The behavior is set, but it needs an event, or trigger.

Setting an event/trigger

The Popup Message needs an event or trigger to know when to appear. In this case, you'll set it to appear when the user clicks on the Validate button.

1   In the top-left corner of the Behaviors panel, click on the Show All Events button. The Show All Events button provides a complete (and very long) list of all possible triggers for this behavior.

2   The default event for a button element is the onClick event, which triggers the behavior when the button is clicked. Clicking on this setting displays a drop-down menu listing different event options. Explore these on your own, returning to the onClick event when finished.

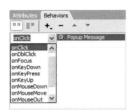

There are a number of choices for the event that triggers your specific behavior.

The button behavior you've applied is now ready for previewing.

Previewing the button behavior

Whenever you create interactive features like a popup message, it's important to test them out in a browser to make sure they're working.

1   Use the Browser Preview button to access your web browser, and select it to preview the open page.

2   Press on the Validate button at the bottom of your form. The popup message you set earlier appears.

Use this feature to warn your viewers, or to guide them in a certain direction.

Depending on the security configurations of your browser, you may be prompted to allow blocked content. If you'd like to change your preferences to avoid conflicts with scripts created in the Behaviors panel, refer to your browser's documentation for instructions on changing the default settings.

3   Press OK to close the message, and close or minimize your browser window.

To further explore the Behaviors panel and its features, you'll add a Form Validation behavior to the same button.

Validating form fields

Because it's a behavior you usually want performed when a user submits his form data to you, the Validate Form action is most often applied to the Submit button in a form. For this lesson, you'll apply this action to the Validate button you created, change its position in the behavior order, delete it, and reapply it to the correct button.

1   In the Document window, select the Validate button at the bottom of your form. The Behaviors panel should display the Popup Message action you added in the last exercise.

2   At the top of the Behaviors panel, click the plus button (**+**), and select Validate Form from the drop-down menu that appears. The Validate Form dialog box opens.

3   In the Validate Form dialog box, enter the following settings:

- Choose Name, the first entry in the Fields list. The Fields list is a compilation of all the names you assigned to the form fields you added to the form earlier in this lesson. (This is one reason why it's so important to name your fields.)

- Click in the Required checkbox to require data entry into this field before the user can submit the form.

- Click on the Anything radio button so the field accepts any alphanumeric entry. For the Name field, leave this button checked.

- Click on the Number radio button so the field accepts only numerical data. For the Name field, leave this button unchecked.

- To make the behavior check for an @ symbol within the entered data, click on the Email address radio button. For the Name field, leave this button unchecked.

- To make the behavior check for a number within a specific range, enter that range in the Number From fields. For the Name field, leave this button unchecked and the fields empty.

Specify which form elements get validated, and what is accepted.

4   Press OK to close the Validate Form dialog box.

5 Choose File > Save, then preview the form page in your browser. Leave the Name field blank, and click on the Validate button at the bottom of your form.

Unfortunately, the Popup Message behavior you added earlier runs before the Validate Form behavior, requiring you to close the Popup Message window to see the results of your validation.

The popup message appears but doesn't go away on its own.

Next, you'll adjust the Validate Form behavior to correct these errors.

Changing a form field's behavior order

To keep the popup message from appearing before the results of your validation you'll need to change the Validate Form behavior's position in the behavior order, delete it, and reapply it to the correct button.

1 In the Dreamweaver Document window, click on the Validate button to select it.

2 The Behaviors panel shows two actions, Popup Message and Validate Form, which share the same event, or trigger.

Use the Behaviors panel to reorder behaviors and make them behave differently for the viewer.

3 Click on the Validate Form behavior to select it, and click the up arrow at the top of the panel to move it to a position above the Popup Message behavior. This makes the Validate Form action run first, but the Popup Message still appears after the validation window is closed.

4 Because it makes more sense for the Validate Form behavior to be applied to the Submit button, click on the minus button to delete it from the behaviors associated with the Validate button.

5 Click on the Submit button at the bottom of your form to select it. Repeat the steps in the preceding exercise to add the validation action to the Submit button.

Now it's time to see the fruits of your labor.

Verifying field contents

Now that you've adjusted the Validate Form behavior, you'll need to make sure the form functions like you expect it to.

1   Preview the open page in your browser, and click on the Validate button. This should now display only the popup message. Close it.

2   Click on the Submit button. Even though the data is not actually submitted (for lack of a CGI script), the Validate Form warns you that required fields have not been filled.

The Validate Form behavior functions as you originally intended, thanks to some editing in the Behaviors panel.

You've successfully added validation to your form, and completed this lesson in the process.

Self study

Using your new knowledge of building and editing web forms in Dreamweaver, try some of the following tasks to build on your experience:

1   Edit the Validate Form behavior you applied to the Submit button in the last exercise. Apply validation to the other text fields in your form, providing checks for the specific content to be filled out in each field. Preview the page in your browser to ensure that the validation works.

2   Create an internal CSS that redefines the *<input>* tag. Set the background color of each form field to light gray to match your page's color scheme. Experiment with the other styling options available to you in the CSS Rule Definition dialog box to further style your form elements.

3   Explore the other form field elements in the Forms category of the Insert toolbar. Add a hidden field to return the creation date of the form when it is submitted, while keeping this information hidden from the user. Add an Image field to turn a placed image into a button with a behavior attached. Group your form fields into labeled sections, using the Fieldset button.

Review

Questions

1 Why is it important to add a form element when building a web form in Dreamweaver?

2 When should you use a radio button group, as opposed to a set of checkboxes, in a form?

3 How does CSS add creativity and efficiency to the form creation process?

4 What do you need to collect the form data that a user enters into your form?

5 Where would you access the different JavaScript actions that can be applied to a button in Dreamweaver?

Answers

1 The form element serves as a container for the fields you'll be adding to the form. If you simply add form fields to a page in Dreamweaver, the user's browser won't know what to do with the user's information when he clicks the Submit button. To identify this information as part of a package, and to specify the route that information should take when submitted, you need to create a Dreamweaver form.

2 The difference between adding checkboxes and radio buttons in a form is that from a group of radio buttons, only a single option can be selected. Checkboxes allow the selection of multiple options.

3 Because CSS allows you to apply several formatting attributes with a single mouse click, both static and dynamic content (such as form fields) can be successfully and creatively styled using CSS. CSS also streamlines your workflow by allowing you to revisit CSS files and change the included style rules once you've completed the initial styling.

4 You can't collect form data without using a server-side script or application such as CGI, JSP, or ASP to process the data. CGI scripts are the most popular form of server-side scripting mechanism to process form data. Several web sites offer free CGI scripts you can use. Your site's ISP may also provide CGI scripts for you.

5 The Behaviors panel provides a means for you to add JavaScript code to your page without actually having to type in the code. The code it inserts adds interactivity to your site, and is usually triggered by some user action. For example, when the user clicks on or hovers over a link, the behavior performs a task. Behaviors are commonly used to add rollovers, open new windows, check for plug-ins, and add navigation elements. You use the Behaviors panel to add, modify, remove, or reorder behaviors.

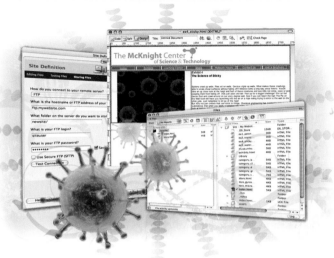

What you'll learn in this lesson:

- Uploading and managing files
- Optimizing pages for performance and search engines
- Using Site Reports
- Using the CSS Advisor & Browser Compatibility Check

Managing Your Web Site:
Reports, Optimization & Maintenance

When it's time to release your web site to the world, you'll want to take some last steps to make sure your site looks and works its best. Dreamweaver has a powerful set of reports, link checkers, and problem-solving tools to locate and fix any potential issues before final upload. When you're ready, the built-in FTP and synchronization features of the Files panel will get you up and running.

Starting up

Before starting, make sure that your tools and panels are consistent by resetting your workspace. See "Resetting the Dreamweaver workspace" on page 3.

You will work with several files from the dw13lessons folder in this lesson. Make sure that you have loaded the dwlessons folder onto your hard drive from the supplied DVD. See "Loading lesson files" on page 3.

Before you begin, you need to create a site definition that points to the dw13lessons folder from the included DVD that contains resources you need for these lessons. Go to Site > New Site, or, for details on creating a site definition, refer to Lesson 2, "Creating a New Site."

See Lesson 13 in action!

Use the accompanying video to gain a better understanding of how to use some of the features shown in this lesson. Open the Dynamic_Learning_DW_CS3.swf file located in the Videos folder and select Lesson 13 to view the video training file for this lesson.

Working with the Files panel

You've already used the Files panel throughout this book to locate and open files within your site projects. In addition to serving as a useful file browser, the Files panel also serves as a full-featured file transfer application and synchronization tool. From the Files panel, you can upload your site to a web server, synchronize local and remote files, and manage files and notes between multiple designers.

Creating a remote connection

The Files panel uploads, retrieves, and synchronizes files between your local site and a web server. Typically, this is done via FTP (File Transfer Protocol), which connects to and allows interaction between your local machine and a web server. Before you can transfer files, you'll first need to establish a remote connection to the web server that stores your web site files. You will not be able to proceed with this portion of the lesson if you do not have FTP information available for a web server. If you do not have this information or do not have a connection to the Internet, you may skip to the *Testing Site Integrity* exercise in this lesson and proceed from there.

To get started, make sure you have:

- **The FTP address of web server and specific directory**. This would be provided by your web hosting provider as part of your account details, or from your company or organization's IT department. A typical FTP address will look like *ftp.mysite.com*.

- **A user login and password for access to the server**. Most web servers require a user login and password for access. This information should be available from your web hosting provider as part of your account details, or from your organization's IT department.

- **The specific directory to which your files should be uploaded**. In many cases, this is the main directory or folder that appears when you connect to your web server. However, in certain cases, you'll need to upload files to a specific directory other than the main directory.

- **The web address (URL) or IP address where you can view your uploaded files on the server**. Sample addresses would be *http://www.mysite.com/*, *http://www.mysite.com/2007/*, or *http://100.0.0.1*.

1   To create a remote connection, choose Site > Manage Sites. The Manage Sites dialog
    box appears.

Select your site definition and choose Edit to add remote connection information.

2   Select the Lesson 13 site definition (you set this up at the beginning of the lesson) and click
    Edit. If you haven't created a site definition for this lesson, make sure you do so now, as
    discussed in Lesson 2, "Creating a Site Definition."

3   The Site Definition dialog box appears. If necessary, click the Basic tab at the top to view
    the dialog box in Basic mode. Press the Next button at the bottom until you advance to the
    Sharing Files panel.

4   Locate the drop-down menu below *How do you connect to your remote server?*, and
    choose FTP. Several fields appear below the drop-down menu, where you can fill in
    your information.

5   Enter your specific FTP information in the text fields, as shown in the example
    figure below. In this example, the folder was defined, however this is optional.

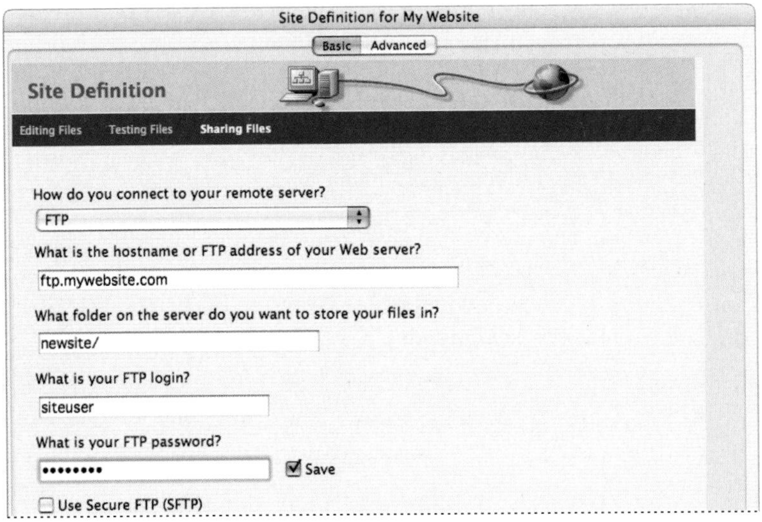

*Sample remote connection information. Your information should include an ftp address, login, and password,
with a possible folder name.*

6   Click the Test Connection button at the bottom of the panel to verify that Dreamweaver can connect to your server. If the information you've provided is valid, a dialog box will appear, confirming that Dreamweaver has successfully connected to your web server.

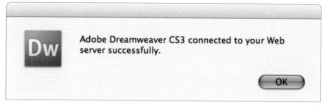

A dialog box will let you know if your connection was successful. If you receive an FTP error, double-check your FTP information, and make any necessary corrections.

7   Press the Next button at the bottom of the panel to advance to the Sharing Files, Part 2 panel. Press Next again to accept the default settings in this panel. When the Summary appears, Press Done to exit the dialog box and save your new connection information.

If you receive an FTP error dialog box, verify the FTP address, login, password, and directory; make any necessary corrections. You will need a live Internet connection to perform this test!

Certain servers may require a passive FTP connection to connect successfully. If you are certain your FTP information is correct, but experience a long delay or failure when connecting, check the Use Passive FTP checkbox on the Sharing panel and try again.

Viewing files on a remote web server

Once you've established a connection to your web server, you can expand the Files panel for a split view that displays both your remote and local files. You can easily drag and drop between both sides to upload or download files and update existing files.

1   If necessary, choose Window > Files to open the Files panel. Click the Expand button (⊞) at the top of the Files panel to ungroup and expand it to full view.

2   Locate and click the Connect button (🔌) above the left-hand column at the top of the panel. Dreamweaver will attempt to connect to your remote server, and, if successful, will display all of its files on the left side of the Files panel

It's important to note that web servers can be configured in many different ways and you may need to edit your site settings again once you have made a successful connection (in particular, the folder information.) A discussion of the different ways that web servers might be configured is outside the scope of this book; if you have specific questions regarding your site, you should contact an IT professional or your web hosting company.

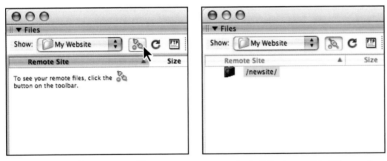

Click the Connect button to view files on your remote server in the left column of the Files panel.

Transferring files to and from a remote server with Get and Put

The built-in FTP and file transfer functionality of the Files panel makes it a snap to place files on your remote server or download files onto your local machine. This can be accomplished using the Get and Put buttons, or by dragging and dropping files between the Remote and Local file listings in the Files panel. Please note again, this exercise involves publishing our sample documents to a remote server therefore publishing them to the Internet; be very careful not to overwrite any pre-existing files that may be crucial to your web site.

1   Make sure you've connected to the remote server as described in the previous exercise, and that you can see your remote files in the left-hand column of the Files panel.

2   Select the index.html file from the local file listing on the right side of your Files panel, and press the Put button (⬆) at the top of the panel.

Select a file and click the Put button to upload it to the remote server.

Alternatively, you can click and drag a file from the right (local) column to the left (remote) column.

Drag a file from the right column to the left to upload it to the remote server.

To get (download) a file from the remote server:

1 Make sure you've connected to the remote server as described in the previous exercise, and that you can see your remote files in the left-hand column of the Files panel.

2 Select a file from the remote file listing on the left side of your Files panel, and press the Get button (⬇) at the top of the panel.

   Alternatively, you can click and drag a file from the left (remote) column to the right (local) column. Note that a dialog box may appear, asking if you'd like to overwrite your local copy if the file already exists in your local file listing.

You can update the local or remote file listing at any time by clicking the Refresh button (↻) at the top of the Files panel.

Using Check In/Check Out and design notes

If you're collaborating with others on a project, you'll want to set up an environment where everyone can edit files independently without overlapping or overwriting someone else's work. For these situations, the Check In/Out and design notes features can help manage workflow and communicate with others on a Dreamweaver site project.

Check In & Check Out

Dreamweaver's Check In/Check Out feature is a way of letting others know that you are working on a file and don't want it disturbed. When Check In/Check Out is enabled, a document that you're editing becomes locked on the remote server to prevent others from modifying the same file at the same time. If you attempt to open a file that's been checked out by another user, you'll see a warning that lets you know that the file is in use and who is currently working with it. Check In/Check Out doesn't require any additional software to run, and other Dreamweaver users can check out files if they also have Check In/Check Out enabled in their site definition.

> *The Check In/Check Out system does not work with a Testing Server. To transfer files to and from a testing server (if one is set up), use the standard Get and Put commands.*

1   Choose Site > Manage Sites. Select the Dreamweaver site that you want to enable Check In/Check Out for and choose Edit.

2   In Basic View, choose Yes, enable check in and check out under the Sharing Files, Part 2 panel. If you want to make sure a file is properly checked out when you open it, make sure the checkbox next to Dreamweaver should check it out is checked. If you want to work with a read-only copy, select I want to view a read-only copy.

In Advanced view, select Enable file check in/check out under the Remote Info panel. In both views, you'll be prompted to enter your name and email address. This information will appear to users who attempt to download or update a file that you currently have checked out.

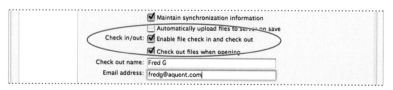

Enable check in/check out in the Site Definition panel to manage workflow between several users.

How does Check In/Check Out work?

Dreamweaver creates a lock (LCK) file for every document that is checked out; this basic text file contains the name and email address of the user who has checked out the file. LCK files are written to both the remote server and local folder using the same name as the active file. When files are checked back in, the LCK files are deleted from both the remote server and local folder.

Although LCK files are not visible in the Files panel, they work behind the scenes to let Dreamweaver know what's checked out and what isn't. Checked-out files appear on both the local and remote file listings with a check mark next to them. Note that a colleague not using Dreamweaver can potentially overwrite a file that's checked out—however, LCK files are visible in applications other than Dreamweaver, and their appearance alone can help avoid any overwriting issues.

A user will be allowed to override your lock and switch check-out status to themselves. Make sure you establish rules with others about how to share and manage locked files.

Checking files in and out

When you check a file out, you are downloading it from the remote server to your local root folder, and placing a lock on the remote copy. Both your local copy and the remote copy appear with check marks next to them, which indicates that the file is currently checked out for editing. When you check a file back in, you are uploading the modified version to the remote server, and removing any locks currently on it.

1   Launch the Files panel and click the Expand button to expand it so that you can see both your local and remote files listed.

2   Select the file in your local folder that you want to check out, and use the Check Out button (⬇) at the top of the panel. Note that Dreamweaver will overwrite your local copy of the file, since it needs to get the remote file from the server. The local and remote versions of the file will appear with check marks next to them in the Files panel.

3   Open the checked file from your Local files panel for editing. Make any necessary changes to the file, then save and close it.

4   From the Files panel, select the file again in the local Files panel and check it back in, using the Check In button (🖢) at the top of the panel. The file will be uploaded to—and unlocked on—the remote server.

Check files out before modifying them so that others won't accidentally overwrite your work at the same time.

Your local copy becomes read-only, and appears with a padlock next to it. Next time you open the file for editing, Dreamweaver will automatically check out and get the latest copy from the server.

Using design notes

Design notes store additional information about a file or media object in your Dreamweaver site. These notes can be for your own use, or can be shared with others using the same root folder. Design notes can be set to appear automatically when the file is opened, making it easy to display up-to-date information to others working on the same site. All design notes are stored as separate files in a _notes folder inside of your site's root directory.

What can be put in design notes?

Design notes can contain any information that is important to the file or project; you can store design instructions, updates about the project, or contact information for project managers and supervisors. You can also store sensitive information that you ideally would not want in the file itself, such as the name of the last designer to work on the file or the location of important assets. You can even set the status of the file to indicate what stage of the revision the file is in.

1 To create a design note, under the Files panel, open a file from the current site.

2 Choose File > Design Notes. The Design Notes dialog box will appear.

File	Edit	View	Insert	Mc

New...   ⌘N
Open...   ⌘O
Browse in Bridge...   ⌥⌘O
Open Recent   ▶
Open in Frame...   ⇧⌘O
Close   ⌘W
Close All   ⇧⌘W

Preview in Browser   ▶
Check Page   ▶
Validate   ▶
Compare with Remote
Design Notes...

*With a file open, select File > Design Notes to add or
modify existing design notes for that specific file.*

3 Type a message in the Notes field. To insert the current date stamp, click the calendar button (▦) above the Notes field. If you want the note displayed when the file is next opened, check Show when file is opened.

4 Use the Status menu to set the document status; this can be useful in letting other collaborators know the revision stage of the current document.

5 Press OK to create the design note.

To view a design note, choose File > Design Notes when a file is open in the Document window. As mentioned earlier, you can also choose to have design notes automatically appear when the file is first opened.

Design notes can also be created or viewed directly from the Files panel; right-click (Windows) or Ctrl+Click (Mac OS) a document in the files list and choose Design Notes from the contextual menu.

Sharing design notes

By default, design notes are only stored in the local site folder, and are not automatically copied to the remote server. However, you can share design notes with other collaborators by having Dreamweaver automatically upload and update them on the remote server.

1 Choose Site > Manage Sites. Select your site from the Sites panel and choose Edit.

2 In Advanced view, choose Design Notes from the left.

3 Under the Design Notes panel, check Upload Design Notes for sharing. Design notes will now be copied and updated on the remote server so that other users can share them.

Set up Design Notes for sharing so that other Dreamweaver users can see and modify design notes on the remote server.

Displaying design notes in the Files panel

A convenient way to view and access design notes is by enabling the design notes column in the Files panel. An icon that can be used to open and edit design notes accompanies documents that have an associated design note. This feature also allows you to see all available design notes at a glance.

1 Choose Site > Manage Sites. Select your site from the Sites panel and choose Edit. In Advanced view, choose File View Columns from the left.

2 Under File View Columns, select the Notes item from the list and check Show under the Options group.

3 Choose OK to update the site definition, then press Done to close the Manage Sites dialog box. A Notes column will appear in the Files panel; a Notes icon (📄) is displayed next to each file that currently is associated with a design note.

Use the Site Definition panel's File View Columns category to show design notes in both the local and remote file listings.

Testing site integrity

Catching potential issues on a page before your visitors do is key in ensuring success from the start. Broken links, display issues, or unreadable pages can make the difference between a great first impression and a poor one. To look for and address problems before you publish your site, Dreamweaver provides many useful tools that can point out potential hazards and, in some cases, help you find the solution.

Using Check Links

The Check Links feature detects any broken links between pages in your local site and will identify orphaned files that are not linked to or used by any document within the site.

1   From the Files panel, double-click and open the index.html document.

2   Choose File > Check Page > Links.

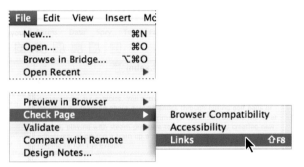

Choose File > Check Page > Links to check for broken links in the current document.

3   The Link Checker panel appears; you will see one listing here. A link to the exhibits.html page is misspelled; you need to fix the error.

4   Click on the link name under the Broken Links column. The link name becomes editable.

5   Click on the folder icon to the far right. A select file window appears. Select the file **exhibits.html** and then press choose. In the Link Checker tab press Enter (Windows) or Return (Mac OS) and the Broken Link disappears.

Retype the link or browse for the correct file using the folder icon to the right.

6   Close the Link Checker panel, and save and close the current document.

Checking links sitewide

Check Links can be used on a single document, multiple documents (via the Files panel), or an entire local site at once.

1 Choose Site > Check Links Sitewide.

2 The Link Checker panel appears; by default, any broken links will be displayed. You should see roughly 12 links here, all referencing the same incorrect link to category_books_cds.html.

Choose Site > Check Links Sitewide to check for broken links throughout the current local site. The Link Checker panel opens and displays any broken links found.

3 To view external links, choose External Links from the Show drop-down menu at the top of the panel. Note: External links are displayed but aren't validated by Dreamweaver. The Link Checker can only validate links between local documents and files.

4 To view orphaned files, choose Orphaned Files from the Show drop-down menu at the top of the panel. Orphaned files are files that are not currently being linked to in your site. You will not be doing anything with these files at this moment.

5 Choose Broken Links from the Show drop-down menu to return to the broken links report. Click on the first of the broken links shown to edit it. Enter **category_bookscds.html** to correct the link, then press Enter (Windows) or Return (Mac OS).

Adjust a link directly from the Link Checker panel to correct it sitewide.

6 A dialog box appears, asking if you'd like to make the same correction throughout the entire current local site. Press Yes.

Viewing Link Checker results

If and when the Link Checker returns results, you'll be able to jump to any problem document to view and fix any issues. The Link Checker panel's Show menu (located at the top of the panel) toggles between three different Link Checker reports: Broken Links, Orphaned Files, and External Links.

Broken Links lists links that point to files not found within the local site. To jump to a page that contains a broken link, double-click the file name shown in the left column of the Link Checker panel. To correct a link directly from the Link Checker panel, click the link shown under the Broken Links column of the panel to edit it. Type in the proper page name or use the folder to browse to the proper file. If you edit a broken link this way, Dreamweaver can apply the same correction throughout other pages on your site.

Orphaned Files are any pages, images, or media files not linked to, referenced, or used by any files in your site. This report can be useful in identifying unused files that can be cleaned up from the local site, or pages that should be linked to (like a site map) but were overlooked.

External Links lists any links to outside web sites, pages, or files, and like the Broken Links panel, allows you to directly edit them or jump to the page that contains them. It's important to note, however, that Dreamweaver does not validate external links—you will still be responsible for double-checking these links on your own. You'll also notice that email (mailto:) links are included in this list.

Generating site reports

Dreamweaver's site reports feature is an indispensable asset for detecting potential design and accessibility issues before publishing your site to the Web. Reports can be generated in several categories to give you a virtual picture of health and the opportunity to locate and fix minor or major issues across an entire Dreamweaver site. These issues can include missing alternate text or titles, CSS issues, and recommendations for better accessibility practices, based on the W3C's WCAG (Web Consortium Accessibility Guidelines).

Reports can be generated for a single page, selected documents, or for the entire current local site. Any results will open and display in the Results panel, where you can see a list of issues and the pages on which they are located.

1   To run a site report, choose Site > Reports. The Reports dialog box will open, displaying two categories of reports: Workflow and HTML. Note: It is not necessary to have a document open in order to run sitewide reports.

Workflow reports display information about design notes, check in and check out operations, and recently modified files. HTML reports display potential design, accessibility, and display issues, based on best practices and W3C/WCAG accessibility guidelines.

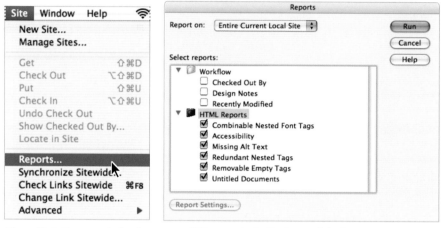

Choose Site > Reports, and select the reports you'd like to run in the Site Reports dialog box.

2   In the Reports panel, check all the reports under the HTML category. At the top of the panel, select Entire Current Local Site from the Report on drop-down menu.

3   Click Run in the top right corner of the Reports panel. The Results panel will appear, displaying any potential issues. Note that depending on the size of your site and number of issues found, it may take a few moments for all results to display.

4   Leave the Results panel open; you'll learn how to read and address issues in the
next exercise.

	File	Line	Description
⊗	✕ Templates:product_detail.dwt	27	Use percentage values for table sizes [WCAG 3.4 P2] -- FAILED -- WIDTH attribute specifies a fixed width for ta
ⓘ	✕ Templates:product_detail.dwt	28	Use percentage values for table sizes [WCAG 3.4 P2] -- FAILED -- WIDTH attribute specifies a fixed width for ta
▣	✕ Templates:product_detail.dwt	8	Use relative units in CSS [WCAG 3.4 P2] -- FAILED --
	? Templates:product_detail.dwt	8	Use relative units in CSS [WCAG 3.4 P2] -- MANUAL --
	? Templates:product_detail.dwt	8	Use relative units in CSS box properties [WCAG 3.4 P2] -- MANUAL --
	✕ Templates:product_detail.dwt	2	Use header elements [WCAG 3.5 P2] -- FAILED --
	? Templates:product_detail.dwt	2	Mark up quotations [WCAG 3.7 P2] -- MANUAL --
	? Templates:product_detail.dwt	13	Layout tables should make sense when linearized [WCAG 5.3 P2] -- MANUAL --
	? Templates:product_detail.dwt	15	Layout tables should make sense when linearized [WCAG 5.3 P2] -- MANUAL --
	? Templates:product_detail.dwt	20	Layout tables should make sense when linearized [WCAG 5.3 P2] -- MANUAL --
	? Templates:product_detail.dwt	55	Layout tables should make sense when linearized [WCAG 5.3 P2] -- MANUAL --
	? Templates:product_detail.dwt	2	GIFs should not cause the screen to blink [WCAG 7.2 P2] -- MANUAL --
	? Templates:product_detail.dwt	2	GIFs should not cause movement [WCAG 7.3 P2] -- MANUAL --
	? Templates:product_detail.dwt	2	Use last appropriate W3C technologies [WCAG 11.1 P2] -- MANUAL --
	✕ Templates:product_detail.dwt	17	Avoid deprecated features of W3C technologies [WCAG 11.2 P2] -- FAILED --
	? Templates:product_detail.dwt	2	Divide information into appropriate manageable groups [WCAG 12.3 P2] -- MANUAL --

The Results panel displays issues found across your entire current local site.

Understanding report results

At first glance, you may be overwhelmed at the amount of information returned by site reports.
Keep in mind that many of the listings returned are recommendations or possible issues that
should be looked into. Learning to read these site reports a little more closely will enable you to
decide which items are crucial to your site's performance, requiring immediate action. Listings
are displayed with three distinct icons.

ICON	NAME	USE
?	Question Mark	These listings suggest possible accessibility issues that should be investigated. Many of these issues will have a reference to a specific W3C/WCAG guideline.
✕	Red X	These listings indicate a failure to meet a certain guideline or requirement. Possible listings could include missing header information, deprecated HTML markup, or page titles that are not defined properly.
⚠	Warning Sign	Warnings indicate missing information that may be potentially detrimental to a site's performance, such as missing ALT text for images.

Addressing a listed item

After you've sifted through the report results, you'll want to use the Results panel to address items listed in the Site Reports tab.

1. Go to the Site Reports tab on the Results panel. Click the Description column header to sort the results. Scroll to the very bottom of the page until you see several listings accompanied by warning signs.

2. Find the listing for the store.html document, and click the More Info button on the left edge of the Results panel for a detailed description and recommended course of action. The Description dialog box shows that an image on this page is missing the ALT attribute and alternate text.

File	Line	Description
toys_gyroscope.html	6	Warning: Document uses default title 'Untitled Document'
ex5_water.html	5	Warning: Document uses default title 'Untitled Document'
category_bookscds.html	6	Warning: Document uses default title 'Untitled Document'
toys_microscope.html	6	Warning: Document uses default title 'Untitled Document'
ex1_aeronautics.html	5	Warning: Document uses default title 'Untitled Document'
index.html	5	Warning: Document uses default title 'Untitled Document'
ex2_trains.html	5	Warning: Document uses default title 'Untitled Document'
category_toys.html	6	Warning: Document uses default title 'Untitled Document'
ex4_sticky.html	5	Warning: Document uses default title 'Untitled Document'
ex1_aeronautics.html	28	Warning: Missing "alt" attribute
ex2_trains.html	28	Warning: Missing "alt" attribute
store.html	66	Warning: Missing "alt" attribute
ex4_sticky.html	28	Warning: Missing "alt" attribute
index.html	12	Warning: Missing "alt" attribute
ex5_water.html	28	Warning: Missing "alt" attribute

Select a listing and click the Info button to display a detailed description about the issue found.

3. Press OK to exit the Description dialog box and return to the Site Reports tab of the Results panel. Double-click the store.html listing to open the page for editing. The line where the issue begins should appear highlighted in Split view.

4. Select the large image in the middle of the page (giftcardpromo.jpg), and, in the Property inspector, enter **MKI Gift Cards are now available!** in the Alt field and press Enter (Windows) or Return (Mac OS).

Select the problem image and enter text in the Alt field to rectify the problem.

5. Save and close the page, and close the Results panel.

A full listing of accessibility guidelines, or WCAG (Web Content Accessibility Guidelines), for web page designers and developers are available at the World Wide Web Consortium (W3C) web site at http://www.w3.org/

Saving reports

In a case such as this when you have numerous warnings or suggestions, you might want to save them for future reference. Reports can be saved as XML for import into databases, existing template files, and archival. You can sort report results using the Results panel before saving them.

1 If necessary, choose Window > Results to open the Results panel. When the Results panel appears, click on the Site Reports tab to view the most current report results.

2 Click on any column header to sort reports by type, page name, line number, and description.

3 Click the Save report button (⊟) on the left edge of the Results panel. When the Save Report dialog box appears, assign the report a name, and choose a location for the file.

The Browser Compatibility Check (BCC)

When you format page content or create layouts with CSS, you'll want to be certain that your pages appear consistently across a variety of browsers. Some combinations of HTML and CSS can unearth some nasty display bugs in specific browsers. In fact, some browsers may not support certain CSS properties at all. To seek out and fix any potential CSS display problems, you'll use Dreamweaver's new Browser Compatibility Check reports in conjunction with the CSS Advisor.

The CSS Advisor

A new addition to the reporting tools in Dreamweaver CS3 is the CSS Advisor, which provides descriptions and solutions for CSS problems found during the Browser Compatibility Check. Located in the lower right-hand corner of the Browser Compatibility Check panel, the CSS Advisor will provide a direct link to the CSS Advisor section of Adobe's web site to find a fix for any CSS issues found and displayed in the Results panel.

1 To use the CSS Advisor, from the Files panel, locate and open the ex5_water.html document for editing.

2 Choose File > Check Page > Browser Compatibility.

Choose File > Check Page > Browser Compatibility to run the Browser Compatibility Check for this document.

3 The Results panel opens and displays any errors or issues in the Browser Compatibility Check tab. Items returned indicate any potential CSS display issues; each result is accompanied by a confidence rating icon which tells you how likely it is that the problem will occur. This page should return one error.

4 The panel on the right shows that a CSS filter applied on this page is incompatible with several browsers.

The Browser Compatibility Check tab on the Results panel displays a single error and description.

5 To jump to the Adobe CSS Advisor section of the Adobe web site for details and solutions to this issue, select the listing and click the Info button (⊕) on the left, or click the link shown in the lower right-hand corner of the Results panel (it should read Learn more about CSS support in the browsers at *Adobe.com*).

By default, the BCC checks for issues in the following browsers: Firefox 1.5; Internet Explorer (Windows) 6.0 and 7.0; Internet Explorer (Macintosh) 5.2; Netscape Navigator 8.0; Opera 8.0 and 9.0; and Safari 2.0. You can modify the target browsers and versions by choosing Settings from the green Run button (▶) on the BCC panel.

Optimizing pages for launch

Although page optimization is discussed at this point in the book, it is by no means an afterthought. A big part of preparing a site for success involves making it accessible to users with special needs, such as those who are visually impaired, or preparing it for indexing by various search engines. In addition to clean design and well-written content, pages can be optimized through the use of keywords, descriptions, and often-overlooked tag attributes, such as alternate text (alt) for images and a page's Title area. Combined, these pieces of information facilitate site usability and visibility in several essential ways.

Search engine visibility and SEO (Search Engine Optimization)

A big part of a web site's success stems from its visibility. Visibility comes through good advertising, networking with other sites, and, above all, proper indexing and listings on the Web's major search engines. Search engines can be a key to generating business and visits to your site, but only if your web site can be easily found. Major search engines such as Google (which powers AOL, MySpace, and Netscape searches), Yahoo! (which powers AltaVista and others), and LiveSearch (formerly MSN Search) use a variety of factors to index and generate listings for web sites. Many of these factors start at home, or more appropriately, on your home page.

Titling your documents with the *<title>* tag

Each document's head area contains a *<title>* tag, which Dreamweaver automatically inserts with any new HTML/ XHTML document. At its most basic, the *<title>* tag sets a display title for a page that appears at the top of the browser window. You can modify the *<title>* tag contents using the Title text field that sits at the top of your Document window. By default, each new document is issued the default title of Untitled Document. The *<title>* tag and its contents, however, can be a powerful and effective way to assist search engines in indexing your page.

What makes a good title?

A good document title ideally should include keywords that describe your site's main service, locale, and the category of business or information. In addition to the obvious—your company's name—think about the categories you would want your site to appear under on a web directory or as the result of a web search. For instance, the McKnight Institute would ideally want users looking for science museums or exhibits in the Philadelphia, Pennsylvania, area to find them first. A possible title could be: The McKnight Institute: Science Museum, Educational Exhibits and Attractions, Philadelphia, Pennsylvania.

This title contains several important keywords that describe the Institute's offerings, and features the Institute's name and location. In addition, re-shuffling these phrases and words produces several other search terms that could be beneficial to the Institute, such as:

* Science Exhibits

* Philadelphia Museum

* Pennsylvania Attractions

Avoid the rookie mistake of including only your company name in the document title. Remember, web searchers who haven't used your business before will only search by terms that apply to the service they are seeking (i.e. Wedding photographers Washington D.C.). Even the most recognized names on the Web, such as Ebay and Amazon, include generic search terms in their page titles.

To add a title to your web page:

1   From the Files panel, select and open the index.html document to open it for editing.

2   Locate the Title text field at the top of the Document window. It currently displays the default title of Untitled Document. Select its contents and enter **The McKnight Institute: Science Museum, Educational Exhibits and Attractions, Philadelphia, Pennsylvania** and hit Return or Enter.

Add a well-constructed title to the index.html page to make it more search engine and bookmark friendly.

3   Choose File > Save to save the document, and then choose File > Preview In Browser > [Default browser] to open the document in your system's primary browser.

4   Note the title that now appears in the bar at the top of the browser window. Close the browser window and return to Dreamweaver.

The most basic purpose of the <title> tag is to display a title at the top of the browser window. If used properly, it can also be used as a powerful hook for search engines.

While there is technically no limit to title length, the W3C's WCAG (Web Consortium Accessibility Guide) recommends that page titles be a maximum of 64 characters to be considered 'well-defined.' Titles exceeding this length may generate warnings in the Site Reports Results panel. Longer titles may also appear truncated (cut off) when displayed in some browser windows.

Bookmark-ability: another benefit of the <*title*> tag

It's common for users to bookmark a site or specific page they've found so they can easily return to it. Every browser features a bookmark feature, which allows users to mark and display favorite sites in an organized list; sometimes favorite sites are listed in a bookmarks bar on the browser window itself.

The document title determines the text that appears with a bookmark, so it's important to consider this when creating a good document title. Using a vague or non-descriptive title (or even worse, the default Untitled Document text) can make it impossible for a user to remember which bookmark is yours. A good title will appear as a descriptive bookmark in a browser's Favorites list or Bookmarks bar.

Adding meta keywords and descriptions

While SEO (Search Engine Optimization) is a broad topic that's far beyond the scope of this book, good SEO methods begin at the design level. Search engines use a variety of factors to rank and list web pages. Keywords and descriptions can help specify the search terms that are associated with your site and how it's listed. The HTML <*meta*> tag enables you to associate any page with a specific list of search terms, as well as a brief description of the page or the web site itself. Like the <*title*> tag, <*meta*> tags are placed in the <*head*> section of a page, and can be added from the Common Insert bar at the top of your workspace.

1   If it's not already open, open the index.html document for editing.

2   From the Common Insert bar, choose the Keywords button from the Head tags group.

3   When the Keywords dialog box appears, add a comma-separated list of search keywords that you'd like associated with this page, or the site in general. While there is no general consensus on the limit of how many keywords you can use, common sense says that you should be able to categorize your site in roughly 20 keywords or less. For example, enter: **The McKnight Institute, science museum, technology exhibits, attractions, family attractions, philadelphia, pennsylvania museums**. Press OK to add the keywords.

From the Common category of the Insert bar, choose the Keywords object from the Head tags group and enter a list of keywords in the resulting dialog box.

4   Now you'll add a description that a search engine can use to summarize your page when creating a listing for it. Choose the Description button from the Head tags group on the Common Insert bar.

5   When the Description dialog box appears, type in a brief descriptive paragraph (fewer than 250 characters, including spaces). For example, enter: **The McKnight Center is a family-oriented education center and museum that explores the history of technology and scientific discovery through hands-on exhibits and events**. Press OK.

Add a short description that search engines can use to display a caption for your site listing.

6   Choose File > Save, then choose File > Close to close the file.

Describing images with alternate text

Each image placed in your page can feature alternate text, which describes that image and also can act as a placeholder in its absence. Alternate text is added with the alt attribute of the *<img>* tag, and, for each image, alternate text can be specified using the Alt field located on the Property inspector. In the past, alternate text was used as a placeholder for an image that failed to load, or for larger images downloading through slow dial-up connections.

With increased download speeds and the widespread availability of high-speed Internet access, this usage of the Alt attribute has taken a backburner to two more popular uses: accessibility and search engine visibility. Accessibility is an important part of web page design, and refers to a page or collective web site's usability by people with disabilities. Alternate text provides a way for disability assistants such as voice browsers, screen readers, and other specialized browsers to interpret and describe images and graphics included on a page. Blind or visually impaired users frequently make use of screen readers to 'speak' the contents of a web page out loud.

Search engines such as Google Images make use of alternate text to provide information about image listings. The more accurate and concise the description, the more likely it is that users will find what they are looking for on your site. Also, well-indexed images are another hook that allows users to find your site—for example, a user searching for an image of a scientific nature may discover many of the images on the MKI site via an image search.

1   To add alt text to your page, first locate and open the ex4_sticky.html page from the Files panel.

2   Select the single image located in the middle of the page (stick.jpg). If necessary, choose Window > Properties to open the Property inspector.

3   On the Property inspector, locate the Alt text field. Enter the words **The Science of Sticky Exhibit at MKI**, and press Return or Enter. Leave the image selected.

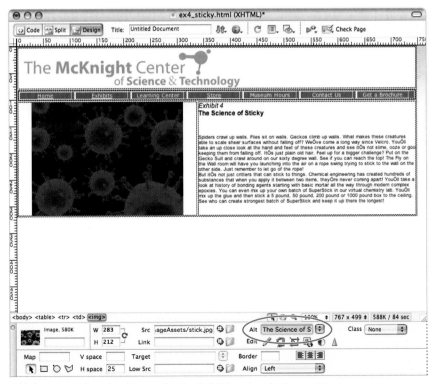

Add alternate text for a selected image using the Alt field located on the Property inspector.

4   Switch to Code view by clicking the Code button in the upper left-hand corner of the Document window. Note the highlighted section of code, which should include an *<img>* tag. The tag will appear with an alt attribute with your new text set as its value.

```
21      <td width="100" bgcolor="#CC9933" class="topmenu"><div align="center">Museum Hours</div></td>
22      <td width="100" bgcolor="#CC9933" class="topmenu"><div align="center">Contact Us</div></td>
23      <td width="100" bgcolor="#CC9933" class="topmenu"><div align="center">Get a Brochure</div></td>
24     </tr>
25     </table></td>
26    </tr>
27    <tr>
28     <td colspan="2"><img src="assets/imageAssets/stick.jpg" alt="The Science of Sticky Exhibit at MKI " width="283" height="212"
       hspace="25" align="left" /></td>
29     <td align="left" valign="top"><p><font size="3" face="Arial, Helvetica, sans-serif"><em>Exhibit
30   4</em><br />
31   <strong>The Science of Sticky</strong></font></p>
32       <p><font size="2" face="Arial, Helvetica, sans-serif"><br />
33       Spiders crawl up walls. Flies sit on walls. Geckos climb up walls. What makes
34       these creatures able to scale shear surfaces without falling off? Weâve come
35       a long way since Velcro. Youâll take an up close look at the hand and feet
36       of these creatures and see itâs not slime, ooze or goo keeping them from
37       falling off. Itâs just plain old hair. Feel up for a bigger challenge?
```

The newly added alternate text, shown in Code view. Alternate text is added via the <img> tag's alt attribute.

5   Click the Design button at the top of the Document window to return to Design view, and choose File > Save to save your page.

Rather than manually searching for missing titles or alternate text, use Dreamweaver's site reports, as shown earlier in this lesson, to generate listings of instances of missing alternate text throughout your site.

Launching your site

Before launching your site to the public—and to ensure that your site looks and works its best—take a moment to go over this pre-flight checklist:

Site Launch Checklist

☐   Enter FTP or upload information and test your FTP connection.

☐   Check links sitewide and repair missing/broken links and images

☐   Run site reports and address crucial issues. Put special emphasis on:

   ☐   Missing document titles

   ☐   Missing alt text

   ☐   Invalid markup that may cause display issues

☐   Open the homepage (index.html, et al) and navigate through your site, using menus, links in copy, and linked images to check page flow. Do this in several browsers, and, if possible, on both Windows and Macintosh platforms.

☐   View your homepage and major section pages in a web browser in the three most common screen resolutions: 640x480, 800x600, and 1024x768.

Uploading your site

At this point, if you have been following along without having access to a remote ftp server, you will now require one to continue this lesson.

1   If you're ready to upload your site to the remote web server, make sure that the Files panel is open (Window > Files).

2   Click the Expand button (⊞) at the top of the Files panel to display it in 2-column expanded view.

3   Click the Connect button (⚙) above the left (remote view) column to connect to your remote web server. Note: You will need to have created a valid connection, as described earlier in the lesson.

Once a successful connection is made, the remote files (if any) will display in the left-hand column.

4   In the right column, click and select the Folder icon at the very top of the file listing. This should be the root folder, and will display the current site definition title (Site Dreamweaver Lesson 13, for example).

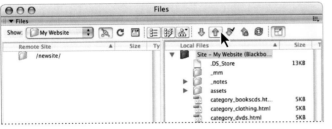

Select the root folder of your local site and click the Put button to upload the entire site to the web server.

5   Click the Put button at the top of the Files panel to copy the entire current local site and all included files to the current directory on the remote server. A dialog box will appear that reads, *Are you sure you wish to put the entire site?*

6   Press OK to begin copying the files to remote server. A progress bar will continue to display until all files have been successfully copied.

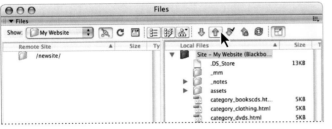

The entire web site has been successfully uploaded to the server, and displays in the remote view on the left.

Getting help and using the reference guides

Whether you are seeking a solution to a Dreamweaver-specific problem, or looking up the appropriate CSS rule to format a page item, you can use Dreamweaver's built-in Help system and integrated reference guides. In addition, the Help menu provides direct links to many online resources and Adobe support areas where you can seek help from Adobe professionals and the Dreamweaver user community.

1 To access the Help system, choose Help > Dreamweaver Help. The Adobe Help Viewer panel appears.

2 Enter a search term at the top of the panel, or browse by topic on the left-hand side of the panel.

3 For more help options and a searchable knowledge base, choose Help > Dreamweaver Support Center. For the Dreamweaver support forums, choose Help > Adobe Online Forums.

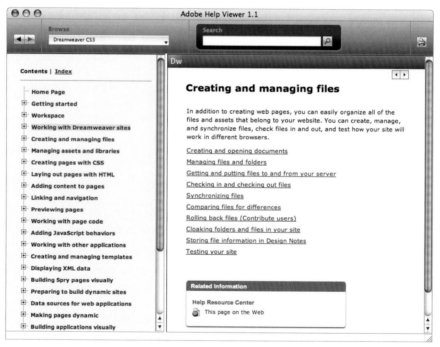

The Help menu (left), and the Adobe Help Viewer (right).

The Reference panel

Dreamweaver's Reference panel is like a full library of O'Reilly technical books, including reference guides for HTML, CSS, JavaScript, and Dreamweaver-friendly, server-side languages such as ColdFusion and JSP.

1   To open the Reference panel, choose Window > Reference.

2   From the menu at the top left corner of the panel, select a reference guide from the Book menu.

3   Click on a specific topic or term in the drop-down menu that appears within the book you've chosen.

Dreamweaver's built-in O'Reilly reference guides are like having a library of books right at your fingertips.

Use the built-in O'Reilly HTML Reference for a full listing of HTML tags, their attributes, and appropriate usage. Use the O'Reilly CSS Reference for a listing of CSS properties and values.

Suggested next steps

Congratulations on launching your first Dreamweaver site project! There's nothing more exciting than having your hard work on the Web, and available for the world to see. The important thing to remember is that your web site should not be static; part of maintaining a successful web site requires continuously evolving it to meet the needs of your viewers and keeping the content fresh and new.

Whether your site is for business, pleasure, or self-promotion, make sure to solicit feedback from friends, family, and colleagues after you've launched. Alert a small and trusted group about the launch by sending out an email, mailing a postcard, or posting a notice on a blog (sometimes this is referred to as the 'beta' stage). Feedback and constructive criticism (a little praise is okay, too) are the best ways to objectively know what needs improvement. You'll probably receive more feedback and suggestions you can handle, so focus on points that are common across multiple users, and address any major issues before making a more public launch (for instance, to your entire client base).

Focus on focus groups

Focus groups are an excellent way to get non-biased feedback on a major new site or product launch, and have been a regular practice in product marketing and research for years. A focus group is composed of a group of individuals who are brought together to analyze, try out, and comment on a specific product—in this case, your web site—for the purpose of obtaining feedback and testing the product's effectiveness.

Groups can be guided through certain portions or processes on the site, or may be encouraged to navigate it on their own. Afterwards, they are polled with specific questions about their experience, and the results are put together to form a picture of the site's usability, effectiveness, and impact. This may include questions such as:

- Did you feel the web site was easy to navigate? On a scale from 1-10, how you would rate the difficulty level in locating specific pages or topics?

- Did the design, including graphics and color themes, effectively help communicate the web site's offerings?

- On a scale from 1-10, how would you rate the quality of the written content on the site?

Focus groups are often interactive, encouraging participants to talk with each other and share their opinions. In some cases, a moderator may be used to regulate group discussions and hand out questionnaires. Participants can be composed of a focused demographic group (for instance, 25- to 35-year-old technology professionals) or can represent a diverse professional and demographic range.

Focus groups are reasonable for any size company to organize—even if it's just you and five friends—and are a highly effective way to find out what's currently working and what's not. Give it a try; you may find the results encouraging, surprising, or even slightly discouraging. The trick is to use this feedback wisely towards the main purpose of making a better web site, and you'll be glad you did.

Web site design resources

There is a vast amount of information and many tutorial-based web sites covering topics from web page standards to advanced CSS design. Here is a small sampling of some useful sites that can help you take your skills and knowledge further. Use these in conjunction with Dreamweaver's built-in reference guides and Adobe's online support forums:

W3C (World Wide Web Consortium) – http://www.w3.org

W3Schools – http://www.w3schools.com

A List Apart – http://alistapart.com/

Adobe's Dreamweaver Developer Center - http://www.adobe.com/devnet/dreamweaver/

CSS Zengarden - http://www.csszengarden.com/

maxdesign - http://css.maxdesign.com.au/

CSSplay - http://www.cssplay.co.uk/www

Self study

1 Import a site from a previous lesson from this book or import your own site and run a site report for broken links, orphaned files, etc.

2 Investigate Dreamweaver's CSS Advisor by examining various files from this lesson and previous lessons. Using the CSS Advisor is a great way to learn more about CSS and browser compatibility issues.

Review

Questions

1 What does FTP stand for, and what is it used for?

2 What three purposes do document titles serve, and why are they important?

3 What are three possible pre-flight checklist items you need to address before launching a web site?

Answers

1 File Transfer Protocol. FTP is used to connect to and transfer files between your local machine and a web server.

2 Document titles display a title at the top of the browser window, display in a user's bookmarks bar, and are an important hook for search engines.

3 **a.** Enter and test your FTP connection information in the Site Definition panel.

b. Run site reports to rectify any potential design or accessibility issues, such as missing alternate text for images or empty document titles.

c. Run the Link Checker sitewide to check for broken links between pages or incorrect image references.

Index

A

\<a\> tag, 115, 118
Absolute hyperlinks, 75
Absolute positioning, 175, 177
   in AP Elements panel, 196
Active links, 53
Adobe Bridge CS3®, 19
Adobe Device Central, 18
Adobe Flash®
   ActionScript, 33
   animations, inserting, 246
   content, creating, 249
Adobe Photoshop®, 1, 8
   Optimization panel, 13
Adobe Premiere Pro®, 259
Advanced site-creation options, 42
AJAX (Asynchronous JavaScript and XML), 10
Alt attribute, 81, 377-378, 384-385
Animation, 246
AP Div, 167-168
   drawing, 168-170, 211
   in AP Elements panel, 196
   modifying properties of, 177-180
   positioning content with, 167
   selecting, 187, 196
AP Elements panel, 196
Apple Final Cut Pro, 259
Apply Source Formatting, 323
Arial, Helvetica, sans-serif, 69
Assets panel, 141, 145
   Library items list, 281-286
   Templates list, 288-289

Attach External Style Sheet, 348

B

Background color
   HTML, 311-312
   in CSS, 125, 349-350
   in tables, 151-152
   setting, with Page Properties dialog 50-52
Background image, 51
Background option, 51
Behaviors, 12, 353-358
   Behaviors panel, 12, 353-355, 359
\<b\> tag, 24, 109, 115
Block
   elements, vs. inline, 186
   options, 109
\<body\> tag, 26, 31, 106, 124
   editing, 311
Border
   for images, 81-82
   HTML attribute, 28
   in CSS, 165, 180, 190-191
   indicating link, 83
   in tables, 138
   properties, in frames and framesets, 225, 226, 229
   repositioning, 236
   settings, 164
   using, 138, 165, 235
Boxes, *See also Divs*, 164, 165, 167, 186
   compared to tables, 167
   creating, with Draw AP Div, 168
   creating, with Insert Div, 182-185
   ID rules for, 171-172
   inline vs. block, 186

   modifying properties of, 177-180
   overlap, 180-182
   positioning, 175-176
   selecting, 169
   styling, 186-195
   visibility, 196
Box Model, *See CSS Box Model*
\<br\> tag, 30, 31, 312
Bridge, *See Adobe Bridge*
Browse Report, 321
Browsers
   Alt text and, 385
   Bookmarks, 383
   Display bugs, 379
   Fonts and, 69
   Link method support, 348
   Previewing behaviors, 355
   Previewing pages, 72
   Role of, 23
Browser Compatibility Check, 8, 17, 167, 379-380
Bulleted lists, 77-78, 93-96, 194
Buttons, *See also Flash buttons*
   radio, 334, 335, 338, 339
   submit and reset, 346-347

C

.css file, *See also External style sheet*, 98, 119-120
   creating new, 124-125
Cascading
   defined, 92
   Documents, 216
Cascading Style Sheets, *See CSS*
Case sensitivity, 29, 43

Dynamic Learning: Dreamweaver CS3

Where innovation, creativity, and technology converge.

There's a revolution in how the world engages ideas and information. As our culture becomes more visual and information-rich, anyone can create and share effective, interactive, and extraordinary visual and aural communications. Through our books, videos, Web sites and newsletters, O'Reilly spreads the knowledge of the creative innovators at the heart of this revolution, helping you to put their knowledge and ideas to work in your projects.

To find out more, visit us at digitalmedia.oreilly.com

Capture. Design. Build. Edit. Play.   digitalmedia.oreilly.com

Want to learn
Adobe Creative Suite 3?

Don't just get a book.

Introducing O'Reilly Dynamic Learning—a comprehensive, self-paced training system that includes books, video tutorials, online resources, and instructor guides. Written by product experts and trainers who have produced many of Adobe's training titles, the books are organized into practical, easy-to-follow lessons that cover everything you need to know about the applications in CS3.

Look for the complete Dynamic Learning series at your favorite bookseller, or online at www.oreilly.com/store

 oreilly.com/store/series/dynamiclearning